KETO AIR FRYER
COOKBOOK

600 Foolproof Ketogenic Air Fryer Recipes
for Quick Weight Loss

Bennie John

CONTENTS

SNACKS & APPETIZERS...39

POULTRY RECIPES 100

MEAT RECIPES 130

VEGAN & VEGETARIAN RECIPES

DESERTS 178

INTRODUCTION

The recipes in this book are meant to be straightforward and delicious while also being healthy. My goal is for you to be able to get a healthy meal on the table in about 30 minutes or less without having to spend a ton of time or money at the grocery store.

You will find some recipes to be longer than an hour, which is mostly related to their refrigeration time, and this is fine for a good turnout.

On the other hand, every recipe in this book can be prepared quickly from readily available ingredients at the grocery store. Do a read through the methods and make sure to understand the processes before you start cooking. It will make you enjoy the cooking process better.

WHAT IS THE KETO DIET?

It is merely a less or no-carb form of eating where starchy and high carb foods are swapped for other ingredients; these low carb foods tend to yield better results.

A high carb diet is one that has 20% and more of complex carbohydrates in its content. Digestion is more difficult with such foods as the body has to struggle to break the complex substances into smaller units. In the end, your body holds up food longer than necessary in the body.

High carb diets are major contributors to weight gain and likely problems as well as sugar, causing diseases like diabetes. Going ketogenic is a sure way to prevent these health problems, and they come with a feel-good factor.

Top 5 Ketogenic Diet Benefits.

1. Weight Loss

You will mainly not be feeding on starchy or complex carb foods when dieting, so the body naturally can break down foods like protein and fat quickly.

Starchy foods do not digest well and fast. They stay in the body for longer, yielding to bloating and weight gain.

2. Heart Health Improvement

When dieting right on a ketogenic diet, that is, not falling onto high levels of bad fat, the amount of bad cholesterol in the body reduces significantly. Good cholesterol then aids the heart in functioning just right.

3. Aids with brain functioning

The high protein content in the keto diet offers neuroprotective benefits to the brain, which goes to prevent brain diseases and sleeping disorders. A dedicated keto lifestyle strengthens the brain's muscles over time, which leads to cognitive functioning and alertness.

4. A suppressed appetite

Sugar is known to make you hungrier faster, which results in easy weight gains from very frequent feeding. On the keto diet, the body feeds on protein and good fat, which have the tendencies of filling the stomach up for a long while. A consistent ketosis diet gradually allows you to eat smaller amounts of food hence a significant weight loss.

5. Improves women health

Sounds fantastic, and this is true. A high carb diet can affect those with the polycystic ovarian syndrome (PCOS) negatively, which is a disorder that causes enlarged ovaries with cysts.

Eating lots of vegetables and more protein allows the hormones to regulate blood glucose levels, which normalizes PCOS to will enable the body to ovulate on time, hence fertility.

What can you eat while you're on a Keto diet?

You are meant to cut down on carbs when on a keto diet and eat more proteins, however, in moderation. Ketosis foods could seem very light in the beginning, and you may be tempted to munch on something more substantial, which often contains carbs. Make sure to remove all of such temptations to make your dieting successful. Some foods to keep are:

- **Vegetables with no starch** – These include a lot of green vegetables than root ones. These foods have little to no carb contents in them and are the safest options to eat. Some types are asparagus, leafy greens, broccoli, radishes, zucchinis, and lots of avocados.

- **Grass-fed meats** – Beef, lamb, pork derived from animals that fed only on grass keeps their meat healthy. Meats mainly do not contain any carbs making it very safe to add to your meals. These types of meat are also less fatty and have the right amounts of protein for the perfect dieting needs.

- **Fish and seafood** – Depending on what name suits you right, these are animals that grow in the sea, which feed on protein. They have zero amount of carbs, making them a run to option. Most often, people may be uncomfortable with the smell of seafood; hence it is best to go for a recipe that has good flavoring to get these smells off. This book shares excellent recipes for this purpose.

- **Healthy fats** – It is not wrong to have fatty foods on a keto diet, but the ones with bad fats like fried foods is not a great idea. Aim for seafood, cheese, creams, fatty fish, nuts like hazelnuts, pecans, walnuts, pine nuts, brazil nuts, and seeds like sesame seeds, pumpkin seeds, and flaxseeds which have healthy fats and do not lead to weight gain and its accompanying problems. Use olive oil mostly for frying or stewing as it contains very little fat.

Also, make sure not to use low-fat creams as they often contain high carb contents to replace the fat content.

What you can't eat while you're on a keto diet?

Make sure to eat these kinds of foods in limited or no quantities.

- **Fruits** – They are very high in sugars, stay away from them except avocados. Eat lots of avocados.

- **Root vegetables** – Like potatoes, cabbages, carrots, artichokes, fennel bulbs, these have higher contents of carbs. You can have them, but they should be in small quantities.

- **Tubers and Grains** – These are very high in starch and complex carbs. Block them out of your keto diet.

- **Wines, Sweet Drinks, and Sweets** – Wines can be used for cooking but in minimal quantities. Sweet drinks, however, should be blocked as the sugar in them is a high carb ingredient.

WHAT IS AN AIR FRYER?

We all want to eat, and the first thing we do is to draw out a Whole Meal plan because we are aiming at cutting down the fats, which is good, but we forget about the cooking process.

The Air Fryer is modern cooking equipment that cooks food with little to no fat using a hot air blowing technique. It comes with a fryer basket were food placed and set to cook under hot air to cook it faster than an oven and crispier.

This method of cooking has proven to be one of the healthiest forms of cooking in existence, and in combination with the keto recipes that we share, the goal to live healthier is made easier.

Seven Benefits of the Air Fryer

The benefits of this cooking device are in a wide range, and I will share the most important ones.

Time-Saving

For busy moms, hungry girls, and impatient cooks, this is the device to go for. It gets foods ready in just a few minutes while yielding fantastic results.

Weight Watching

Just because it cooks with no to little fat, your chances of adding on more weight can be controlled easily.

Easy to Use

You don't have to deal with several buttons to get it working. The cooking settings are very straightforward to apply. With the recipe in hand, select the temperature and time level, and you're good to go.

Easy to Clean

Who loves cleaning devices with complicated designs? Not me! The Air Fryer comes with a good set up that allows you to clean the fryer basket and food trapper very easily. Just wash them with wipes and dry them with a napkin. That easy!

Multiple Cooking Options

You can bake, fry, roast, sauté, and grill with the Air Fryer and guess what you can choose not to oil your food when doing any of these. Meaning, you will not have to fill your kitchen with the different appliances to cook variety.

Space Saver

Many Air Fryers are designed to save space. They can fit in almost every area and are light to move around. You can have it set on the dinner table and dish food out from it onto the family's plates.

<u>Energy Saving</u>

They do not heat spaces and use lesser electricity than an electric oven. If you're not up for the heat in summer, this is one that will serve you well.

How to Use an Air Fryer?

In 5 to 6 steps, you should be able to use an air fryer for the best result and long-lasting use.

Shake the fryer basket once or twice when making smaller foods like croquettes, wings, and meatballs. It ensures that the food is well cooked.

Never overcrowd the fryer basket when cooking. Work in batches for optimum results.

If there's a need to oil your foods, **always** go for cooking sprays as they are lighter and will not clog the holes of the fryer basket or make them greasy.

When cooking foods that have been marinated for a while, **pat them dry** before placing them in the fryer basket else the liquid will drop into the residue trapper and create the other mess.

Use heatproof bowls when there's a need to use a container in the air fryer.

Just **clean** the air fryer with a wet napkin or soak the fryer basket in soapy water before scrubbing or washing in the dishwasher.

Is an Air Fryer Good for a Keto Diet?

Yes, and yes! It is one of the best for it. You can cook all kinds of vegetables and meats in the Air Fryer, and they will turn out excellently. Its use of less to no fat makes it all the better to use when making keto foods leaving out the trouble of taking in more fats.

However, sauces and highly liquid dishes may not be made in the Air Fryer because of the design of the fryer basket, which has holes in it. You are better off making dryer or solid foods with it or else prepare saucy foods in a heatproof dish placed in the fryer basket. I added some recipes to show you how to do this.

Now, onto the recipes, have a great time making and enjoying these tasty dishes.

MORNING RECIPES

Avocado & Cauliflower Casserole

Total Time: 35 min | **Serves:** 4 | **Per serving:** Cal 510; Net Carbs 2.4g; Fat 38g; Protein 27g

Ingredients

6 large eggs, beaten
¼ cup heavy cream
1 ½ cups chopped cauliflower
¼ tsp red pepper flakes

½ tsp dried parsley
Salt and black pepper to taste
1 cup Cheddar cheese, shredded
1 avocado, peeled, pitted, sliced

8 tbsp sour cream
2 scallions, cut on the bias
12 bacon slices, chopped

Directions

Preheat the Air Fryer to 330°F. Combine the eggs, heavy cream, and cauliflower in a bowl. Spread the mixture on a greased baking dish and sprinkle with red pepper flakes, parsley, salt, and pepper. Bake for 10 minutes. Open the fryer and scatter the cheese over the eggs. Cook for 10 minutes until the eggs are set and the cheese is golden.

Meanwhile, fry the bacon in a skillet over medium heat for 5 minutes until crispy; set aside. When cooking is complete, remove the baking dish. Scatter the bacon and scallions over and arrange the avocado slices on top. Slice into 4 portions and serve drizzled with sour cream. Enjoy!

Chicken Sausage & Ricotta Calzones

Total Time: 30 min | **Serves:** 4 | **Per serving:** Cal 558; Net Carbs 2.1g; Fat 19.2g; Protein 1.6g

Ingredients

½ lb cooked chicken sausage, crumbled
1 ½ cups mozzarella cheese, grated
½ cup almond flour
1 oz cream cheese

1 whole egg, beaten
4 eggs, scrambled
½ cup ricotta cheese, crumbled

Salt and black pepper to taste

Directions

Preheat the Air Fryer to 375°F. Microwave the mozzarella, almond flour, and cream cheese for 50 seconds. Remove, add the beaten egg, and stir until a smooth ball is formed. Place the dough on a parchment sheet and cover it with another sheet. With a rolling pin, roll out the dough to a ¼-inch thickness.

Cut the dough into 4 pieces. Mix the chicken sausage, ricotta cheese, scrambled eggs, salt, and pepper in a bowl. Divide the filling onto one side of each of the rectangles, fold the empty side over the filling, and seal the edges. Transfer them to a foil-lined baking pan and place in the air fryer basket. Bake for 14-16 minutes, flipping them over halfway through cooking until golden and puffed. Serve immediately.

Cheesy Egg Scramble Bake

Total Time: 20 min | **Serves:** 3 | **Per serving:** Cal 360; Net Carbs 0.6g; Fat 28g; Protein 19.4g

Ingredients

3 large eggs, beaten
2 tsp butter, melted

2 tbsp shredded sharp cheddar cheese
Salt and black pepper to taste

¼ tsp green bell pepper flakes

Directions

Preheat the Air Fryer to 400°F. Pour the eggs into a greased baking pan and insert the pan in the air fryer basket. Bake for 5 minutes. Stir the eggs, drizzle the butter all over and top with cheese. Cook for 5 more minutes, stirring once. Remove and fluff the eggs with a fork. Sprinkle with salt, pepper, and green bell pepper flakes. Serve.

Cheesy Bell Pepper Eggs

Total Time: 25 min | **Serves**: 4 | **Per serving**: Cal 316; Net Carbs 2.9g; Fat 19g; Protein 25g

Ingredients

4 green bell peppers, tops and seeds removed

3 oz cooked ham, chopped

1 shallot, chopped

8 large eggs, beaten

1 cup Monterey Jack cheese, grated

Salt and black pepper to taste

Directions

Preheat the Air Fryer to 390°F. In a bowl, combine the ham, shallot, eggs, salt, and pepper. Fill the pepper with the mixture and top with the cheese. Arrange the stuffed peppers on the greased air fryer basket. Bake for 14-16 minutes, turning once until the peppers are soft and the eggs are set. Serve immediately.

Bacon Spaghetti Squash Fritters

Total Time: 25 min | **Serves**: 4 | **Per serving**: Cal 130; Net Carbs 2.1g; Fat 9.8g; Protein 2g

Ingredients

3 bacon slices, cooked and chopped

2 cups cooked spaghetti squash

2 tbsp butter, softened

1 large egg

¼ cup almond flour

2 green onions, sliced

½ tsp garlic powder

1 tsp dried parsley

Directions

Preheat the Air Fryer to 390°F. Spread the cooked spaghetti squash between several sheets of kitchen towels and pat dry. Transfer to a mixing bowl and add the remaining ingredients; mix to combine. Divide the mixture into 4 balls, flatten them slightly to form patties, and transfer to the foil-lined air fryer basket. AirFry for 8-10 minutes. Flip halfway through the cooking time. Serve warm and enjoy!

Effortless Veggie Frittata

Total Time: 30 min | **Serves**: 4 | **Per serving**: Cal 165; Net Carbs 1.5g; Fat 12.1g; Protein 10g

Ingredients

6 fresh eggs

3 tbsp milk

Salt and black pepper to taste

½ cup broccoli, chopped

¼ cup yellow onion, chopped

¼ cup green bell pepper, chopped

Directions

Preheat the Air Fryer to 350°F. Add the broccoli, onion, and green bell peppers to a greased pan and Bake in the fryer for 5-6 minutes. In a bowl, whisk the eggs with milk, salt, and pepper and pour over the veggies. Return the pan to the fryer and cook for 10-12 more minutes. Serve sliced into wedges.

Mexican-Style Jalapeño Egg Cups

Total Time: 20 min | **Serves**: 3 | **Per serving**: Cal 352; Net Carbs 1.3g; Fat 25g; Protein 20.9g

Ingredients

6 fresh eggs

¼ cup pickled jalapeños, chopped

3 oz ricotta cheese, softened

⅓ cup sharp cheddar cheese, grated

¼ tsp Mexican oregano

Salt and black pepper to taste

Directions

Preheat the Air Fryer to 350°F. Whisk the eggs with salt and pepper and spoon them into 3 greased ramekins. In a bowl, mix well the remaining ingredients and top the eggs with the mixture. Put the ramekins in the air fryer basket. Bake for 10-12 minutes until set. Let cool slightly, then serve. Enjoy!

Cheese & Sausage Cocktail Meatballs

Total Time: 25 min | **Serves**: 4 | **Per serving**: Cal 422; Net Carbs 1.5g; Fat 32g; Protein 23g

Ingredients

1 pound ground Italian sausage	1 oz cream cheese, softened	Salt and black pepper to taste
½ cup mozzarella cheese, shredded	1 large egg	½ tsp chili powder

Directions

Preheat the Air Fryer to 390°F. In a bowl, combine all the ingredients. Shape the mixture into 1-inch meatballs. Place them in the air fryer basket and AirFry for 12 minutes, shaking once. Serve with toothpicks.

Avocado Topped Cauliflower Cakes

Total Time: 25 min | **Serves**: 2 | **Per serving**: Cal 276; Net Carbs 3.8g; Fat 16g; Protein 14g

Ingredients

1 tbsp butter, melted	1 large egg, beaten	1 ripe medium avocado, mashed
¼ cup almond flour	½ cup cheddar cheese, shredded	½ tsp garlic powder
5 oz cauliflower rice	1 spring onion, finely chopped	Salt and black pepper to taste

Directions

Preheat the Air Fryer to 390°F. Place the cauliflower in a bowl and mix with the egg, cheddar cheese, spring onion, garlic powder, salt, and pepper. Form the mixture into 2 patties and coat with almond flour on all sides. Transfer the cakes to the greased air fryer basket and brush them with butter on both sides. AirFry for 6-8 minutes, flipping once until they're cooked through and golden. Spread the mashed avocado on the cakes and serve immediately.

Parsley, Egg & Bacon Roll-Ups

Total Time: 30 min | **Serves**: 4 | **Per serving**: Cal 458; Net Carbs 2.9g; Fat 32g; Protein 28g

Ingredients

1 cup sharp cheddar cheese, shredded

2 tbsp butter	6 eggs, beaten	12 bacon slices
¼ cup onions, chopped	1 tbsp parsley, chopped	½ cup mild salsa
½ green bell pepper, chopped	Salt and black pepper to taste	

Directions

Preheat the Air Fryer to 360°F. Melt the butter in a pan over medium heat and stir-fry the onion and bell pepper for 4 minutes until softened. Pour the eggs over; scramble for 4 minutes until fluffy, and no visible liquid egg remains. Turn off the heat. Sprinkle with salt, pepper, and parsley. Place 3 overlapping bacon slices on a cutting board.

Spoon ¼ of the scrambled eggs on top and sprinkle with cheese. Roll up tightly and secure with a toothpick. Repeat until you run out of ingredients. Arrange the rolls on the air fryer basket. Bake for 15 minutes. Turn the rolls halfway through cooking and cook until the rolls are crispy on all sides. Serve with salsa and enjoy!

Italian Cinnamon Roll Sticks

Total Time: 25 min | **Serves**: 4 | **Per serving**: Cal 230; Net Carbs 1g; Fat 19.2g; Protein 10g

Ingredients

1 cup mozzarella cheese, shredded	½ tsp baking soda	1 large egg
1 oz mascarpone cheese	½ cup granular erythritol	2 tbsp unsalted butter, melted
⅓ cup almond flour	1 tsp vanilla extract	½ tsp ground cinnamon
¼ tsp salt	¼ tsp Amaretto liqueur	3 tbsp powdered erythritol

Directions

Preheat the Air Fryer to 390°F. Microwave the mozzarella and mascarpone cheeses for 40-50 seconds. In a bowl, combine almond flour, baking soda, salt, 2 tbsp of granular erythritol, and vanilla. Add in the cheese mixture and stir until a soft dough forms. Add in the egg and mix well.

Transfer the dough to a flat surface and roll it out with a rolling pin. Cut it into 8 (1-inch) pieces. Whisk butter, Amaretto, cinnamon, and remaining granular erythritol. Arrange the sticks on a greased baking pan and brush them with some of the butter mixture. Place the pan in the basket and Bake for 8 minutes, flipping and brushing once with the remaining butter. Dust the sticks with powdered erythritol and serve.

Healthy Pumpkin Spice Cupcakes

Total Time: 25 min | **Serves:** 6 | **Per serving:** Cal 207; Net Carbs 1.4g; Fat 18.1g; Protein 6g

Ingredients

½ lemon, zested
1 cup almond flour
¼ tsp salt
½ cup swerve

½ tsp baking powder
¼ cup butter, at room temperature
¼ cup canned pumpkin
¼ tsp ground cinnamon

¼ tsp pumpkin pie spice
¼ tsp ground nutmeg
1 tsp vanilla extract
2 large eggs

Directions

Preheat the Air Fryer to 350°F. Grease a muffin tin with a nonstick cooking spray. In a mixing bowl, combine all the ingredients and stir well. Divide the batter between the muffin cups; place them in the air fryer basket. Bake for 14-16 minutes or until a toothpick inserted in the center comes out dry. Serve.

Breakfast Bacon & Egg Muffins

Total Time: 20 min | **Serves:** 3 | **Per serving:** Cal 380; Net Carbs 1.9g; Fat 23.9g; Protein 29g

Ingredients

6 bacon slices
6 fresh eggs, beaten
3 tbsp sour cream

¼ red bell peppers, chopped
¼ green bell pepper, chopped
1 green onion, chopped

⅓ cup cheddar cheese, shredded
Salt and black pepper to taste

Directions

Preheat the Air Fryer to 350°F. Line the bottom and sides of 3 muffin cups with bacon slices, ensuring that all sides are covered. In a bowl, mix the eggs, sour cream, red peppers, green pepper, green onion, salt, and pepper and spoon the mixture onto the cups. Sprinkle the cheddar cheese on top. Place the cups in the air fryer basket and Bake for 10-12 minutes until set. Let cool for a few minutes, then serve in the ramekins.

Cinnamon Sponge Cake

Total Time: 20 min | **Serves:** 4 | **Per serving:** Cal 152; Net Carbs 0.7g; Fat 13g; Protein 5.4g

Ingredients

¼ tsp salt
½ cup almond flour
¼ cup powdered erythritol

½ tsp baking powder
2 tbsp vegetable oil
½ cup almond milk

1 large egg, beaten
¼ tsp vanilla extract
½ tsp ground cinnamon

Directions

Preheat the Air Fryer to 310°F. Grease a baking pan with cooking spray. In a bowl, combine the dry ingredients. In another bowl, mix the eggs, oil, vanilla, and almond milk. Pour the wet mixture into the dry ingredients and whisk until there are no lumps in the batter. Pour it into the pan and insert into the air fryer basket. AirFry for 20-25 minutes or until a toothpick inserted in the center comes out dry. Serve.

Chorizo Stuffed Poblanos

Total Time: 30 min | **Serves:** 4 | **Per serving:** Cal 490; Net Carbs 2.7g; Fat 36g; Protein 23g

Ingredients

8 tbsp Monterey Jack cheese, shredded

4 large poblano peppers, stems and seeds removed

¼ cup canned green chiles and tomatoes, drained

1 tbsp olive oil

½ pound chorizo sausage

4 large eggs, beaten

4 oz cream cheese, softened

½ tsp cayenne pepper

½ cup sour cream

Directions

Preheat the Air Fryer to 350°F. Heat the olive oil in a skillet over medium heat and cook the chorizo sausage for 5-6 minutes until browned; set aside. Pour the eggs in the skillet and scramble them for 3-4 minutes until they begin to set. Add the cream cheese, tomatoes, cayenne pepper, and chiles to the cooked chorizo; mix well.

Fold in the eggs. Divide the filling among the poblano peppers and sprinkle the cheese on top. Arrange the peppers on the greased baking dish and Bake for 14-16 minutes until the peppers are tender and the cheese is golden brown. Drizzle with sour cream and serve immediately.

Classic Pecan Cake

Total Time: 40 min | **Serves:** 6 | **Per serving:** Cal 260; Net Carbs 1.2g; Fat 23.8g; Protein 6.9g

Ingredients

¼ tsp salt

1 cup almond flour

½ cup powdered erythritol

2 tbsp ground golden flaxseed

2 tsp baking powder

½ tsp grated nutmeg

2 tsp orange zest

1 tsp vanilla extract

¼ cup butter, melted

¼ cup buttermilk

2 large eggs

¼ cup pecans, chopped

Directions

Preheat the Air Fryer to 310°F. Grease a baking pan with a nonstick cooking spray. In a bowl, place the salt, almond flour, erythritol, flaxseed, baking powder, nutmeg, and orange zest and stir to combine. In another bowl, whisk the eggs until pale and frothy. Stir in the butter, vanilla, and buttermilk.

Add the wet mixture to the dry mix and fold in the pecans. Spoon the batter into the pan and insert into the air fryer basket. Bake for 22-25 minutes or until a toothpick inserted in the center comes out dry. Serve.

Lime Cake

Total Time: 25 min | **Serves:** 6 | **Per serving:** Cal 202; Net Carbs 0.8g; Fat 18g; Protein 6.4g

Ingredients

¼ tsp salt

1 cup almond flour

½ cup powdered erythritol

½ tsp baking powder

¼ cup butter, melted

¼ cup unsweetened almond milk

2 large eggs

1 tsp vanilla extract

¼ tsp banana extract

1 lime, zested and juiced

1 tsp poppy seeds

Directions

Preheat the Air Fryer to 310°F. Grease a baking pan with cooking spray. In a bowl, place the salt, almond flour, erythritol, baking powder, and lime zest and stir to combine. In another bowl, whisk the eggs, butter, vanilla, banana extract, milk, and lime juice. Pour the wet mixture into the dry ingredients and fold in the poppy seeds.

Scrape the batter into the prepared baking pan and insert it into the air fryer basket. Bake for 12-14 minutes or until a toothpick inserted in the center comes out dry. Serve chilled. Enjoy!

Veggie Cheese Quiche

Total Time: 50 min | **Serves:** 2 | **Per serving:** Cal 316; Net Carbs 1g; Fat 24g; Protein 10g

Ingredients

4 eggs
1 cup almond milk
2 medium broccoli, cut into florets
2 medium tomatoes, diced

4 medium carrots, diced
¼ cup feta cheese, crumbled
1 cup cheddar cheese, grated
Salt and black pepper to taste

1 tsp parsley, chopped
1 tsp dried thyme

Directions

Put the broccoli and carrots in a food steamer and cook until soft, about 10 minutes. In a jug, crack in the eggs, add the parsley, salt, pepper, and thyme. Using a whisk, beat the eggs while adding the almond milk gradually until a pale mixture is attained. Once the broccoli and carrots are ready, strain them through a sieve and set aside.

In a baking dish, add the carrots and broccoli. Put the tomatoes on top, then the feta and cheddar cheese following. Leave a little cheddar cheese. Pour the egg mixture over the layering and top with the remaining cheddar cheese. Place the dish in the Air Fryer and Bake at 350°F for 20 minutes. Remove the dish. Serve sliced.

Classic French Toast Sticks

Total Time: 13 min | **Serves:** 3 | **Per serving:** Cal 165; Net Carbs 3.5g; Fat 13g; Protein 7.2g

Ingredients

5 zero-carb bread slices
3 eggs

1 ½ tbsp butter
½ tsp cinnamon powder

A pinch of nutmeg powder
A pinch of clove powder

Directions

Preheat the Air Fryer to 350°F. In a bowl, add the clove powder, eggs, nutmeg powder, and cinnamon powder. Beat well using a whisk. Apply butter on both sides of the bread slices and cut them into 4 strips. Dip them in the egg mixture and arrange them on the air fryer basket in one layer. AirFry for 2 minutes.

Once ready, pull out the air fryer basket and spray the toasts with cooking spray. Flip the toasts and spray the other side with cooking spray. Slide the air fryer basket back into the Air Fryer and continue cooking for 4 minutes. Once the toasts are golden brown, remove them onto a serving platter. Dust with cinnamon and serve.

Crispy Hash Browns

Total Time: 45 min | **Serves:** 3 | **Per serving:** Cal 312; Net Carbs 1.6g; Fat 15g; Protein 16g

Ingredients

7 radishes, shredded
Salt and black pepper to taste
1 tsp garlic powder

1 tsp chili flakes
1 tsp onion powder
1 egg, beaten

1 tbsp olive oil

Directions

Place a skillet over medium heat on a stovetop, add the olive oil and radishes. Sauté until turn evenly golden, about 7-8 minutes. Transfer to a bowl and let them cool completely. Then, add in the egg, pepper, salt, chili flakes, onion powder, and garlic powder. Mix well. On a flat plate, spread the mixture and pat firmly with your fingers. Refrigerate for 20 minutes and preheat the Air Fryer to 350°F. Remove from the fridge.

Use a knife to divide it into equal sizes. Grease the basket of the Air Fryer with cooking spray and place the patties in the basket. Close the Air Fryer and cook them at 350°F for 15 minutes. Open the Air Fryer and turn the hash browns with a spatula. Cook further for 6 minutes. Serve with sunshine eggs.

Cheesy Buffalo Egg Cups

Total Time: 25 min | **Serves:** 3 | **Per serving:** Cal 356; Net Carbs 1.6g; Fat 21.9g; Protein 21g

Ingredients

1 tbsp olive oil

3 fresh eggs

3 oz cream cheese

3 tbsp buffalo wing sauce

⅓ cup blue cheese, crumbled

Salt and black pepper to taste

Directions

Preheat the Air Fryer to 350°F. Grease 3 baking cups with olive oil. Microwave the blue cheese, cream cheese, and buffalo sauce for 20-30 seconds in a microwave-safe bowl. Remove and stir to combine. Divide the mixture between the cups. Carefully crack an egg into the middle of each cup and sprinkle with salt and pepper. Place the cups in the air fryer basket and Bake for 12-14 minutes until the yolks are set. Let cool for 5 minutes and serve.

Cauliflower & Parmesan Hash Browns

Total Time: 25 min | **Serves:** 4 | **Per serving:** Cal 152; Net Carbs 1.7g; Fat 9.8g; Protein 9.8g

Ingredients

2 tbsp scallions, chopped

Salt and black pepper to taste

1 head cauliflower, cut into florets

1 large egg

1 cup Parmesan cheese, shredded

1 tbsp butter, melted

Directions

Preheat the Air Fryer to 390°F. Blanch the cauliflower in salted boiling water for 5-6 minutes. Drain well and let it cool. Pulse in a food processor. Transfer to a bowl and mix in the egg, scallions, salt, pepper, and Parmesan.

Form the mixture into hash brown shapes. Arrange them on the greased air fryer basket. Brush them with butter and AirFry for 10-12 minutes, flipping them halfway through cooking until golden brown. Serve and enjoy!

No Water Hard-Boiled Eggs

Total Time: 20 min | **Serves:** 4 | **Per serving:** Cal 78; Net Carbs 0.7g; Fat 4.5g; Protein 6g

Ingredients

4 fresh eggs

Salt and hot paprika to taste

Directions

Preheat the Air Fryer to 250°F. Arrange the eggs on the air fryer basket and cook for 15-17 minutes. Once done, run them under cold water and peel right away. Slice the eggs in half lengthwise and season with salt and paprika.

Almond Blueberry Tart

Total Time: 40 min | **Serves:** 10 | **Per serving:** Cal 210; Net Carbs 10.2g; Fat 16g; Protein 3.4g

Ingredients

½ cup ground almonds

3 ½ cups almond flour

1 tsp baking powder

1 tsp ground cinnamon

3 eggs, lightly beaten

½ cup coconut oil

⅓ cup almond milk

2 tsp vanilla extract

2 cups blueberries

Directions

Spray a baking pan that fits in your air fryer with cooking spray. In a bowl, add almonds, almond flour, baking powder, and cinnamon and stir well. In another bowl, whisk eggs, oil, almond milk, and vanilla extract.

Stir the wet ingredients into the oat mixture. Fold in the blueberries. Pour the mixture into the baking pan and place it in the preheated to 330°F Air Fryer. Bake for 30 minutes. When ready, check if the bars are nice and soft.

Buttered Eggs in Hole

Total Time: 11 min | **Serves**: 2 | **Per serving**: Cal 220; Net Carbs 1g; Fat 16g; Protein 8g

Ingredients

2 low-carb bread slices
2 eggs

Salt and black pepper to taste
2 tbsp butter

Directions

Place a 3 X 3 cm heatproof bowl in the air fryer basket and brush with butter. Make a hole in the middle of the bread slices with a bread knife and place in the heatproof bowl in 2 batches. Break an egg into the center of each hole. Season with salt and pepper. Close the Air Fryer and cook for 4 minutes at 330°F. Turn the bread with a spatula and cook for another 4 minutes.

Keto Brown Bread

Total Time: 2 hrs 40 min | **Serves**: 4 | **Per serving**: Cal 396; Net Carbs 2.8g; Fat 36g; Protein 13g

Ingredients

8 oz almond flour
1 oz liquid stevia

1 egg, beaten
2 tbsp butter

Directions

Combine flour, stevia, and 3 oz of water. Keep mixing the components with your hands. Add the butter and knead the mixture very well. Let bread dough rest, keep warm and covered, for about 2 hours until it grows in size.

Divide the dough into small balls of 1 oz each and place them in the baking paper. Brush the balls with the egg. Let the dough rest again for 30 minutes. Place dough balls in a tray. Cook in the Air Fryer at 330°F until brown.

Homemade Bacon "Nachos"

Total Time: 20 min | **Serves**: 3 | **Per serving**: Cal 90; Net Carbs 0g; Fat 6g; Protein 6g

Ingredients

6 sugar-free bacon slices

½ tsp taco seasoning

Directions

Preheat the Air Fryer to 400°F. Cut the bacon slices into triangles and arrange them on the greased air fryer basket. Bake for 12 minutes, flipping once until crispy. Remove and sprinkle with taco seasoning.

Almond Raspberry Pancakes

Total Time: 15 min | **Serves**: 4 | **Per serving**: Cal 483; Net Carbs 10.8 g; Fat 15.6g; Protein 17g

Ingredients

2 cups almond flour
1 cup almond milk
3 eggs, beaten

1 tsp baking powder
1 ½ tsp vanilla extract
½ cup frozen raspberries, thawed

2 tbsp liquid stevia
Pinch of salt

Directions

Preheat the air fryer to 390°F. In a bowl, mix the almond flour, baking powder, salt, almond milk, eggs, vanilla extract, and stevia until smooth. Stir in the raspberries. Do it gently to avoid coloring the batter.

Grease a baking dish with cooking spray. Drop the batter onto the dish. Just make sure to leave some space between the pancakes. Bake for 10 minutes. Serve warm and enjoy!

Nut Choco Muffins

Total Time: 40 min | **Serves:** 6 | **Per serving:** Cal 306; Net Carbs 7.2g; Fat 32g; Protein 6g

Ingredients

½ cup butter, melted
½ cup powdered erythritol
2 eggs, lightly beaten
1 cup strawberries, mashed

1 tsp vanilla extract
2 cups almond flour
1 tsp baking powder
½ tsp baking soda

1 tsp ground cinnamon
½ cup hazelnuts, chopped
½ cup dark chocolate chips, unsweetened

Directions

Spray 6-hole muffin with cooking spray. In a bowl, whisk butter, erythritol, eggs, strawberries, and vanilla until well combined. Sift in almond flour, baking powder, baking soda, and cinnamon without overmixing.

Stir in the hazelnuts and chocolate. Pour the mixture into the muffin holes and place in the air fryer. Bake for 30 minutes at 350°F, checking at the around 20-minute mark. Serve chilled and enjoy!

Dijon Beet & Feta Salad

Total Time: 50 min | **Serves:** 4 | **Per serving:** Cal 225; Net Carbs 6.2g; Fat 16g; Protein 7g

Ingredients

4 large beets, stems trimmed
2 tbsp olive oil
Salt and pepper, to taste
3 tbsp red wine vinegar

¼ cup red onion, minced
2 cloves garlic, minced
1 ½ tbsp Dijon mustard
½ tbsp liquid stevia

1 tbsp fresh parsley, minced
½ tbsp fresh thyme leaves, minced
2 cups mixed baby lettuces
¾ cup feta cheese, crumbled

Directions

Preheat the Air Fryer to 390°F. Place the beets on aluminum foil and drizzle with oil. Season with salt and pepper. Close up with aluminum foil the beets. Transfer to the Air Fryer and AirFry for 45 minutes. Remove and let cool.

In a bowl, mix red onion, garlic, mustard, vinegar, and stevia. Whisk the ingredients until they are combined. Stir in the herbs and season with salt and pepper. When the beets are chilled, cut them into slices of half an inch. Arrange on a platter, top with feta cheese, and scatter the dressing over. Garnish with baby lettuce and serve.

Welsh-Style Rarebit

Total Time: 15 min | **Serves:** 2 | **Per serving:** Cal 405; Net Carbs 4.5g; Fat 27g; Protein 26g

Ingredients

4 zero-carb bread slices
1 tsp smoked paprika

2 eggs
1 tsp Dijon mustard

4 ½ oz cheddar cheese, grated
Salt and black pepper to taste

Directions

Whisk the eggs. Stir in mustard, cheddar cheese, and paprika. Season with salt and pepper. Spread the mixture on the toasts. Bake the bread in the air fryer for 10 minutes at 360°F.

Basic Crunchy Granola

Total Time: 15 min | **Serves:** 6 | **Per serving:** Cal 615; Net Carbs 2.8g; Fat 56g; Protein 10g

Ingredients

2 cups pecans, chopped
1 cup unsweetened coconut flakes
1 cup almond slivers
⅓ cup pumpkin seeds

¼ tsp coarse sea salt
¼ cup golden flaxseed
¼ cup sugar-free chocolate chips
¼ cup granular erythritol

2 tbsp unsalted butter
1 tsp ground cinnamon

Directions

Preheat the Air Fryer to 330°F. Thoroughly combine all ingredients and spread the mixture on a baking dish. Put the dish in the air fryer basket and Bake for 5-8 minutes, shaking once. Let cool completely and serve.

Breakfast Sausage & Egg Casserole

Total Time: 20 min | **Serves**: 6 | **Per serving**: Cal 494; Net Carbs 5.3g; Fat 41g; Protein 26g

Ingredients

1 lb breakfast sausage, minced
6 eggs
2 tbsp olive oil
1 red pepper, diced
1 green pepper, diced
1 yellow pepper, diced
1 onion, diced
2 cups cheddar cheese, shredded
Salt and black pepper to taste
Fresh parsley to garnish

Directions

Warm olive oil in a skillet over medium heat, add the sausage, and cook until brown, stirring occasionally. Once done, drain any excess fat derived from cooking; set aside. Arrange the sausage on the bottom of a greased casserole dish. Top with onion, red pepper, green pepper, and yellow pepper. Spread the cheese on top.

Beat the eggs and season with salt and black pepper. Pour the mixture over the casserole. Place the casserole dish in the air fryer basket, close the Air Fryer and bake at 355°F for 13-15 minutes. Serve garnished with fresh parsley.

Parsnips Hash Browns

Total Time: 45 min | **Serves**: 3 | **Per serving**: Cal 312; Net Carbs 1.6g; Fat 15g; Protein 16g

Ingredients

2 parsnips, shredded
Salt and black pepper to taste
1 tsp garlic powder
1 tsp chili flakes
1 tsp onion powder
1 egg, beaten
1 tbsp olive oil

Directions

Warm the olive oil in a skillet over medium heat and sauté the parsnips for 7-8 minutes until golden. Remove to a bowl and let cool. Combine the cooled parsnips with the egg, pepper, salt, chili flakes, onion powder, and garlic powder. On a flat plate, pour the mixture and transfer it to the fridge. Let it sit for 20 minutes.

Preheat the Air Fryer to 350°F. Remove from the fridge and cut into equal slices. Grease the basket with cooking spray and place the slices in the basket. AirFry for 15 minutes. Open the Air Fryer and flip them. Cook for another 6 minutes. Serve with sunshine eggs.

Traditional English Toast

Total Time: 15 min | **Serves**: 3 | **Per serving**: Cal 245; Net Carbs 7.2g; Fat 10.5g; Protein 11g

Ingredients

6 zero-carb bread slices
2 eggs
¼ cup heavy cream
⅓ cup powdered erythritol mixed
with 1 tsp ground cinnamon
6 tbsp sugar-free caramel topping

Directions

In a bowl, whisk eggs and cream. Dip each piece of bread into the egg and cream. Dip the bread into the cinnamon mixture until well-coated. On a clean board, lay the coated slices and spread three slices with about 2 tbsp of caramel topping each around the center. Place the remaining three slices on top to form three sandwiches.

Spray the air fryer basket with cooking spray. Arrange the sandwiches into the fryer and cook for 10 minutes at 340°F, turning once halfway through cooking.

Vanilla Coconut Scones

Total Time: 30 min | **Serves:** 4 | **Per serving:** Cal 167; Net Carbs 4.2g; Fat 15.4g; Protein 3.4g

Ingredients

2 cups almond flour
⅓ cup stevia
2 tsp baking powder

½ cup almonds, sliced
¾ cup coconut, shredded
¼ cup cold butter, cut into cubes

½ cup almond milk
1 egg
1 tsp vanilla extract

Directions

Line air fryer basket with baking paper. Mix together almond flour, stevia, baking powder, almonds, and coconut. Rub the butter into the dry ingredients with hands to form a sandy, crumbly texture.

Whisk egg, almond milk, and vanilla extract. Pour into the dry ingredients and stir to combine. Sprinkle a working board with almond flour, lay the dough and give it a few kneads. Shape into a rectangle and cut into 9 squares. Arrange the squares in the air fryer basket and cook for 14 minutes at 390°F.

Hot Egg Avocado Salad

Total Time: 7 min | **Serves:** 3 | **Per serving:** Cal 472; Net Carbs 4.2g; Fat 41g; Protein 17g;

Ingredients

6 cooked eggs
2 avocados, peeled and chopped
2 cups tomatoes, chopped

½ cup red onion, chopped
Salt and black pepper to taste
2 tbsp keto mayo

2 tbsp sour cream
1 tbsp lemon juice
6 drops hot sauce

Directions

In the basket of the Air Fryer, place thinly sliced eggs. Add the tomatoes, red onion, salt, and pepper. Set the timer to 7 minutes and the heat to 340°F. When ready, transfer the ingredients into a bowl. Stir in the mayo, the sour cream, the lemon juice, and the hot sauce. Garnish with avocado. Serve and enjoy!

Bacon & Chives Egg Cups

Total Time: 30 min | **Serves:** 10 | **Per serving:** Cal 245; Net Carbs 1.5g; Fat 21g; Protein 14g

Ingredients

10 eggs, lightly beaten
10 bacon rashers, chopped

½ cup chives, chopped
1 brown onion, chopped

1 cup cheddar cheese, grated
Salt and black pepper to taste

Directions

Spray a 10-hole muffin pan with cooking spray. In a bowl, add eggs, bacon, chives, onion, cheese, salt, and pepper; stir to combine. Pour into muffin pans and place inside the fryer. Cook for 12 minutes at 330°F until nice and set.

Spinach & Ham Eggs

Total Time: 8 min | **Serves:** 3 | **Per serving:** Cal 223; Net Carbs 3.1g; Fat 13g; Protein 18g

Ingredients

1 lb spinach
4 oz sliced ham

4 eggs
1 tbsp olive oil

4 tbsp water
Salt and black pepper to taste

Directions

Preheat the Air Fryer to 360°F. Butter 4 ramekins. In each ramekin, place the spinach, one egg, an ounce of ham, a tablespoon of water, salt, and pepper. Line the ramekins in the Air Fryer's basket. Set the timer to 10 minutes (6-7 minutes for runny eggs). Serve and enjoy!

Yellow Bell Peppers & Asparagus Salad

Total Time: 10 min | **Serves:** 3 | **Per serving:** Cal 232; Net Carbs 6.2g; Fat 16g; Protein 10g

Ingredients

1 lb asparagus, trimmed and cubed
2 yellow bell peppers, cut and cubed
¼ cup almonds, toasted

½ cup Parmesan cheese, grated
2 tbsp olive oil
2 tbsp Dijon mustard

2 cloves garlic, minced
2 tbsp lime juice
1 tbsp hot sauce

Directions

Preheat the Air Fryer to 390°F. Mix the asparagus and the bell peppers with 1 tbsp of olive oil. Cook them for 10 minutes in the Air Fryer Remove from the heat and add the almonds and Parmesan cheese. In another bowl, mix 1 tbsp of olive oil, mustard, garlic, lime juice, and hot sauce. Pour over the vegetables and serve.

Grandma's Zucchini Cakes

Total Time: 20 min | **Serves:** 4 | **Per serving:** Cal 357; Net Carbs 7.6g; Fat 25g; Protein 18g

Ingredients

1 ½ cups almond flour
1 tsp cinnamon
3 eggs
2 tsp baking powder

2 tbsp stevia
1 cup almond milk
2 tbsp butter, melted
1 tbsp yogurt

½ cup zucchini, shredded
Pinch of salt
2 tbsp cream cheese

Directions

Preheat the air fryer to 350°F. In a bowl, whisk the eggs along with the stevia, salt, cinnamon, cream cheese, almond flour, and baking powder. In another bowl, combine all liquid ingredients. Combine dry and liquid mixtures; stir in zucchini. Line the muffin tins and pour the batter into the tins. Cook for 12 minutes. Serve.

Sausage Thai Omelet

Total Time: 20 min | **Serves:** 3 | **Per serving:** Cal 253; Net Carbs 2.2g; Fat 11g; Protein 11g

Ingredients

4 eggs
2 tbsp fish sauce
2 tbsp white pepper powder
Juice from ½ lime

2 cloves garlic, minced
1 minced shallot
½ cup sausage, finely cut
1 handful fresh spinach

1 fresh green onion, chopped
2 tsp cilantro, chopped

Directions

Preheat the air fryer to 350°F. Crack the eggs into a large bowl. Add in fish sauce and pepper. Whisk until bubbles start to appear in the mixture. Add the remaining ingredients and keep whisking until well combined. Pour the mixture into a baking pan and place it in the air fryer basket. Bake for 10 minutes. Sprinkle with cilantro and serve.

Buttered Scrambled Eggs

Total Time: 6 min | **Serves:** 1 | **Per serving:** Cal 180; Net Carbs 0.2g; Fat 14g; Protein 11g

Ingredients

2 eggs

¼ oz butter, melted

Salt and black pepper to taste

Directions

Preheat the Air Fryer to 350°F. Break and whisk the eggs. Brush the air fryer basket with butter and add the beaten eggs. Bake for 6 minutes. Sprinkle with salt and pepper and serve immediately.

Modern Pumpkin Pie

Total Time: 30 min | **Serves:** 4 | **Per serving:** Cal 267; Net Carbs 3.2g; Fat 19g; Protein 8g

Ingredients

2 large eggs, beaten
¼ cup water

¼ cup pumpkin purée
¼ tsp pumpkin pie spices

4 slices low-carb bread
¼ cup butter

Directions

Preheat the Air Fryer to 350°F. In a large bowl, mix the eggs, the water, the pumpkin, and the pie spice. Whisk until you obtain a smooth mixture. Dip both sides of the bread in the egg mixture. Place the rack inside the air fryer basket. Bake for 10 minutes. Brush the pumpkin pie with butter and let it cool slightly. Serve and enjoy!

Mozzarella & Ham Sandwiches

Total Time: 25 min | **Serves:** 2 | **Per serving:** Cal 275; Net Carbs 6.2g; Fat 13g; Protein 18g

Ingredients

4 zero-carb bread slices
2 tbsp mayonnaise
2 slices ham

2 lettuce leaves
1 tomato, sliced
2 slices mozzarella cheese

Salt and black pepper to taste

Directions

On a clean board, lay the zero-carb bread slices and spread with mayonnaise. Top 2 of the slices with ham, lettuce, tomato, and mozzarella cheese. Season with salt and pepper. Top with the remaining two slices to form two sandwiches. Spray with cooking spray and transfer to the air fryer. Cook for 14 minutes at 340°F, flipping once halfway through cooking. Serve hot!

Roasted Balsamic Radishes with Mozzarella

Total Time: 35 min | **Serves:** 4 | **Per serving:** Cal 235; Net Carbs 2.6g; Fat 15g; Protein 19g

Ingredients

1 lb radishes with their tops
2 tbsp olive oil

Salt and black pepper to taste
½ lb mozzarella cheese

2 tbsp balsamic vinegar

Directions

Preheat the air fryer to 350°F. Trim the wilted stems from the radishes and cut them into quarters. Place the radishes in the air fryer basket and coat them with oil, salt, and pepper. Roast them for 10-12 minutes, shaking halfway through the cooking time. Remove to a plate and drizzle with balsamic vinegar. Top with cheese to serve.

Roasted Cabbage Salad

Total Time: 30 min | **Serves:** 3 | **Per serving:** Cal 145; Net Carbs 5.2g; Fat 10g; Protein 3g

Ingredients

2 tbsp olive oil
½ head green cabbage cut into 4

wedges
A pinch of garlic powder

A pinch of red pepper flakes
2 small halved lemons

Directions

Preheat the Air Fryer to 390°F. Brush the sides of each of the cabbage wedges with olive oil. Sprinkle with garlic powder and add a pinch of red pepper flakes and salt. Roast the cabbage wedges in the Air Fryer for 30 minutes. Make sure to flip them at least once. Squeeze lemon juice and enjoy its delicious taste!

Prosciutto & Mozzarella Egg Cups

Total Time: 20 min | **Serves:** 2 | **Per serving:** Cal 291; Net Carbs 5.9g; Fat 20.5g; Protein 13g

Ingredients

2 zero-carbs bread slices
2 prosciutto slices, chopped
2 eggs

4 tomato slices
¼ tsp balsamic vinegar
2 tbsp grated mozzarella cheese

¼ tsp stevia
2 tbsp mayonnaise

Directions

Preheat the air fryer to 320 degrees.

Grease 2 ramekins. Place one bread slice in the bottom of each ramekin. Top with tomato slices, mozzarella, and chopped prosciutto. Crack the eggs on top. Drizzle with stevia and balsamic vinegar. Bake for 10 minutes or until until golden and set. Top with mayonnaise. Let them cool slightly before releasing from the ramekins. Serve.

Raspberry & Almond Muffins

Total Time: 15 min | **Serves:** 4 | **Per serving:** Cal 75; Net Carbs 0.6g; Fat 7g; Protein 1.3g

Ingredients

¼ cup ground almonds
½ cup raspberries
1 cup almond flour

1 tbsp baking powder
A pinch of salt
1 egg

1 tbsp liquid stevia
¾ cup almond milk

Directions

Preheat the Air Fryer to 300°F. Combine the flour, ground almonds, raspberries, and baking powder in a bowl. In another bowl, whisk the eggs with stevia until thick. Pour in the almond milk and stir. Divide the batter between 4 ramekins. Bake in the Air Fryer for 15 minutes until a toothpick inserted comes out dry and clean. Serve chilled.

Feta Frittata with Chorizo Sausage

Total Time: 12 min | **Serves:** 2 | **Per serving:** Cal 354; Net Carbs 7.4 g; Fat 22g; Protein 20g

Ingredients

3 eggs
1 large turnip, boiled and cubed
½ cup feta cheese, crumbled

1 tbsp parsley, chopped
½ chorizo sausage, sliced
3 tbsp olive oil

Salt and black pepper to taste

Directions

Pour the olive oil into the air fryer and preheat it to 330°F. Cook the chorizo just so it becomes slightly browned. Beat the eggs with some salt and pepper in a bowl. Stir in all of the remaining ingredients. Pour the mixture into the air fryer and cook for 6 minutes. Serve and enjoy!

Basil & Kale Omelet

Total Time: 15 min | **Serves:** 1 | **Per serving:** Cal 294; Net Carbs 3.9g; Fat 19.5g; Protein 24.7 g

Ingredients

3 eggs
3 tbsp cottage cheese

3 tbsp kale, chopped
½ tbsp basil, chopped

Salt and black pepper to taste
1 tsp olive oil

Directions

Preheat the Air Fryer to 380°F. Beat the eggs with salt and pepper in a bowl. Stir in the rest of the ingredients. Spoon the mixture into a greased baking pan and bake for 6-8 minutes until set and golden. Serve and enjoy!

Morning Muffins

Total Time: 20 min | **Serves:** 4 | **Per serving:** Cal 214; Net Carbs 6.3g; Fat 17g; Protein 3g

Ingredients

1 ¼ cups almond flour
¼ cup mashed strawberries
¼ cup powdered erythritol

1 tsp almond milk
1 tbsp walnuts, chopped
½ tsp baking powder

¼ cup butter, room temperature

Directions

Preheat the air fryer to 320°F. Place the erythritol, walnuts, strawberries, and butter in a bowl; mix to combine. In another bowl, combine the almond flour and baking powder. Combine the two mixtures together and stir in the milk. Spoon the batter into a greased muffin tin. Bake in your air fryer for 10-15 minutes. Serve and enjoy!

Cheesy Parsnip & Spinach Frittata

Total Time: 35 min | **Serves:** 4 | **Per serving:** Cal 235; Net Carbs 8.2g; Fat 9.5g; Protein 17.4g

Ingredients

2 cups parsnip cubes, boiled, soft
2 cups spinach, chopped
5 eggs, lightly beaten

¼ cup heavy cream
1 cup mozzarella cheese, grated
½ cup parsley, chopped

Fresh thyme, chopped
Salt and black pepper to taste

Directions

Spray the air fryer's basket with oil. Arrange the parsnip cubes inside. Whisk eggs, cream, spinach, mozzarella, parsley, thyme, salt, and pepper and pour over the parsnips. Cook for 16 minutes at 400°F, until nice and golden.

Blackberry Bars with Almonds

Total Time: 40 min | **Serves:** 6 | **Per serving:** Cal 210; Net Carbs 10.2g; Fat 16g; Protein 3.4g

Ingredients

2 cups blackberries
½ cup ground almonds
3 ½ cups almond flour

1 tsp baking powder
1 tsp ground cinnamon
3 eggs, lightly beaten

½ cup coconut oil
⅓ cup almond milk
2 tsp vanilla extract

Directions

Preheat the Air Fryer to 300°F. In a bowl, stir the almonds, baking powder, almond flour, and cinnamon. In a second bowl, beat the eggs, oil, almond milk, and vanilla. Stir in the almond mixture and fold in the blackberries. Pour the mixture into a greased baking pan. Bake for 30 minutes. Allow to cool completely. Cut into bars. Serve.

Breakfast Eggs

Total Time: 15 min | **Serves:** 2 | **Per serving:** Cal 220; Net Carbs 1g; Fat 16g; Protein 8g

Ingredients

2 ham slices
2 zero-carb bread slices

2 eggs
Salt and black pepper to taste

2 tbsp butter

Directions

Preheat the Air Fryer to 330°F. Place a heatproof bowl in the fryer and grease with butter. Grease the bread slices with butter and cover each one with a piece of ham. Crack an egg into the center of each slice and season with salt and pepper. Cook for 4 minutes. Serve and enjoy!

Blueberry Cake with Chocolate

Total Time: 40 min | **Serves:** 8 | **Per serving:** Cal 317; Net Carbs 9.2g; Fat 24g; Protein 6g

Ingredients

1 ½ cups hazelnut flour
½ tsp salt
⅓ cup cocoa powder
2 tsp baking powder
¼ cup stevia

¾ cup butter
2 tsp vanilla extract
1 cup almond milk
1 tsp baking soda
2 eggs

1 cup blueberries
1 cup dark chocolate chips, unsweetened

Directions

Combine the hazelnut flour, salt, cocoa powder, and baking powder in a bowl. In a microwave-safe bowl, combine the stevia, butter, vanilla, almond milk, and baking soda. Heat for 60 seconds. Let cool.

Beat the eggs into the mixture. Combine the wet ingredients with the dry ones and toss to coat. Add in the blueberries and chocolate chips. Pour the mixture into the tin and bake in the Air Fryer at 350°F for 30 minutes.

Healthy Almond Bread

Total Time: 40 min | **Serves:** 6 | **Per serving:** Cal 215; Net Carbs 0.6g; Fat 22g; Protein 6.5g

Ingredients

¾ cup almond flour
1 tbsp baking powder
½ tsp almond extract

6 eggs
½ tbsp erythritol
A pinch of salt

½ cup olive oil

Directions

Preheat the Air Fryer to 325°F. In a bowl, mix the almond flour with baking powder. Set aside. In a second bowl, whisk the eggs, almond extract, oil, erythritol, and a pinch of salt. Put in the dry ingredients and stir. Pour the mixture into a greased baking pan and place in the air fryer and cook for 35 minutes. Serve and enjoy!

Chocolate & Blueberry Sandwiches

Total Time: 30 min | **Serves:** 2 | **Per serving:** Cal 256; Net Carbs 9.6g; Fat 15g; Protein 14g

Ingredients

1 tbsp mascarpone
4 zero-carb bread slices

6 oz dark chocolate, chopped
1 cup blueberries

Directions

Brush the bread slices with mascarpone. Arrange the chocolate and blueberries on 2 pieces of bread. Top with the remaining 2 slices. Place the sandwiches in the air fryer basket and cook for 14 minutes, flipping once. Serve.

Green Onion & Cheese Omelet

Total Time: 15 min | **Serves:** 1 | **Per serving:** Cal 347.3; Net Carbs 6 g; Fat 23.2 g; Protein 13g

Ingredients

2 eggs
2 tbsp cheddar cheese, grated

1 tsp soy sauce, sugar-free
1 green onion, sliced

¼ tsp pepper
1 tbsp olive oil

Directions

Preheat the air fryer to 350°F. Whisk the eggs along with the pepper and soy sauce. Heat the olive oil and add the egg mixture and the onion. Cook for 8-10 minutes. Top with the grated cheddar cheese. Serve and enjoy!

Mediterranean Quiche

Total Time: 40 min | **Serves:** 2 | **Per serving:** Cal 540; Net Carbs 7.4g; Fat 44g; Protein 25.8g

Ingredients

4 eggs
½ cup chopped tomatoes
1 cup feta cheese, crumbled
1 tbsp basil, chopped

1 tbsp oregano, chopped
¼ cup kalamata olives, chopped
¼ cup onion, chopped
2 tbsp olive oil

½ cup almond milk
Salt and black pepper to taste

Directions

Preheat the air fryer to 340°F. Brush a pie pan with olive oil. Beat the eggs along with almond milk, salt, and pepper. Stir in all of the remaining ingredients. Pour the egg mixture into the pan. Cook for 30 minutes. Serve.

Steamed Asparagus Omelet

Total Time: 8 min | **Serves:** 2 | **Per serving:** Cal 287; Net Carbs 2g; Fat 23g; Protein 15g

Ingredients

3 eggs
1 tbsp Parmesan cheese

2 tbsp warm water
A pinch of salt

A pinch of black pepper
5 steamed asparagus tips

Directions

Whisk eggs, cheese, water, salt, and pepper in a bowl. Spray a pan with cooking spray. Pour the egg mixture into the pan and add the asparagus. Cook in the air fryer for 5 minutes at 320°F. Serve and enjoy!

Tuscan Omelet

Total Time: 10 min | **Serves:** 2 | **Per serving:** Cal 328; Net Carbs 6.2g; Fat 24g; Protein 21g

Ingredients

4 eggs, lightly beaten
2 tbsp heavy cream
2 cups spinach, chopped

1 cup mushrooms, chopped
3 oz feta cheese, crumbled
A handful of fresh parsley, chopped

Salt and black pepper to taste

Directions

Spray your air fryer basket with oil spray. In a bowl, whisk eggs and until combined. Stir in heavy cream, spinach, mushrooms, feta, parsley, salt and pepper. Pour into the basket and cook for 6 minutes at 350°F. Serve immediately with a touch of tangy tomato relish.

Cardamom French Toasts

Total Time: 13 min | **Serves:** 3 | **Per serving:** Cal 335; Net Carbs 3.5g; Fat 22.3g; Protein 25.3g

Ingredients

½ tsp cardamom powder
5 zero-carb bread slices

3 eggs
1 ½ tbsp butter

½ tsp clove powder
2 tbsp heavy whipping cream

Directions

Preheat Air Fryer to 350°F. In a bowl, whisk clove powder, eggs, and cardamom powder. Brush both sides of the bread with butter and cut into 4 strips. Dip in the egg mixture.

Place it in the fryer and cook for 2 minutes. Once ready, take out the basket, turn the toast, and spray with oil on the other side. Back the basket to the fryer and cook for another 4 minutes until golden brown. Transfer to a plate and top with heavy whipping cream to serve.

Vanilla Peanut Butter Cake

Total Time: 20 min | **Serves:** 8 | **Per serving:** Cal 287; Net Carbs 0.8g; Fat 31g; Protein 4g

Ingredients

1 cup butter
2 tbsp peanut butter
¼ cup xylitol

1 tbsp pure vanilla extract
6 egg yolks
3 cups almond flour

¼ tsp salt
1 egg, beaten

Directions

Preheat the Air Fryer to 350°F. With an electric mixer, blitz the butter, peanut butter and xylitol until fluffy. Add in almond flour, vanilla, egg yolks, and salt. Pour the mixture into a greased baking pan. Transfer to the fridge for 15 minutes. Brush the mixture with beaten eggs and place in the air fryer basket. Bake for 35 minutes. Serve chilled.

Morning Eggs with Ground Beef

Total Time: 20 min | **Serves:** 6 | **Per serving:** Cal 494; Net Carbs 5.3g; Fat 41g; Protein 26g

Ingredients

1 lb ground beef
6 eggs
2 tbsp olive oil
1 red pepper, diced

1 green pepper, diced
1 yellow pepper, diced
1 onion, diced
2 cups cheddar cheese, shredded

Salt and black pepper to taste
Fresh parsley to garnish

Directions

Preheat the Air Fryer to 355°F. In a skillet over medium heat, warm the olive oil and brown the ground beef. Blot the excess fat and set aside. Grease a casserole with oil and place the beef on the bottom.

Put in the onion, red, green and yellow pepper and top with cheddar cheese. Whisk the eggs with salt and black pepper and pour over the casserole. Cook for 13-15 minutes. Serve garnished with parsley.

Sweet Potato French Toast

Total Time: 26 min | **Serves:** 4 | **Per serving:** Cal 267; Net Carbs 3.2g; Fat 19g; Protein 8g

Ingredients

¼ cup mashed sweet potatoes
2 large eggs, beaten

¼ cup water
¼ tsp ground clove

4 zero-carb bread slices
¼ cup butter

Directions

Preheat Air Fryer to 340°F. Whisk the eggs, water, mashed sweet potatoes, and ground clove until smooth. Dip each bread slice into the egg mixture and place in the basket. Cook for 10 minutes. Serve with butter.

Mustard & Mozzarella Breakfast

Total Time: 15 min | **Serves:** 2 | **Per serving:** Cal 405; Net Carbs 4.5g; Fat 27g; Protein 26g

Ingredients

4 ½ oz mozzarella cheese, grated
3 zero-carb bread slices

1 tsp paprika
2 eggs

1 tsp Dijon mustard
Salt and black pepper to taste

Directions

Preheat the Air Fryer to 360°F. Toast the bread slices in the air fryer until it's to your liking. Beat the eggs in a bowl and add the mustard, mozzarella cheese, and paprika and stir to combine. Sprinkle with salt and pepper. Arrange the toasted bread slices on a baking pan and pour the egg mixture over. Cook for 10 minutes. Serve warm.

Classic Scramble Eggs with Prosciutto

Total Time: 6 min | **Serves:** 1 | **Per serving:** Cal 180; Net Carbs 0.2g; Fat 14g; Protein 11g

Ingredients

2 eggs
1 prosciutto slice

¼ oz butter, melted
Salt and black pepper to taste

Directions

Preheat the Air Fryer to 240°F. Grease the air fryer basket with butter. Crack and beat the eggs. Season with salt and pepper. Add in prosciutto. Place the eggs in the basket and cook for 6 minutes. Serve and enjoy!

Cinnamon Almond Mini Cakes

Total Time: 30 min | **Serves:** 4 | **Per serving:** Cal 167; Net Carbs 4.2g; Fat 15.4g; Protein 3.4g

Ingredients

¼ teaspoon ground cinnamon
2 cups almond flour
⅓ cup stevia
2 tsp baking powder

1 cup almonds, sliced
¼ cup cold butter, cubed
½ cup almond milk
1 egg

1 tsp vanilla extract
Pinch of salt

Directions

Preheat the Air Fryer to 390°F. Line the basket with baking paper. Combine the almond flour, stevia, baking powder and almonds. Add in the butter and mix to create a crumbly texture. Beat the egg, almond milk, vanilla extract, cinnamon, and salt. Stir with the almond mix.

Rub a flat surface with almond flour and lay the dough. Knead them a few times and form a rectangle. Cut into 9 squares. Place the squares in the basket and cook for 14 minutes. Serve right away.

Kale & Bacon Quiche

Total Time: 8 min | **Serves:** 3 | **Per serving:** Cal 223; Net Carbs 3.1g; Fat 13g; Protein 18g

Ingredients

1 lb kale
4 oz sliced bacon

4 eggs
1 tbsp olive oil

4 tbsp water
Salt and black pepper to taste

Directions

Preheat Air Fryer to 360°F. Grease 4 ramekins with olive oil. Put in each ramekin the kale, one egg, 1 ounce of bacon, and 1 tbsp of water. Season with salt and pepper. Place in the fryer and cook for 10 minutes. Enjoy!

Spinach & Chorizo Omelet

Total Time: 20 min | **Serves:** 2 | **Per serving:** Cal 253; Net Carbs 2.2g; Fat 11g; Protein 11g

Ingredients

½ chorizo, chopped
4 eggs
2 tbsp tamari sauce
White pepper to taste

Juice from ½ lime
2 cloves garlic, minced
1 minced shallot
1 handful fresh spinach

1 fresh green onion, chopped
1 tbsp parsley, chopped

Directions

Preheat the Air Fryer to 360°F. In a bowl, beat the eggs, tamari sauce, and white pepper. Stir in the remaining ingredients until well mixed. Pour the mixture into a greased baking dish. Bake for 6-8 minutes. Serve and enjoy!

Macadamia Muffins with Chocolate Chips

Total Time: 40 min | **Serves:** 6 | **Per serving:** Cal 306; Net Carbs 7.2g; Fat 32g; Protein 6g

Ingredients

½ cup macadamia nuts, chopped
½ cup butter, melted
½ cup powdered erythritol
2 eggs, lightly beaten

1 cup strawberries, mashed
1 tsp vanilla extract
2 cups almond flour
1 tsp baking powder

½ tsp baking soda
1 tsp ground cinnamon
½ cup dark chocolate chips, unsweetened

Directions

Preheat the Air Fryer to 350°F. Grease 10-hole muffin with cooking spray. In a bowl, beat the butter, erythritol, eggs, strawberries, and vanilla. Add in the almond flour, baking powder, baking soda, and cinnamon. Stir well without overmixing. Put in the macadamia nuts and chocolate chips and stir. Pour the mixture into the muffin holes and place in the fryer. Cook for 30 minutes. Serve and enjoy!

Chives Omelet with Grated Cheddar

Total Time: 15 min | **Serves:** 1 | **Per serving:** Cal 347.3; Net Carbs 6 g; Fat 23.2 g; Protein 13g

Ingredients

2 chives, chopped
2 eggs

2 tbsp cheddar cheese, grated
1 tsp soy sauce, sugar-free

¼ tsp pepper
1 tbsp olive oil

Directions

Preheat the Air Fryer to 350°F. Beat the eggs with pepper and soy sauce. Heat the olive oil in the fryer basket and pour in the egg mixture. Add in the chives and cook for 8-10 minutes. Serve topped with grated cheddar cheese.

Funny Strawberry Pancakes

Total Time: 15 min | **Serves:** 4 | **Per serving:** Cal 483; Net Carbs 10.8 g; Fat 15.6g; Protein 17g

Ingredients

½ cup strawberries
2 cups almond flour
1 cup almond milk

3 eggs, beaten
1 tsp baking powder
1 cup erythritol, powdered

1 ½ tsp almond extract
2 tbsp liquid stevia

Directions

Preheat the Air Fryer to 390°F. Combine the almond flour, baking powder, almond milk, eggs, almond extract, stevia, and erythritol until smooth in a bowl. Add in the strawberries. Grease a baking dish with cooking spray. Pour in the mixture and cook for 10 minutes. Repeat the process until no batter is left. Serve and enjoy!

Sweet Mixed Nuts

Total Time: 15 min / **Serves:** 5 | **Per serving:** Cal 147; Net Carbs 10g; Fat 12g; Protein 3g

Ingredients

2 cups mixed nuts of choice
2 tbsp xylitol

2 tbsp egg whites
2 tsp allspice

Directions

In a bowl, combine xylitol and allspice. In a second bowl, combine the mixed nuts and egg whites. Stir the allspice mixture into the nuts. Grease the air fryer basket with cooking spray. Put in the nuts and cook for 10 minutes, shaking once. Leave to cool before serving. Enjoy!

Sweet Toasts

Total Time: 15 min | **Serves:** 3 | **Per serving:** Cal 245; Net Carbs 7.2g; Fat 10.5g; Protein 11g

Ingredients

⅓ cup powdered erythritol mixed with 1 tsp cinnamon
6 zero-carb bread slices   ¼ cup heavy cream
2 eggs   6 tbsp sugar-free maple syrup

Directions

Preheat the Air Fryer to 340°F. Beat the eggs with heavy cream. Dip each bread slice in the egg mixture, then in the cinnamon mixture until coat. Place the coated slices on a flat surface and dress 3 slices with the maple syrup. Place the remaining slices on top. Grease the air fryer basket with cooking spray. Place the sandwiches in the fryer and cook for 10 minutes. Turn once during cooking time. Serve and enjoy!

Cheese & Turkey Bacon Sandwiches

Total Time: 25 min | **Serves:** 2 | **Per serving:** Cal 275; Net Carbs 6.2g; Fat 13g; Protein 18g

Ingredients

2 slices turkey bacon   2 lettuce leaves   Salt and black pepper to taste
4 zero-carb bread slices   1 tomato, sliced
2 tbsp mayonnaise   2 slices cheddar cheese

Directions

Preheat the Air Fryer to 340°F. Place the bread slices on a clean surface and spread with mayonnaise. Place one of the bacon slices, lettuce, tomato and cheddar on two of the slices. Sprinkle with salt and pepper. Top with the remaining slices. Spray with cooking spray. Place the sandwiches in the fryer; cook for 14 minutes. Turn once.

Pumpkin Mini Cakes

Total Time: 20 min | **Serves:** 4 | **Per serving:** Cal 357; Net Carbs 7.6g; Fat 25g; Protein 18g

Ingredients

½ cup pumpkin, shredded   2 tsp baking powder   1 tbsp yogurt
1 ½ cups almond flour   2 tbsp stevia   Pinch of salt
1 tsp cinnamon   1 cup almond milk   2 tbsp cream cheese
3 eggs   2 tbsp butter, melted

Directions

Preheat the Air Fryer to 350°F.

In a bowl, beat eggs with stevia, salt, cinnamon, cream cheese, almond flour, and baking powder. In a second bowl, mix all the liquid ingredients. Combine the dry and liquid mixtures. Stir in pumpkin. Pour the mixture into the muffin tins. Bake for 15 minutes until a toothpick inserted comes out dry and clean. Serve cooled and enjoy!

Pecan & Raspberry Muffins

Total Time: 20 min | **Serves:** 4 | **Per serving:** Cal 214; Net Carbs 6.3g; Fat 17g; Protein 3g

Ingredients

¼ cup mashed raspberries   1 tsp almond milk   ¼ cup butter, room temperature
1 ¼ cups almond flour   1 tbsp pecans, chopped
¼ cup powdered erythritol   ½ tsp baking powder

Directions

Preheat the Air Fryer to 320°F. In a bowl, combine the erythritol, pecans, raspberries, and butter. In a second bowl, mix the almond flour and baking powder. Combine together the flour mixture and raspberry mixture. Add in the almond milk and stir. Grease a muffin tin with butter. Spoon the mixture in the tin. Bake for 15 minutes.

Tofu & Kale Omelet

Total Time: 15 min | **Serves:** 1 | **Per serving:** Cal 294; Net Carbs 3.9g; Fat 19.5g; Protein 24.7 g

Ingredients

3 tbsp tofu
3 eggs

3 tbsp kale, chopped
½ tbsp parsley, chopped

Salt and black pepper to taste
1 tsp olive oil

Directions

Preheat the Air Fryer to 360°F. In a bowl, whisk the eggs with salt and pepper. Add in the remaining ingredients and stir. Pour the mixture in a baking dish. Bake for 6-8 minutes until golden and set. Serve and enjoy!

Grilled Ham Sandwiches

Total Time: 10 min | **Serves:** 1 | **Per serving:** Cal 452; Net Carbs 2.3g; Fat 32g; Protein 17g

Ingredients

2 slices ham

2 tsp butter

2 zero-carb bread slices

Directions

Preheat Air Fryer to 370°F. Brush bread slices with butter. Put 1 ham slice on each bread slice and top with another piece of bread. Place in the fryer and cook for 8 minutes, turning once. Slice diagonally and serve.

Baked Tomato Cups

Total Time: 12 min | **Serves:** 3 | **Per serving:** Cal 131; Net Carbs 2g; Fat 5g; Protein 13g

Ingredients

1 cup cheddar cheese, shredded
3 large tomatoes, halved

Salt and black pepper to taste
2 tbsp herbs de Provençe

3 bacon slices, chopped

Directions

Preheat the Air Fryer to 320°F. Remove the pulp and seeds of the tomatoes; season with salt and pepper. Season with herbs and fill them with cheese and bacon. Place in the air fryer and cook for 8 minutes. Serve hot.

Mozzarella & Celery Frittata

Total Time: 35 min | **Serves:** 4 | **Per serving:** Cal 235; Net Carbs 8.2g; Fat 9.5g; Protein 17.4g

Ingredients

¼ celery root, cubed, boiled, soft
2 cups spinach, chopped
5 eggs, lightly beaten

¼ cup heavy cream
1 cup mozzarella cheese, grated
½ cup parsley, chopped

Fresh thyme, chopped
Salt and black pepper to taste

Directions

Preheat the Air Fryer to 400°F. Grease the air fryer basket with oil. Place the celery cubes in the basket. Beat the eggs with heavy cream, spinach, mozzarella cheese, parsley, thyme, salt, and pepper. Pour the egg mixture over the celery and Bake for 16 minutes until nice and golden. Serve and enjoy!

Goat Cheese & Olive Quiche

Total Time: 40 min | **Serves:** 2 | **Per serving:** Cal 540; Net Carbs 7.4g; Fat 44g; Protein 25.8g

Ingredients

1 cup goat cheese, crumbled
4 eggs
½ cup chopped tomatoes
1 tbsp basil, chopped

1 tbsp oregano, chopped
¼ cup black olives, chopped
¼ cup onion, chopped
2 tbsp olive oil

½ cup almond milk
Salt and black pepper to taste

Directions

Preheat the Air Fryer to 340°F. Grease a pie pan with olive oil. Whisk the eggs with almond milk, salt, and pepper. Add in the remaining ingredients and stir. Pour the mixture into the pan and cook for 30 minutes. Enjoy!

Italian Fritatta

Total Time: 10 min | **Serves:** 2 | **Per serving:** Cal 328; Net Carbs 6.2g; Fat 24g; Protein 21g

Ingredients

2 cups Swiss chard, chopped
4 eggs, lightly beaten
2 tbsp heavy cream

1 cup mushrooms, chopped
3 oz ricotta cheese, crumbled
A handful of fresh parsley, chopped

Salt and black pepper to taste

Directions

Preheat the Air Fryer to 350°F. Grease the air fryer basket with oil spray. In a bowl, beat the eggs. Add in the Swiss chard, mushrooms, heavy cream, ricotta cheese, parsley, salt, and pepper and stir. Spoon the mixture into a greased baking pan. Bake for 6 minutes. Garnish with tomato relish if desired. Serve immediately.

Turnip & Salami Frittata

Total Time: 12 min | **Serves:** 2 | **Per serving:** Cal 354; Net Carbs 7.4 g; Fat 22g; Protein 20g

Ingredients

½ salami, sliced
3 eggs

1 large turnip, boiled and cubed
½ cup feta cheese, crumbled

3 tbsp olive oil
Salt and black pepper to taste

Directions

Preheat the Air Fryer to 330°F. Grease the air fryer basket with olive oil. Place the salami in the fryer and cook until it becomes slightly browned. Whisk the eggs with salt and pepper. Add in the remaining ingredients and stir. Pour the mixture over the salami and cook for 6 minutes. Serve and enjoy!

Simple Hazelnut Cake

Total Time: 45 min | **Serves:** 6 | **Per serving:** Cal 183; Net Carbs 0.5g; Fat 21g; Protein 1.7g

Ingredients

1 cup toasted hazelnuts, chopped
1 cup butter

½ cup liquid stevia
4 large eggs

2 cups almond flour

Directions

Preheat the Air Fryer to 350°F. Grease and flour a jelly roll pan. In a bowl, place the butter, toasted hazelnuts, and stevia and mix until the mixture becomes light and soft. Beat in the eggs, one by one. Add in the almond flour and mix until smooth. Place the dough in the roll pan and Bake for 40 minutes. Serve and enjoy!

SNACKS & APPETIZERS

Cheese-Stuffed Meatballs

Total Time: 30 min | **Serves**: 4 | **Per serving**: Cal 445; Net Carbs 1.9g; Fat 30g; Protein 29.9g

Ingredients

½ lb ground beef
½ lb ground pork
¼ cup almond flour
1 tsp dried parsley

½ tsp garlic powder
¼ tsp shallot powder
1 egg
3 oz Monterey Jack cheese, cubed

½ cup sugar-free pasta sauce
¼ cup grated Parmesan cheese
Salt and black pepper to taste

Directions

Preheat the Air Fryer to 360°F. In a bowl, combine the ground beef, ground pork, almond flour, parsley, garlic powder, shallot powder, egg, salt, and pepper and knead with your hands. Shape the mixture into meatballs.

Place a cheese cube in the middle of each ball. Seal the meat around the cheese. Repeat with the remaining ingredients. Arrange the meatballs in the air fryer basket and AirFry for 14-16 minutes or until cooked through and golden. Remove the meatballs to a platter, pour over pasta sauce, and sprinkle with parmesan cheese. Serve.

Party Pepperoni Pizza Rolls

Total Time: 25 min + chilling time | **Serves**: 6 | **Per serving**: Cal 330; Net Carbs 0.8g; Fat 23.8g; Protein 21g

Ingredients

½ cup almond flour
2 cups mozzarella cheese, shredded
2 large eggs, beaten

72 pepperoni slices
24 mozzarella cheese sticks
2 tbsp butter, melted

¼ tsp paprika
½ tsp dried oregano
2 tbsp grated Pecorino cheese

Directions

Microwave the mozzarella cheese and almond flour for 50-60 seconds. Remove, add the beaten egg, and stir the mixture until a smooth ball is formed. Place the dough on a parchment sheet and cover it with another sheet. With a rolling pin, roll the dough out to ¼-inch thickness. Cut the dough into 24 rectangles. Divide the pepperoni slices and mozzarella sticks onto one side of each of the rectangles, roll up jelly-roll style using wet hands, and pinch the edge to seal. Transfer them to the refrigerator and chill for 20 minutes.

Preheat the Air Fryer to 360°F. Arrange the rolls on a foil-lined air fryer basket. AirFry for 10-12 minutes, flipping them halfway through cooking, until golden and crisp. Remove the rolls and brush them with butter. Sprinkle with oregano, paprika, and Pecorino cheese. Serve immediately.

Cheese Pork Rind Nachos

Total Time: 10 min | **Serves**: 2 | **Per serving**: Cal 390; Net Carbs 0.9g; Fat 27g; Protein 29.9g

Ingredients

4 oz cooked chicken, shredded
1 oz pork rinds
½ cup cheddar cheese, shredded

¼ tsp cumin
1 jalapeño pepper, sliced
1 avocado, sliced

¼ cup sour cream
½ cup hot sauce
Salt and black pepper to taste

Directions

Preheat the Air Fryer to 340°F. Add the pork rinds to a baking pan. Top with chicken, cheddar cheese, salt, pepper, and cumin. Place the pan in the air fryer basket and Bake for 4-6 minutes until the cheese melts. Remove and pour the sour cream and hot sauce over the meal. Top with avocado slices and jalapeño pepper and serve.

Homemade Beef Jerky

Total Time: 25 min + marinating time | **Serves**: 6 | **Per serving**: Cal 80; Net Carbs 0.2g; Fat 3.2g; Protein 9.9g

Ingredients

1 lb flank steak, thinly sliced
¼ cup soy sauce
2 tsp Worcestershire sauce

¼ tsp ancho chili powder
¼ tsp garlic powder
¼ tsp onion powder

¼ tsp smoked paprika

Directions

Add all the ingredients, except for the steak, to a large bowl and stir well. Add in the steak and toss to coat. Cover with plastic wrap and place in the refrigerator to marinate for at least 2 hours.

Preheat the Air Fryer to 380°F. Arrange the beef slices on the air fryer basket in a single layer. Work in batches if necessary. Cook for 14-16 minutes. Let cool slightly and serve.

Barbecue Roasted Almonds

Total Time: 15 min | **Serves**: 6 | **Per serving**: Cal 180; Net Carbs 1.2g; Fat 16g; Protein 6g

Ingredients

Salt and black pepper to taste
1 ½ cup raw almonds
1 ½ tbsp olive oil

1 tsp chili powder
¼ tsp cumin
¼ tsp smoked paprika

¼ tsp onion powder
¼ tsp garlic powder
¼ tsp cayenne pepper

Directions

Preheat the Air Fryer to 330°F. In a mixing bowl, place all the ingredients and toss to coat. Transfer the almonds to the air fryer basket. Cook for 6-8 minutes, shaking the basket once or twice. Let cool. Serve.

No-Crust Meat Lovers Pizza

Total Time: 20 min | **Serves**: 1 | **Per serving**: Cal 465; Net Carbs 1.8g; Fat 34g; Protein 28g

Ingredients

1 tsp olive oil
½ cup mozzarella cheese, shredded
6 pepperoni slices

¼ cup cooked ground sausage
2 bacon slices, cooked and crumbled
1 tbsp Parmesan cheese, grated

2 tbsp sugar-free pizza sauce
3 black olives
½ tsp dried oregano

Directions

Preheat the Air Fryer to 390°F. Spread the mozzarella cheese onto a cake pan. Sprinkle with olive oil and oregano. Top with pepperoni, sausage, and bacon. Scatter the Parmesan over the top. Place the pan in the air fryer and Bake for 5 minutes until golden and bubbling. Allow to cool slightly. Top with olives and serve with pizza sauce.

Homemade Cheese Bread

Total Time: 20 min | **Serves**: 4 | **Per serving**: Cal 260; Net Carbs 3.4g; Fat 17g; Protein 19g

Ingredients

1 tsp butter, melted
2 cups shredded mozzarella cheese

½ cup grated Parmesan cheese
2 eggs

½ tsp garlic powder
2 green onions, chopped

Directions

Preheat the Air Fryer to 340°F. In a mixing bowl, thoroughly combine all the ingredients. Transfer to a foil-lined baking pan and mold the mixture into a round bread shape. Place in the air fryer basket and cook for about 10 minutes, flipping once. Allow the bread to cool slightly. Serve and enjoy!

Hot & Spicy Spinach Artichoke Dip

Total Time: 20 min | **Serves**: 6 | **Per serving**: Cal 225; Net Carbs 3.1g; Fat 16g; Protein 9.8g

Ingredients

2 cups canned artichoke hearts, chopped

1 tbsp avocado oil	¼ cup mayonnaise	¼ cup Parmesan cheese, grated
10 oz frozen spinach, thawed	¼ cup sour cream	1 cup Monterey Jack cheese, shredded
¼ cup pickled jalapeños, chopped	½ tsp garlic powder	
8 oz cream cheese, softened	½ tsp cayenne pepper	

Directions

Preheat the Air Fryer to 390°F. In a mixing bowl, thoroughly combine all the ingredients. Transfer the to a baking dish and insert the dish in the frying basket. Bake for about 10 minutes or until brown and bubbling. Serve warm.

Sweet Mini Pepper Poppers

Total Time: 25 min | **Serves**: 4 | **Per serving**: Cal 178; Net Carbs 2.1g; Fat 13.2g; Protein 7.5g

Ingredients

8 assorted mini sweet peppers	4 bacon slices, cooked and crumbled	Salt and black pepper to taste
4 oz cream cheese, softened	¼ cup cheddar cheese, shredded	¼ tsp garlic powder

Directions

Preheat the Air Fryer to 390°F. Cut the peppers a quarter way from the head down and lengthwise. Remove the membrane and seeds. Season the peppers with garlic powder, black pepper, and salt. Place them in the air fryer basket. Divide the cream cheese between the peppers and top with bacon and cheddar cheese. Bake for 6-8 minutes or until the peppers are tender and the top is golden brown. Serve.

Onion Rings Wrapped in Bacon

Total Time: 15 min | **Serves**: 4 | **Per serving**: Cal 102; Net Carbs 2.1g; Fat 6g; Protein 7.3g

Ingredients

1 yellow onion, sliced into rings	8 bacon slices	¼ tsp chili powder
1 tbsp sriracha sauce	Salt and black pepper to taste	¼ tsp granulated garlic

Directions

Preheat the Air Fryer to 350°F. Season the onion rings with salt, black pepper, granulated garlic, and chili powder and brush them with sriracha sauce. Wrap doubled-up rings with bacon and transfer them to the greased frying basket. AirFry for 10-12 minutes or until golden and crispy. Serve and enjoy!

Spicy Bacon-Wrapped Brussels Sprouts

Total Time: 25 min | **Serves**: 4 | **Per serving**: Cal 245; Net Carbs 1.5g; Fat 18g; Protein 14g

Ingredients

12 bacon strips	2 tbsp sugar-free maple syrup	1 lemon, zested
12 Brussels sprouts, trimmed	1 tsp cayenne pepper	

Directions

Preheat the Air Fryer to 380°F. Lay the strips of bacon on a working surface. Brush them with maple syrup and sprinkle with cayenne pepper and lemon zest. Place a Brussels sprout on one end of each strip and roll them over. Arrange the wrapped sprouts on the frying basket and AirFry for 14-16 minutes until the bacon is crispy. Serve.

Chicken Wings Alla Parmigiana

Total Time: 30 min | **Serves:** 4 | **Per serving:** Cal 568; Net Carbs 0g; Fat 42g; Protein 42g

Ingredients

2 lb chicken wings
Salt and black pepper to taste
1 garlic clove, minced

¼ cup olive oil
½ tsp chili oil
⅓ cup Parmesan cheese, grated

¼ tsp dried thyme

Directions

Preheat the Air Fryer to 390°F. In a mixing bowl, thoroughly combine the olive oil, chili oil, garlic, salt, pepper, and thyme. Add in the wings and toss to combine. Transfer them to the air fryer basket and AirFry for 23 minutes, tossing the basket once or twice. Once the time is over, sprinkle the Parmesan over the wings. Serve warm.

Classic Cheesy Jalapeños

Total Time: 30 min | **Serves:** 4 | **Per serving:** Cal 148; Net Carbs 1.7g; Fat 19g; Protein 14g

Ingredients

6 jalapeños, halved lengthwise, seeds and white membranes removed
3 oz cream cheese, softened
⅓ cup cheddar cheese, shredded

¼ tsp garlic powder
¼ tsp chives, chopped

12 bacon slices

Directions

Preheat the Air Fryer to 390°F. In a bowl, combine cream cheese, garlic powder, and chives. Smear the cheese mixture into the jalapeño halves and top with cheddar cheese. Wrap each jalapeño half with a slice of bacon and secure with a toothpick. Arrange them on the frying basket and AirFry for 12 minutes, turning once. Serve warm.

Asparagus Wrapped in Parma Ham

Total Time: 20 min | **Serves:** 4 | **Per serving:** Cal 162; Net Carbs 2.1g; Fat 20g; Protein 14g

Ingredients

12 asparagus spears, trimmed
12 Parma ham slices

1 tbsp olive oil
⅛ tsp red pepper flakes

⅓ cup Parmesan cheese, grated
2 tbsp butter, melted

Directions

Preheat the Air Fryer to 370°F. Wrap each asparagus spear with a slice of Parma ham, drizzle with olive oil and arrange them on the air fryer basket. AirFry for 8-10 minutes. At the 5-minute mark, turn the asparagus over and sprinkle with Parmesan cheese. Cook for another 5 minutes. Serve topped with butter and red pepper flakes.

Jalapeño Cheddar Bread with Bacon

Total Time: 25 min | **Serves:** 4 | **Per serving:** Cal 275; Net Carbs 0.8g; Fat 18g; Protein 20g

Ingredients

2 cups cheddar cheese, shredded
¼ cup Parmesan cheese, grated

¼ cup pickled jalapeños, chopped
2 eggs

4 bacon slices
2 green onions, thinly sliced

Directions

Preheat the Air Fryer to 400°F. Place the bacon in the frying basket and AirFry for 5 minutes, flipping once. Remove and let cool slightly, then chop into small pieces. Mix in the remaining ingredients.

Transfer to a foil-lined baking pan and mold the mixture into a round bread shape. Place in the frying basket, reduce temperature to 330°F, and Bake for 14-16 minutes, flipping once. Let cool slightly and serve.

Awesome Vegetable Croquettes

Total Time: 65 min | **Serves:** 4 | **Per serving:** Cal 224; Net Carbs 8.6g; Fat 14.2g; Protein 10.3g

Ingredients

1 ½ cups pork rinds, crushed
1 lb turnips
2 cups water
¼ cup coconut milk
Salt to taste
2 tsp + 3 tsp butter

2 tsp olive oil
2 red peppers, chopped
½ cup baby spinach, chopped
3 mushrooms, chopped
¼ cup broccoli florets, chopped
1/6 cup sliced green onions

½ red onion, chopped
2 cloves garlic, minced
1 medium carrot, grated
⅓ cup almond flour
1 cup unsweetened almond milk
2 tbsp arrowroot starch

Directions

Boil the turnips in a pot over medium heat until tender and mashable. Drain and pour into a bowl. Add 2 teaspoons of butter, coconut milk, and salt. Mash well and set aside. Melt the remaining butter in a skillet over medium heat. Add the onion, garlic, red peppers, broccoli, carrot, and mushrooms. Stir and cook the veggies for 2 minutes. Add the green onions and spinach. Cook until the spinach wilts. Season salt and stir. Turn the heat off and pour the veggies in the turnip mash. Use the potato masher to mash the veggies into the turnip. Cool.

Using your hands, form balls of the mixture. In 3 separate bowls, pour the pork rinds in one, almond flour in the second bowl, and arrowroot starch, almond milk, and salt in the third bowl. Mix the arrowroot starch with almond milk and salt with a fork. Remove the patties from the fridge.

Preheat the Air Fryer to 390°F. Dredge each veggie mold in almond flour, then in the arrowroot starch mixture, and then in the pork rinds. Place the patties in batches in a single layer in the fryer basket without overlapping. Spray them with olive oil cooking spray and cook them for 2 minutes. Flip and spray with cooking spray and continue cooking for 3 minutes. Remove to a wire rack and serve with tomato sauce.

Spicy Cheeseburger Dip with Bacon

Total Time: 30 min | **Serves:** 6 | **Per serving:** Cal 455; Net Carbs 2.1g; Fat 35g; Protein 22g

Ingredients

½ tsp red pepper flakes
1 cup cream cheese, softened
¼ cup mayonnaise
¼ cup sour cream

¼ cup onion, chopped
2 garlic cloves, minced
1 tbsp Worcestershire sauce
1 ¼ cups mozzarella cheese, shredded

½ lb cooked ground beef
6 bacon slices, cooked and crumbled
2 pickle spears, chopped

Directions

Preheat the Air Fryer to 390°F. Microwave the cream cheese for 40-50 seconds. Remove, add the mayonnaise, sour cream, onion, garlic, Worcestershire sauce, red pepper flakes, and 1 cup of mozzarella cheese and mix to combine. Add the cooked ground beef and bacon. Spread the mixture on a greased baking dish and top with the remaining cheese. Bake in the air fryer for 10-12 minutes or until it is bubbling. Sprinkle with pickles.

Carrot Crisps

Total Time: 20 min | **Serves:** 2 | **Per serving:** Cal 35; Net Carbs 6g; Fat 0g; Protein 1g

Ingredients

3 large carrots, sliced   Salt to taste

Directions

Season carrots with salt to taste. Open the Air Fryer, grease the fryer basket lightly with cooking spray, and add the carrot strips to it. Close the Air Fryer and fry at 350°F for 6 minutes. Pull out the fryer basket, and stir the carrots with a spoon. Cook further for 4 minutes or until crispy. Serve with dipping sauce of your choice.

Bacon & Chicken Wrapped Jalapenos

Total Time: 35 min | **Serves**: 6 | **Per serving**: Cal 523; Net Carbs 8.7g; Fat 42.8g; Protein 49.6g

Ingredients

8 jalapeno peppers, halved
4 chicken breasts, butterflied
6 oz cream cheese

6 oz cheddar cheese
16 slices bacon
1 cup pork rinds, crushed

Salt and black pepper to taste
2 eggs

Directions

Wrap the chicken in cling film and place on a chopping board. Using a rolling pin, pound the chicken evenly to flatten them but not too thin. Afterward, remove the cling film and season the chicken with pepper and salt on both sides. In a bowl, add the cream cheese, cheddar cheese, a pinch each of pepper, and salt. Mix well.

Take each jalapeno and spoon in the cheese mixture to the brim. On a chopping board, flatten each piece of chicken and lay 2 bacon slices each on them. Place a stuffed jalapeno on each laid out chicken and bacon set and wrap the peppers in them. Set aside.

Preheat the Air Fryer to 350°F. Add the eggs to a bowl and pour the pork rinds into another bowl. Also, set a flat plate aside. Take each wrapped jalapeno and dip it into the eggs and then thoroughly in the pork rinds. Place them on the flat plate. Open the Air Fryer and lightly grease the fryer basket with cooking spray.

Arrange 4 to 5 jalapenos in the fryer basket, close the Air Fryer and cook for 7 minutes. Prepare a paper towel-lined plate and set aside. Once the timer beeps, open the Air Fryer, turn the jalapenos, close and cook for 4 minutes. Once ready, remove them onto the paper towel-lined plate and repeat the cooking process for the remaining peppers. Serve with sweet dip.

The Best Zucchini Fries

Total Time: 25 min | **Serves**: 4 | **Per serving**: Cal 367; Net Carbs 5g; Fat 28g; Protein 11g

Ingredients

3 medium zucchini, sliced
2 egg whites

½ cup seasoned pork rinds, crushed
2 tbsp Parmesan cheese, grated

¼ tsp garlic powder
Salt and black pepper to taste

Directions

Preheat your Air Fryer to 425°F. Coat cooling rack with cooking spray and place in your air fryer's cooking basket. In a mixing bowl, beat the egg whites and season with salt and pepper. In another bowl, mix garlic powder, cheese, and pork rinds. Take zucchini slices and dredge them in eggs, followed by pork rinds. Add zucchini to the rack and spray more oil. cook for 20 minutes. Serve and enjoy!

Quick Pork Rind Tortillas

Total Time: 15 min | **Serves**: 4 | **Per serving**: Cal 140; Net Carbs 0.6g; Fat 9.8g; Protein 11g

Ingredients

¾ cup Mexican cheese, shredded
2 tbsp cream cheese

2 tbsp pork rinds, finely ground
1 large egg, beaten

1 tsp taco seasoning
¼ tsp chili powder

Directions

Preheat the Air Fryer to 390°F. Microwave Mexican and cream cheeses for 35 seconds. Remove, add the pork rinds, taco seasoning, chili powder, and egg, and stir the mixture until a smooth ball is formed.

Divide the mixture into 4 balls. Place each ball on a parchment sheet and cover with another sheet. With a rolling pin, roll out the dough to ¼-inch thickness. Repeat until you run out of ingredients. Transfer the tortillas to the greased frying basket and Bake for 6 minutes or until golden and crispy. Serve.

Caper Eggplant with Crispy Mozzarella Crust

Total Time: 30 min | **Serves:** 3 | **Per serving:** Cal 317; Net Carbs 2g; Fat 16.8g; Protein 12g

Ingredients

1 cup eggplants, cubed
¼ cup red pepper, chopped
¼ cup green pepper, chopped
¼ cup yellow onion, chopped
⅓ cup tomatoes, chopped

1 clove garlic, minced
1 tbsp pimiento-stuffed olives, sliced
1 tsp capers
¼ tsp dried basil
¼ tsp dried marjoram

Salt and black pepper to taste
¼ cup mozzarella cheese, grated
1 tbsp pork rinds, crushed

Directions

Preheat the Air Fryer to 300°F. In a bowl, add the eggplant, green pepper, red pepper, onion, tomatoes, olives, garlic, basil marjoram, capers, salt, and pepper. Lightly grease a baking dish with the cooking spray.

Ladle the eggplant mixture into the baking dish and level it using the vessel. Sprinkle the mozzarella cheese on top of it and top it with the pork rinds. Place the dish in the Air Fryer and cook it for 20 minutes.

Crunchy Kale Chips

Total Time: 15 min | **Serves:** 2 | **Per serving:** Cal 167; Net Carbs 2.9g; Fat 15g; Protein 5g

Ingredients

2 tbsp olive oil
4 cups kale, stemmed

1 tsp vegan seasoning
1 tbsp yeast flakes

Sea salt to taste

Directions

In a bowl, mix the oil, the kale and the vegan seasoning. Add the yeast and mix well. Dump the coated kale in the Air fryer basket. Cook for 5 minutes 370°F. Shake after 3 minutes. Serve sprinkled with salt.

Speedy Grilled Cheese

Total Time: 15 min | **Serves:** 1 | **Per serving:** Cal 452; Net Carbs 2.3g; Fat 32g; Protein 17g

Ingredients

2 tsp butter

2 slices zero carb bread

3 slices American cheese

Directions

Preheat the air fryer to 370°F. Spread 1 tsp of butter on the outside of each of the bread. Place the cheese on the inside of one bread slice. Top with the other slice. Cook for 4 minutes. Flip the sandwich over and cook for 4 more minutes. Slice diagonally and serve.

Celery Salmon Balls

Total Time: 15 min | **Serves:** 2 | **Per serving:** Cal 389; Net Carbs 1.6g; Fat 32g; Protein 25g

Ingredients

6 oz tinned salmon
1 large egg
4 tbsp celery, chopped

4 tbsp spring onion, sliced
1 tbsp fresh dill, chopped
½ tbsp garlic powder

5 tbsp pork rinds, crushed
3 tbsp olive oil

Directions

Preheat the Air Fryer to 370°F. In a large bowl, mix salmon, egg, celery, onion, dill, and garlic powder. Shape the mixture into golf ball size balls and roll them in pork rinds. Heat the oil in a skillet. Add the salmon balls and slowly flatten them. Then transfer them to the Air Fryer and fry for about 10 minutes.

Button Mushrooms with Cheese

Total Time: 55 min | **Serves:** 4 | **Per serving:** Cal 378; Net Carbs 7.3g; Fat 20.4g; Protein 38g

Ingredients

2 cups Parmigiano Reggiano cheese, grated
1 lb small button mushrooms
2 cups pork rinds, crushed

2 eggs, beaten
Salt and black pepper to taste

Directions

Preheat the Air Fryer to 360°F. Pour the pork rinds in a bowl, add the salt and pepper and mix well. Pour the cheese into a separate bowl and set aside. Dip each mushroom in the eggs, then in the pork rinds, and then in the cheese. Slide out the fryer basket and add 6 to 10 mushrooms to it. Close the Air Fryer and cook them for 20 minutes. Once ready, remove to a serving plate and repeat the cooking process for the remaining mushrooms.

Parmesan Crusted Pickles

Total Time: 35 min | **Serves:** 4 | **Per serving:** Cal 255; Net Carbs 4.2g; Fat 15.5g; Protein 24.7g

Ingredients

3 cups large dill pickles, sliced
2 eggs

2 tsp water
1 cup Parmesan cheese, grated

1 ½ cups pork rinds, crushed
Black pepper to taste

Directions

Mix the pork rinds and black pepper in a bowl. Beat the eggs with water. Add the cheese to a separate bowl. Line a flat surface with a paper towel and arrange the pickle slices on it to extra as much water from them.

Preheat the Air Fryer to 400°F. Pull out the fryer basket and spray it lightly with cooking spray. Dredge the pickle slices it in the egg mixture, then in pork rinds and then in cheese. Pull out the fryer basket and lay as many coated pickle slices in it without overlapping. Slide the fryer basket back in and cook for 4 minutes. Turn the pickles over. Cook further for 4-5 minutes until crispy. Once ready, remove onto a serving platter and serve with a cheese dip.

Garlic Calamari Rings

Total Time: 18 min | **Serves:** 2 | **Per serving:** Cal 233; Net Carbs 6.1g; Fat 16.5; Protein 15.2g

Ingredients

½ pound calamari, sliced into rings
¾ cup Parmesan cheese, shredded
2 medium eggs, beaten

1 tsp garlic powder
A pinch of salt
1 cup almond flour

1 tsp paprika powder

Directions

Preheat the Air Fryer to 350°F. Add the eggs to a bowl. Set aside. In another bowl, add the cheese, garlic powder, salt, almond flour, and paprika powder. Mix them using a spoon. Dip each calamari ring in egg, then in the cheese mixture, in the egg again and finally in the cheese mixture. Slide out the fryer basket and add the rings to it. Cook them for 8 minutes. Remove them onto a serving platter and serve with a cheese or tomato dip.

Savory Coconut Shrimp

Total Time: 40 min | **Serves:** 5 | **Per serving:** Cal 260; Net Carbs 2g; Fat 14g; Protein 8g

Ingredients

1 lb jumbo shrimp, peeled and deveined
¾ cup unsweetened coconut, grated
1 tbsp erythritol

½ cup pork rinds, crushed
⅓ cup arrowroot starch

½ cup coconut milk

Directions

Pour the arrowroot starch in a zipper bag, add the shrimp, zip the pocket up and shake to coat. Preheat the Air Fryer to 350°F. Mix erythritol and coconut milk in a bowl. In a separate bowl, mix the pork rinds and shredded coconut. Open the zipper bag and remove shrimp while shaking off excess starch on it.

Dip in the coconut milk mixture and then in the pork rinds mixture while pressing loosely to trap enough pork rinds and shredded coconut. Slide out the fryer basket and place the coated shrimp in it without overcrowding. Cook the shrimp for 12 minutes, flipping once until golden brown. Serve the shrimp with a coconut-based dip.

PinWheels

Total Time: 6 min | **Serves:** 4 | **Per serving:** Cal 392; Net Carbs 3.2g; Fat 35g; Protein 15g

Ingredients

2 lb dill pickles
1 lb cream cheese, softened

3 oz ham, sliced
2 almond tortillas

Directions

Preheat the Air Fryer to 340°F. Spread the cream cheese on one side of the tortilla. Put a slice of ham over it. Spread a layer of cheese on top of the ham. Roll 1 pickle up in the tortilla. Place the rolls in the air fryer basket of the Air Fryer and cook for 6 minutes. Serve and enjoy!

Spicy Chicken Wings

Total Time: 45 min | **Serves**: 4 | **Per serving**: Cal 295; Net Carbs 1.8g; Fat 21g; Protein 35g

Ingredients

16 chicken wings
Salt and black pepper to taste

⅓ cup hot sauce
⅓ cup butter

½ tbsp white vinegar

Directions

Preheat the Air Fryer to 360°F. Season the wings with pepper and salt. Slide out the fryer basket, add the wings to it and cook for 35 minutes. Toss them every 5 minutes. Once ready, remove them into a bowl.

Melt the butter in a saucepan over medium heat. Add the butter and melt it. Add the vinegar and hot sauce. Stir and cook for a minute. Turn the heat off. Pour the sauce over the chicken. Toss to coat well. Transfer the chicken to a serving platter. Serve with a side of celery strips and blue cheese dressing.

Avocado Wrapped in Bacon

Total Time: 40 min | **Serves**: 6 | **Per serving**: Cal 193; Net Carbs 2.3g; Fat 18g; Protein 3.4g

Ingredients

12 thick bacon strips
3 avocados

⅓ tsp salt
⅓ tsp chili powder

⅓ tsp cumin powder

Directions

Using a knife, cut open the avocados, remove the seeds and slice them into 24 pieces without the skin. Stretch the bacon strips to elongate them and use a knife to cut in half to make 24 pieces. Wrap the bacon around avocado slices from one end to the other end. Tuck the end of bacon into the wrap.

Arrange the wrapped avocado on a flat surface and sprinkle with salt, chili, and cumin on both sides. Slide out the fryer basket and arrange 4 to 8 wrapped pieces in it. Slide the fryer basket in and cook at 350°F for 8 minutes or until the bacon is browned and crunchy, flipping halfway through to cook evenly. Remove onto a wire rack and repeat the process for the remaining avocado pieces.

Hot Chicken Dip

Total Time: 20 min | **Serves**: 4 | **Per serving**: Cal 470; Net Carbs 7.2g; Fat 32g; Protein 26g

Ingredients

1 cup cooked chicken breasts, chopped
8 oz cream cheese, softened
½ cup buffalo sauce
1 tsp Worcestershire sauce

¼ tsp cayenne pepper
¼ tsp chili powder
⅓ cup ranch dressing
⅓ cup pickled jalapeños, chopped

1 ½ cups Monterey Jack cheese, grated
2 scallions, sliced

Directions

Preheat the Air Fryer to 360°F. In a mixing bowl, whisk the cream cheese, buffalo sauce, Worcestershire sauce, cayenne pepper, chili powder, and ranch dressing. Add in the chicken and jalapeños and stir well. Fold in half of the cheese. Spread the mixture on the bottom of a greased baking dish and top with the remaining cheese. Insert the dish in the frying basket and AirFry for 10-12 minutes until it is bubbling. Sprinkle with scallions and serve.

Tasty Chicken Nuggets

Total Time: 25 min + chilling time | **Serves**: 4 | **Per serving**: Cal 523; Net Carbs 6.9g; Fat 46.1g; Protein 46.9g

Ingredients

2 chicken breasts
2 tbsp paprika
2 cups coconut milk

2 eggs
4 tsp onion powder
1 ½ tsp garlic powder

Salt and black pepper to taste
2 cups almond flour
2 cups pork rinds, crushed

Directions

Cut the chicken into 1-inch chunks. In a small bowl, add the paprika, onion powder, garlic powder, salt, pepper, almond flour, and pork rinds. Mix well. In another bowl, whisk the eggs with coconut milk. Prepare a tray aside. Dip each chicken chunk in the egg mixture. Place them on the tray and refrigerate for 1 hour.

Preheat the Air Fryer to 370°F. Remove the chicken and roll each chunk in the pork rind mixture. Place the crusted chicken in the fryer basket. Spray with cooking spray. AirFry for 4 minutes. Pull out the fryer basket, flip the chicken chunks, spray with cooking spray, and cook further for 4 minutes. Prepare a wire rack and remove the chicken onto it once ready. Serve the nuggets with a tomato dipping sauce or sugar-free ketchup. Yummy!

Paprika Cheesy Sausage Balls

Total Time: 60 min | **Serves**: 6 | **Per serving**: Cal 326; Net Carbs 1g; Fat 26.6g; Protein 19.6g

Ingredients

1 ½ lb ground sausages
2 ¼ cups cheddar cheese, shredded
¾ cups almond flour
½ cup coconut flour

¾ tsp baking soda
4 eggs
¾ cup sour cream
1 tsp dried oregano

1 tsp smoked paprika
2 tsp garlic powder
½ cup melted coconut oil

Directions

Heat a greased pan over medium heat. Add the sausages and brown for 3-4 minutes. Drain the excess fat derived from cooking and set aside. Add the baking soda, almond flour, and coconut flour to a bowl. Set aside.

In another bowl, add the eggs, sour cream, oregano, paprika, coconut oil, and garlic powder. Whisk to combine well. Combine the egg and flour mixtures. Add the cheese and sausages. Fold in and let it sit for 5 minutes to thicken. Rub your hands with coconut oil and mold out bite-size balls out of the batter. Chill for 15 minutes.

Preheat the Air Fryer to 350°F. Remove the sausage balls from the fridge, slide out the fryer basket, and add as much of the balls to it without overcrowding. Slide the fryer basket in and cook them for 10 minutes. Transfer to a serving platter once ready and repeat the cooking process for any remaining balls. Serve with salsa.

Tortilla Chips

Total Time: 55 min | **Serves**: 3 | **Per serving**: Cal 165; Net Carbs 3g; Fat 14.4g; Protein 4.7g

Ingredients

1 cup almond flour
Salt and black pepper to taste
1 tbsp golden flaxseed meal
2 cups cheddar cheese, shredded

Directions

Preheat the Air Fryer to 350°F. Pour the cheddar cheese into a medium-sized microwave-safe dish and melt it in the microwave for 1 minute. Remove the bowl in 15-second intervals to stir the cheese. Once melted, remove the bowl and quickly add the almond flour, salt, flaxseed meal, and pepper. Mix well with a fork.

On a chopping board, place the dough, and knead it with your hands while warm until the ingredients are well combined. Divide the dough into two, and, using a rolling pin, roll them out flat into two rectangles.

Use a pastry cutter to cut out triangle-shaped pieces and line them in 1 layer on a baking dish. Open the Air Fryer and grease the fryer basket lightly with cooking spray. Arrange some triangle chips in 1 layer in the fryer basket without touching or overlapping. Spray with cooking spray. Close the Air Fryer and cook for 8 minutes.

Cilantro Cheese Balls

Total Time: 50 min | **Serves**: 6 | **Per serving**: Cal 176; Net Carbs 5g; Fat 15g; Protein 5g

Ingredients

2 cups crumbled cottage cheese
2 cups Parmesan cheese, grated
2 turnips, peeled and chopped
1 medium onion, finely chopped
1 ½ tsp red chili flakes
1 green chili, finely chopped
Salt to taste
4 tbsp cilantro leaves, chopped
1 cup almond flour
1 cup pork rinds, crushed

Directions

Place the turnips in a pot, add water and bring them to boil over medium heat on a stovetop for 25 to 30 minutes until soft. Drain the turnips and place them in a bowl. With a potato masher, mash the turnips and leave to cool.

Add the cottage cheese, Parmesan cheese, onion, red chili flakes, green chili, salt, cilantro leaves, and almond flour to the turnip mash. Mix the ingredients well and mold out bite-size balls of the mixture. Pour the pork rinds into a bowl and roll each cheese ball lightly in it. Place them on a tray.

Preheat Air Fryer to 350°F. Open it and place 8 to 10 cheese balls in the fryer basket. Cook them for 15 minutes. Once ready, remove to a plate. Repeat the cooking process for the remaining balls. Serve with tomato-based dip.

Chili Calamari with Olives

Total Time: 25 min | **Serves**: 3 | **Per serving**: Cal 218; Net Carbs 5.3g; Fat 16.5g; Protein 4.6g

Ingredients

1 cup pimiento-stuffed green olives, sliced
½ lb calamari rings
2 tbsp cilantro, chopped
2 strips chili pepper, chopped
1 tbsp olive oil
Salt and black pepper to taste

Directions

Add the calamari rings, chili pepper, salt, black pepper, oil, and cilantro in a bowl. Mix and leave the calamari to marinate for 10 minutes. Pour the calamari into an oven-safe bowl, good enough to fit into the fryer basket. Slide the fryer basket out, place the bowl in it, and slide the basket back in. Cook the calamari for 15 minutes at 390°F, stirring every 5 minutes using a spoon. After 15 minutes, open the Air Fryer, and add the olives. Stir, close the Air Fryer and continue cooking for 3 minutes. Once ready, transfer to a serving platter. Serve warm.

Effortless Mozzarella Sticks

Total Time: 2 hrs 20 min | **Serves:** 4 | **Per serving:** Cal 288; Net Carbs 2.9g; Fat 11g; Protein 39g

Ingredients

12 mozzarella string cheese
2 cups ground pork rinds

3 eggs
4 tbsp coconut milk

Directions

Pour the pork rinds into a medium bowl. Crack the eggs into another bowl and beat with the coconut milk. One after the other, dip each cheese sticks in the egg mixture, in the pork rinds, then the egg mixture again, and then in the pork rinds again. Place the coated cheese sticks on a cookie sheet and freeze for 2 hours.

Preheat the Air Fryer to 380°F. Pull out the fryer basket and arrange the cheese sticks in it without overcrowding. Slide the fryer basket back in and cook for 5 minutes, flipping them halfway to brown evenly. Remove them to a plate and repeat the cooking process for the remaining sticks.

Italian Salmon Croquettes

Total Time: 40 min | **Serves:** 6 | **Per serving:** Cal 433; Net Carbs 4.1g; Fat 25g; Protein 48.2g

Ingredients

15 oz tinned salmon, flaked
1 cup grated onion
1 ½ cups grated carrots
3 large eggs

1 ½ tbsp chives, chopped
4 tbsp mayonnaise
4 tbsp pork rinds, crushed
2 ½ tsp Italian seasoning

Salt and black pepper to taste
2 ½ tsp lemon juice

Directions

In a mixing bowl, add the salmon, onion, carrots, eggs, chives, mayonnaise, pork rinds, Italian seasoning, pepper, salt, and lemon juice and mix well. Using your hands, form 2-inch thick oblong balls from the mixture of as much as you can get. Put the croquettes on a flat tray and refrigerate for 45 minutes to make them compact. Pull out the fryer basket and grease with cooking spray.

Preheat the Air Fryer to 380°F. Remove the croquettes from the fridge and arrange them on the greased fryer basket without overcrowding. Re-spray with cooking spray. Slide the fryer basket in and cook for 6 minutes until crispy. Flip the patties, spray with oil, and continue cooking for 4 minutes. Serve with a dill dip.

Chili Cheese Lings

Total Time: 25 min | **Serves:** 4 | **Per serving:** Cal 112; Net Carbs 3.1g; Fat 5.6g; Protein 2.8g

Ingredients

4 tbsp grated cheddar cheese + extra for rolling
1 cup almond flour + extra for kneading
¼ tsp chili powder
½ tsp baking powder

3 tsp butter
A pinch of salt

Directions

Add the cheese, almond flour, baking powder, chili powder, butter, and salt to a bowl. Mix well. The mixture should be crusty. Add some drops of water and mix well to get a dough. Remove the dough to a chopping board. Rub some extra flour in your palms and knead the dough for a while. Sprinkle some more flour on the flat surface and roll the dough out into a thin sheet using a rolling pin. Cut the dough into your desired shapes.

Preheat the Air Fryer to 350°F. Pull out the fryer basket and add the cheese lings. Close the Air Fryer and cook for 2 minutes. Open the Air Fryer, toss the cheese lings, and continue cooking for 3 minutes.

Cauliflower & Mushroom Balls

Total Time: 50 min | **Serves:** 6 | **Per serving:** Cal 95; Net Carbs 3g; Fat 5.8g; Protein 5.6g

Ingredients

½ lb mushrooms, diced
2 tbsp olive oil
1 small red onion, chopped
3 cloves garlic, minced

3 cups cauli rice
2 tbsp vegetable stock
1 cup pork rinds, crushed
1 cup Grana Padano cheese

¼ cup coconut oil
2 sprigs fresh thyme, chopped
Salt and black pepper to taste

Directions

Warm the olive oil in a skillet over medium heat. Add the garlic and onion. Sauté until translucent. Add the mushrooms, stir and cook for about 4 minutes. Add the cauli rice and constantly stir-fry for 5 minutes. Add the stock and thyme and simmer until the cauli rice has absorbed the stock.

Stir in Grana Padano cheese, pepper, and salt. Turn off the heat. Allow the mixture cooling and make bite-size balls of the mix. Place them on a plate and refrigerate them for 30 minutes to harden.

Preheat the Air Fryer to 350°F. In a bowl, add the pork rinds and coconut oil and mix well. Remove the mushroom balls from the refrigerator, stir the pork rind mixture again, and roll the balls in the pork rind mixture. Place the balls in the fryer basket without overcrowding and cook for 15 minutes while tossing every 5 minutes for an even cook. Repeat this process until all the mushroom balls have fried.

Mozzarella & Pepperoni Mushrooms

Total Time: 15 min | **Serves:** 3 | **Per serving:** Cal 340; Net Carbs 3.8g; Fat 19g; Protein 37g

Ingredients

3 portobello mushrooms, stems removed
3 tbsp olive oil
3 tbsp tomato sauce
3 tbsp mozzarella cheese, shredded

12 slices pepperoni
A pinch of salt
A pinch of dried Italian seasonings

1 tsp red pepper flakes
Parmesan cheese, for garnish

Directions

Preheat the Air Fryer to 330°F. Drizzle a little bit of olive oil on each side of the mushroom. Season mushrooms with salt and Italian seasonings. Spread tomato sauce evenly over the mushrooms and top with cheese. Place the stuffed mushrooms in the cooking basket and insert in the Air Fryer.

After 1 minute, remove the basket and add the pepperoni slices on top of the portobello pizza. Place back on the fire and cook for 5 more minutes. Top with grated Parmesan cheese and red pepper flakes.

Air Fried Radish Chips

Total Time: 35 min | **Serves:** 4 | **Per serving:** Cal 48; Net Carbs 0.2g; Fat 2.7g; Protein 0.8g

Ingredients

10 Radishes, leaves removed, cleaned   Salt to taste

Directions

With a mandolin slicer, slice the radishes thinly. Place the radishes in a pot and pour in water to cover them up. Place the pot over medium heat and bring the water to boil until the radishes turn translucent, about 4 minutes.

Drain the radishes through a sieve. Set aside. Open the Air Fryer and grease the fryer basket with cooking spray. Add the radish slices into the fryer basket. Close the air fryer, and cook for 8 minutes at 390°F or a deep golden brown color. Season with salt and serve.

Hot Almond Flour Cheesy Lings

Total Time: 20 min | **Serves:** 4 | **Per serving:** Cal 173; Net Carbs 2.5g; Fat 14g; Protein 6g

Ingredients

1 cup almond flour
1 tsp baking powder

¼ tsp chili powder
1 tsp butter

3 tbsp cheddar cheese, grated
Hot sauce to serve

Directions

Mix the flour and the baking powder. Add chili powder, butter, grated cheese, and a few drops of water to the mixture. Make sure to make a stiff dough. Knead the dough for a while. Sprinkle some flour on the table. Take a rolling pin and roll the dough. Then, cut into any shape wanted. Preheat the Air Fryer to 370°F. Set the time to 4 minutes and line the cheese lings in the basket. Serve with hot sauce.

Cheddar Cheese Croquettes with Prosciutto

Total Time: 45 min | **Serves:** 6 | **Per serving:** Cal 346; Net Carbs 5.2g; Fat 25g; Protein 23g

Ingredients

1 lb cheddar cheese, sliced
12 slices prosciutto

1 cup almond flour
2 eggs, beaten

4 tbsp olive oil
1 cup pork rinds, crushed

Directions

Wrap each slice of cheese with 2 prosciutto slices. Place them in the freezer just enough to set. Preheat your Air Fryer to 380°F. Dip the croquettes into the flour first, then the egg, and then coat them with the pork rinds. Place the olive oil in the Air Fryer basket and cook the croquettes for 7 minutes, or until golden. Serve and enjoy!

Speedy Cheesy Strips

Total Time: 45 min | **Serves:** 3 | **Per serving:** Cal 314; Net Carbs 1.5g; Fat 16g; Protein 36g

Ingredients

8 oz mozzarella cheese
1 tsp garlic powder

1 egg
1 cup pork rinds, crushed

½ tsp salt
2 tbsp olive oil

Directions

Cut the mozzarella into 6 strips. Whisk the egg along with salt and garlic powder. Dip the mozzarella into the egg mixture first and then into the pork rinds. Arrange them on a platter and place in the freezer for about 30 min.

Preheat the Air Fryer to 360°F. Drizzle olive oil into the Air Fryer. Arrange the mozzarella sticks in the Air Fryer and cook for 5 minutes. Flip at least twice to ensure that they will cook evenly on all sides. Serve and enjoy!

Parmesan Asparagus Fries

Total Time: 35 min | **Serves:** 4 | **Per serving:** Cal 213; Net Carbs 4.1g; Fat 12g; Protein 19g

Ingredients

1 lb asparagus spears
¼ cup almond flour

1 cup pork rinds, crushed
½ cup Parmesan cheese, grated

2 eggs, beaten
Salt and black pepper to taste

Directions

Preheat the Air Fryer to 380°F. Combine the pork rinds and the Parmesan cheese in a small bowl. Season with salt and pepper. Line a baking sheet with parchment paper. Dip half of the asparagus spears into the flour, then into the eggs, and finally coat with pork rinds. Arrange them on the sheet and cook for about 9 to 10 minutes. Repeat with the remaining spears. Serve and enjoy!

Almond Onion Rings

Total Time: 20 min | **Serves:** 3 | **Per serving:** Cal 165; Net Carbs 4.7g; Fat 8g; Protein 6g

Ingredients

1 pound onions

1 ½ cups almond flour

1 tbsp baking powder

1 egg

1 cup coconut milk

¾ cup pork rinds, crushed

Directions

Preheat the Air Fryer for 10 minutes, if needed. Cut the onion into slices and then separate them into rings. In a bowl, stir the flour and baking powder. Whisk the eggs and the milk and combine with the flour. Dip the floured onion rings into the batter to coat it. Spread the pork rinds on a plate and dredge all the rings in the rinds. AirFry the rings in the Air Fryer for around 10 minutes at 360°F. Serve and enjoy!

Family Calamari Rings

Total Time: 25 min | **Serves:** 3 | **Per serving:** Cal 128; Net Carbs 0g; Fat 3g; Protein 22g

Ingredients

1 cup pimiento-stuffed green olives, sliced

½ lb calamari rings

½ piece coriander, chopped

2 strips chili pepper, chopped

1 tbsp olive oil

Salt and black pepper to taste

Directions

Add rings, chili pepper, salt, black pepper, oil, and coriander in a bowl. Mix and let marinate for 10 minutes. Pour the calamari into an oven-safe bowl that fits into the fryer basket. Cook for 15 minutes, shaking every 5 minutes using a spoon, at 400 F. After 15 minutes, and add in the olives. Stir, close, and continue to cook for 3 minutes. Once ready, transfer to a serving platter. Serve warm with a side of bread slices and mayonnaise.

Garlic Fried Tomatoes

Total Time: 20 min | **Serves:** 2 | **Per serving:** Cal 135; Net Carbs 6.7g; Fat 5g; Protein 1g

Ingredients

4 tomatoes

1 tbsp olive oil

Salt and black pepper to taste

1 clove garlic, minced

½ tbsp dried thyme

3 tbsp vinegar

Directions

Preheat the Air Fryer to 390°F. Cut the tomatoes in half, and remove the seeds. Put them in a big bowl and toss well with oil, salt, pepper, garlic, and thyme. Place them in the Air Fryer and cook them for 15 minutes. Drizzle with vinegar. Serve and enjoy!

Famous Fried Calamari

Total Time: 15 min | **Serves:** 4 | **Per serving:** Cal 233; Net Carbs 0.7g; Fat 11g; Protein 32g

Ingredients

1 lb calamari (squid), cut in rings

¼ cup almond flour

2 large eggs, beaten

1 cup pork rinds, crushed

Directions

Coat the calamari rings with flour. Dip the calamari in the mixture of the eggs. Then, dip in the pork rinds. Cool in the fridge for 2 hours. Line them in the Air Fryer and apply oil generously. Cook for 10 minutes at 380°F. Serve with garlic mayo or lemon wedges.

Spiced Chicken Sticks

Total Time: 25 min + chilling time | **Serves:** 4 | **Per serving:** Cal 523; Net Carbs 6.9g; Fat 46.1g; Protein 46.9g

Ingredients

2 eggs
2 chicken breasts, sliced
2 tbsp paprika

2 cups coconut milk
4 tsp onion powder
Salt and black pepper to taste

2 cups coconut flour
2 cups pork rinds, crushed

Directions

In a bowl, combine the paprika, onion powder, salt, pepper, coconut flour, and pork rinds. In a separate bowl, break the eggs, pour the coconut milk and whisk until well-combined. Dip the chicken slices in the egg mixture, and transfer to a tray. Let chill in the fridge for 1 hour. Once the time has passed, remove the chunks from the tray. Roll them in the pork mixture.

Preheat your Air Fryer to 370°F. Transfer the chicken to your Air Fryer and grease with cooking spray. Cook for 4 minutes. Remove the basket, toss the chicken, grease them with cooking spray, and cook for an additional 4 minutes. When the nuggets are cooked, transfer to a wire rack. Serve and enjoy!

Crispy Crumbed Chicken Tenderloins

Total Time: 15 min | **Serves:** 4 | **Per serving:** Cal 312; Net Carbs 0.8g; Fat 17g; Protein 21g

Ingredients

2 tbsp oil
2 oz pork rinds, crushed

1 large egg, whisked
6 chicken tenderloins

Directions

Preheat the Air Fryer to 365°F. Combine oil and pork rinds. Keep mixing and stirring until the mixture gets crumbly. Dip the chicken in the egg wash. Dip the chicken in the rinds mix, making sure it is evenly and fully covered. Cook for 12 minutes. Serve the dish and enjoy its crispy taste!

Lemon Bacon Shrimp

Total Time: 20 min + cooling time | **Serves:** 4 | **Per serving:** Cal 125; Net Carbs 1.2g; Fat 10g; Protein 11g

Ingredients

1 ¼ lbs shrimp, peeled, 16 pieces

1 lb bacon, 16 slices

Juice from 1 lemon

Directions

Take a bacon slice and carefully wrap it around one shrimp, starting from the shrimp's head. Put the wrapped shrimp into the fridge for 25 minutes. Preheat the Air Fryer to 390°F. Remove the shrimp from the fridge and arrange them on the greased air fryer basket. Cook them for 6–8 minutes. Sprinkle with lemon juice and serve.

Sweet Baby Carrots

Total Time: 20 min | **Serves:** 4 | **Per serving:** Cal 54; Net Carbs 5g; Fat 5.8g; Protein 2.4g

Ingredients

1 pound baby carrots
1 tsp dried dill

1 tbsp olive oil
1 tbsp stevia

Salt and black pepper to taste

Directions

Preheat your Air Fryer to 350°F. In a mixing bowl, mix oil, carrots and stevia. Gently stir to coat the carrots. Season with dill, pepper, and salt. Place the carrots in your Air fryer basket and cook for 12 minutes.

Tasty Fish Balls

Total Time: 45 min | **Serves:** 6 | **Per serving:** Cal 158; Net Carbs 3.1g; Fat 9.1g; Protein 16.8g

Ingredients

1 cup smoked fish, flaked
2 cups cauli rice
2 eggs, lightly beaten

1 cup Grana Padano cheese, grated
¼ cup thyme, finely chopped
Salt and pepper to taste

1 cup pork rinds, crushed

Directions

In a bowl, add fish, cauli rice, eggs, Grana Padano cheese, thyme, salt and pepper into a bowl and stir to combine. Shape the mixture into 12 even-sized balls. Roll the balls in the pork rinds, then spray with oil. Arrange the balls into the air fryer and cook for 16 minutes at 400°F, shaking once. Serve and enjoy!

Simple Zucchini Fries

Total Time: 15 min | **Serves:** 3 | **Per serving:** Cal 193; Net Carbs 0.3g; Fat 21g; Protein 1g

Ingredients

4 large zucchini
¼ cup almond flour

¼ cup olive oil
Salt to taste

Directions

Preheat the Air Fryer to 390°F. Cut the zucchini to a half-inch by 3 inches. In a large bowl, mix flour, olive oil, ¼ cup water, salt, and zucchini. Mix well and coat the zucchini. Line the zucchini fries in the Air Fryer and AirFry for 15 minutes, flipping once. Serve with Greek yogurt and garlic paste if desired.

Festive Cauli Croquettes

Total Time: 45 min | **Serves:** 4 | **Per serving:** Cal 167; Net Carbs 5.2g; Fat 10g; Protein 12g

Ingredients

2 cups cauli rice
1 brown onion, chopped
2 garlic cloves, chopped

2 eggs, lightly beaten
½ cup Parmesan cheese, grated
Salt and black pepper to taste

½ cup pork rinds, crushed
1 tsp dried mixed herbs

Directions

Combine cauli rice, onion, garlic, eggs, Parmesan cheese, herbs, salt and pepper. Shape into 10 croquettes. Spread the pork rinds onto a plate and coat each croquette in the pork rinds. Spray each croquette with oil. Arrange the croquettes in the air fryer and cook for 16 minutes at 380°F, turning once. They should be golden and crispy.

Goat Cheese & Pancetta Bombs with Plums

Total Time: 25 min | **Serves:** 15 | **Per serving:** Cal 151; Net Carbs 8.2g; Fat 10.5g; Protein 9g

Ingredients

16 oz soft goat cheese
2 tbsp fresh rosemary, finely chopped
1 cup almonds, chopped into small

pieces
Salt and black pepper to taste
15 dried plums, chopped

15 pancetta slices

Directions

Line the air fryer with baking paper. In a bowl, add cheese, rosemary, almonds, salt, pepper, and plums and stir. Roll into balls and wrap with a pancetta slice. Arrange the bombs in the air fryer and cook for 10 minutes at 400°F. Check at the 5-minute mark to avoid overcooking. Serve on a platter with toothpicks!

Delicious Mixed Nuts

Total Time: 25 min | **Serves:** 6 | **Per serving:** Cal 170; Net Carbs 3g; Fat 15g; Protein 6g

Ingredients

½ cup pecans
½ cup walnuts
½ cup almonds

A pinch of ground cayenne pepper
2 tbsp stevia sweetener
2 tbsp egg whites

2 tsp cinnamon powder

Directions

Preheat Air Fryer to 300°F.

Add the pepper, stevia, and cinnamon to a bowl and mix them well. Set aside. In another bowl, pour in the pecans, walnuts, almonds, and egg whites. Mix well. Add the spice mixture to the nuts and give it a good mix.

Lightly grease the fryer basket with cooking spray. Pour in the nuts and Bake them for 10 minutes. Open the Air Fryer, stir the nuts using a wooden vessel, close the Air Fryer, and bake further for 10 minutes. Set a bowl ready and once the timer is done, pour the nuts in the bowl. Let cool before crunching on them as they are.

Ginger Beef Meatballs

Total Time: 25 min | **Serves:** 3 | **Per serving:** Cal 221; Net Carbs 2.4g; Fat 13g; Protein 23g

Ingredients

½ lb ground beef
1 small finger ginger, crushed
1 tbsp hot sauce

3 tbsp vinegar
1 ½ tsp lemon juice
½ cup tomato ketchup, reduced sugar

2 tbsp erythritol
¼ tsp dry mustard
Salt and black pepper to taste

Directions

In a bowl, add the beef, ginger, hot sauce, vinegar, lemon juice, tomato ketchup, erythritol, dry mustard, pepper, and salt and mix well using a spoon. Mold out 2-inch sized balls out of the mixture with your hands. Pull out the fryer basket and add the balls to it without overcrowding. Slide the fryer basket back in and cook the balls at 370°F for 15 minutes. Remove them onto a serving platter and repeat the frying process for any remaining balls.

Southern Fried Beef Liver

Total Time: 15 min | **Serves:** 4 | **Per serving:** Cal 290; Net Carbs 1.4g; Fat 21g; Protein 14g

Ingredients

1 egg
1 lb beef liver, sliced
Salt and black pepper to taste

2 tbsp black truffle oil
½ cup milk
1 cup flour

1 tbsp garlic powder
1 tbsp parsley, chopped

Directions

Preheat the Air Fryer to 340°F. In a bowl, beat the egg and milk. In another bowl, put the flour, garlic powder, parsley, salt and pepper and mix to combine. Dip the liver slices in the egg mixture, then coat with the flour one. Brush them with truffle oil. Place in the air fryer basket and cook for 12 minutes, flipping once. Serve and enjoy!

Smoked Paprika Zucchini Parmesan Chips

Total Time: 25 min | **Serves:** 4 | **Per serving:** Cal 140; Net Carbs 1g; Fat 9g; Protein 4g

Ingredients

3 medium zucchinis
1 cup pork rinds, crushed

2 eggs, beaten
1 cup grated Parmesan cheese

Salt and black pepper to taste
1 tsp smoked paprika

Directions

With a mandolin cutter, slice the zucchinis thinly. Use paper towels to press out excess liquid. In a bowl, add the pork rinds, salt, pepper, cheese, and paprika. Mix well and set aside. Place a wire rack or tray. Set aside.

Now, dip each zucchini slice in egg and then in the cheese mix while pressing to coat them well in cheese. Place them on the wire rack. Spray the slices with cooking spray. Place the slices in the fryer basket in a single layer without overlapping. Close the Air Fryer and cook them at 350°F for 8 minutes for each batch. Sprinkle with salt.

Bread Cheese Sticks

Total Time: 15 min | **Serves:** 3 | **Per serving:** Cal 112; Net Carbs 1g; Fat 10g; Protein 6g

Ingredients

6 (6 oz) bread cheese   2 tbsp butter, melted

Directions

Cut the cheese into equal-sized sticks. Brush with butter. Arrange the coated cheese sticks in a single layer on the fryer basket. Slide in the fryer basket and cook at 390°F for 10 minutes. Flip halfway to brown evenly.

Herby Turnip Chips

Total Time: 25 min | **Serves:** 2 | **Per serving:** Cal 162; Net Carbs 6.2g; Fat 14g; Protein 1.4g

Ingredients

3 turnips, sliced   3 garlic cloves, crushed   oregano, chopped
2 tbsp olive oil   1 tsp each of fresh rosemary, thyme,   Salt and black pepper to taste

Directions

In a bowl, add turnips, oil, garlic, herbs, salt and pepper and toss with hands until well-coated. Arrange the slices in the air fryer basket and cook for 14 minutes at 360°F, shaking it every 4-5 minutes. Enjoy with onion dip.

Crispy Eggplant Fries

Total Time: 20 min | **Serves:** 3 | **Per serving:** Cal 265; Net Carbs 4,2g; Fat 21g; Protein 4g

Ingredients

2 eggplants   ¼ cup almond flour   ¼ cup olive oil

Directions

Preheat the Air Fryer to 390°F. Cut the eggplants in slices of half-inch each. In a big bowl, mix the flour, olive oil, ½ cup of water, and eggplants. Slowly coat the eggplants. Cook for 12 minutes until they start to brown. Repeat this process until all eggplant slices are cooked. Serve with yogurt or tomato sauce if desired.

Cajun Sautéed Shrimp

Total Time: 15 min | **Serves:** 4 | **Per serving:** Cal 73; Net Carbs 0.6g; Fat 4g; Protein 6g

Ingredients

4 oz tiger shrimp, 16 to 20   ½ a tbsp Cajun seasoning   A pinch of sea salt
¼ a tbsp cayenne pepper   ¼ a tbsp smoked paprika   1 tbsp olive oil

Directions

Preheat the Air Fryer to 390°F. In a large mixing bowl, put the ingredients. Coat the shrimp with a little bit of oil and spices. Gently place the shrimp in the cooking basket and cook for 5 minutes. Serve and enjoy!

Salmon with Dill Sauce

Total Time: 20 min | **Serves:** 2 | **Per serving:** Cal 291; Net Carbs 5.6g; Fat 23g; Protein 15g

Ingredients

2 pieces salmon, 6 oz each

2 tbsp olive oil

A pinch of salt

Dill sauce:

½ cup full-fat Greek yogurt

A pinch of salt

½ cup sour cream

2 tbsp fresh dill, finely chopped

Directions

Preheat the Air Fryer to 370°F. Cut the salmon into four equal-sized portions, then drizzle with oil. Season with a pinch of sea salt. Place the salmon into the cooking basket. Cook for 12-14 minutes. For the dill sauce: in a large bowl, combine yogurt, sour cream, chopped dill, and salt until smooth. Top the salmon with sauce and serve.

The Best Chili Rellenos

Total Time: 35 min | **Serves:** 5 | **Per serving:** Cal 258; Net Carbs 2g; Fat 20g; Protein 15g

Ingredients

2 cans green chili peppers

2 large eggs, beaten

½ cup milk

1 cup Monterey Jack Cheese

½ cup water

1 can tomato sauce

1 cup cheddar cheese, shredded

2 tbsp almond flour

Directions

Preheat the Air Fryer to 350°F. Spray a baking dish with the cooking spray. Take half of the chilies and arrange them in the baking dish. Top chilies with cheddar cheese and cover with the remaining chilies. In a bowl, combine the eggs, water, flour, and milk. Pour the mixture over the chilies. AirFry for 25 minutes. Slide out the basket and pour the tomato sauce over the chilies. Cook again for 10 minutes. Top with the Monterey jack cheese to serve.

Rich Eggplant Caviar

Total Time: 25 min | **Serves:** 3 | **Per serving:** Cal 287; Net Carbs 5.2g; Fat 7g; Protein 4g

Ingredients

2 medium eggplants

1 ½ tbsp balsamic vinegar

Salt to taste

½ red onion

1 tbsp olive oil

Directions

Preheat the Air Fryer to 360°F. Wash, then dry the eggplants. Arrange them on the greased air fryer basket and cook them for 16 minutes. Let the eggplants cool down. Blend the onion in a blender. Cut the eggplants in half, lengthwise, and empty their insides with a spoon. Put the inside of the eggplants in the mixer and process everything. Add vinegar, olive oil, and salt, then blend again. Serve chilled with tomato sauceif desired.

Marjoram & Basil Zucchini

Total Time: 30 min | **Serves:** 3 | **Per serving:** Cal 317; Net Carbs 2g; Fat 16.8g; Protein 12g

Ingredients

1 tsp capers

⅓ cup tomatoes, chopped

Salt and black pepper to taste

1 cup zucchini, cubed

1 clove garlic, minced

¼ cup mozzarella cheese, grated

¼ cup red pepper, chopped

1 tbsp pimiento-stuffed olives, sliced

1 tbsp pork rinds, crushed

¼ cup green pepper, chopped

¼ tsp dried basil

¼ cup yellow onion, chopped

¼ tsp dried marjoram

Directions

Preheat your Air Fryer to 300°F. Combine the zucchini, green pepper, red pepper, onion, tomatoes, olives, garlic, basil marjoram, capers, salt, and pepper in a bowl. Grease a baking dish with cooking spray. Spread the zucchini mixture on the bottom of the dish. Top with the mozzarella and the pork rinds. Cook for 20 minutes. Serve.

Lemon Cupcakes with Creamy Glaze

Total Time: 25 min | **Serves:** 5 | **Per serving:** Cal 412; Net Carbs 2g; Fat 25g; Protein 4.6g

Ingredients

Frosting:

1 lemon, juiced	Swerve sweetener to taste	7 oz mascarpone
1 cup unsweetened natural yogurt	1 tbsp lemon zest	

Cupcakes:

2 lemons, quartered	2 tbsp swerve sweetener	½ cup butter, softened
½ cup almond flour + extra for basing	1 tsp baking powder	2 tbsp coconut milk
¼ tsp salt	2 eggs	

Directions

Preheat your Air Fryer to 400°F. In a bowl, combine the yogurt and mascarpone. Stir with a fork until smooth. Add in the lemon juice and zest; mix well. Slowly add in sweetener to taste while stirring until smooth; set aside.

In your food processor, put the lemon quarters and mix until pureed. Add in the almond flour, baking powder, softened butter, coconut milk, eggs, swerve sweetener, and salt. Blend until smooth. Pour into 10 floured cupcake cases. Transfer to the Air Fryer and cook for 7 minutes. Let cool. Decorate with the lemon icing in a swirl.

Thyme Meatballs in Tomato Sauce

Total Time: 25 min | **Serves:** 3 | **Per serving:** Cal 441; Net Carbs 3.2g; Fat 37g; Protein 22g

Ingredients

1 medium onion, chopped	½ tbsp thyme leaves, chopped	Salt and black pepper to taste
12 oz ground beef meat	1 egg	6 oz tomato sauce
1 tbsp fresh parsley, chopped	3 tbsp pork rinds, crushed	

Directions

Place the ingredients, except the tomato sauce into a bowl, and mix well. Shape the mixture into balls. Preheat the Air Fryer to 390°F. Place the meatballs in a baking dish and place in the basket. AirFry for 8-9 minutes. Slide out the basket and pour the tomato sauce over the meatballs. Cook again in the fryer for 4 minutes. Serve and enjoy!

Garlic Roasted Vegetables with Olives

Total Time: 15 min | **Serves:** 4 | **Per serving:** Cal 212; Net Carbs 7.8g; Fat 13g; Protein 10g

Ingredients

1 lb tomatoes	2 cloves garlic	2 oz black olives, sliced
1 bell pepper	½ tbsp salt	3 cooked eggs
1 medium onion	1 tbsp olive oil	

Directions

Line the pepper, tomatoes and onion in the basket. Cook for 5 minutes, then flip around and cook for 5 more minutes, at 300°F. Remove them from the Air Fryer and peel their skin. Place the vegetables, olive oil, and garlic in a blender and sprinkle with salt. Blend to a smooth mixture. Top with the cooked eggs and olives to serve.

Crispy Tofu

Total Time: 25 min | **Serves:** 4 | **Per serving:** Cal 427; Net Carbs 5.1g; Fat 31g; Protein 38g

Ingredients

3 tofu blocks, cut into ½-inch thick
2 tbsp olive oil

½ cup almond flour
½ cup pork rinds, crushed

Salt and black pepper to taste

Directions

Sprinkle oil over tofu and massage gently until well coated. On a plate, mix almond flour, pork rinds, salt and black pepper. Dip each strip into the mixture to coat, spray with oil and arrange the strips in your air fryer lined with baking paper. Cook for 14 minutes at 360°F, turning once halfway through cooking. Serve and enjoy!

Best-Ever Stuffed Mushrooms

Total Time: 30 min | **Serves:** 10 | **Per serving:** Cal 65; Net Carbs 3.2g; Fat 4.5g; Protein 3.4g

Ingredients

10 mushrooms, stems removed
Olive oil to brush the mushrooms

1 cup cauli rice
1 cup Grana Padano cheese, grated

1 tsp dried mixed herbs
Salt and black pepper to taste

Directions

Brush every mushroom with oil and set aside. In a bowl, mix cauli rice, cheese, herbs, salt and pepper. Stuff the mushrooms with the mixture. Arrange the mushrooms in the air fryer and cook for 14 minutes at 360°F until the mushrooms are golden and the cheese has melted. Serve with scattered herbs.

Sweet & Spicy Nut Mix

Total Time: 25 min | **Serves:** 5 | **Per serving:** Cal 147; Net Carbs 10g; Fat 12g; Protein 3g

Ingredients

½ cup pecans
½ cup walnuts
½ cup almonds

A pinch of cayenne pepper
2 tbsp stevia
2 tbsp egg whites

2 tsp cinnamon

Directions

Add the pepper, stevia, and cinnamon to a bowl and mix well; set aside. In another bowl, mix in the pecans, walnuts, almonds, and egg whites. Add the spice mixture to the nuts and give it a good mix. Lightly grease the fryer basket with cooking spray. Pour in the nuts, and cook for 10 minutes. Stir the nuts using a wooden vessel, and cook further for 10 minutes. Pour the nuts into the bowl. Let cool before crunching on them.

Easy Meatballs with Herbs

Total Time: 30 min | **Serves:** 4 | **Per serving:** Cal 483; Net Carbs 8.2g; Fat 23g; Protein 54g

Ingredients

1 lb ground beef
1 onion, finely chopped
3 garlic cloves, finely chopped

2 eggs
1 cup pork rinds, crushed
½ cup fresh mixed herbs

Salt and pepper to taste
Olive oil

Directions

In a bowl, add beef, onion, garlic, eggs, pork rinds, herbs, salt and pepper and mix with hands to combine. Shape into balls and arrange them in the air fryer basket. Drizzle with oil and cook for 16 minutes at 380°F, turning once halfway through cooking.

Calamari with Parsley & Capers

Total Time: 25 min | **Serves**: 3 | **Per serving**: Cal 218; Net Carbs 5.3g; Fat 16.5g; Protein 4.6g

Ingredients

1 cup capers
½ lb calamari rings

2 tbsp parsley, chopped
2 strips chili pepper, chopped

1 tbsp olive oil
Salt and black pepper to taste

Directions

Combine the calamari rings, chili pepper, salt, black pepper, oil, and parsley in a bowl. Mix well, cover, and let them marinate for 10 minutes. Preheat your Air Fryer to 390°F. Place the calamari in an oven-safe bowl and put in the fryer. Cook for 15 minutes, shaking every 5 minutes. After 15 minutes, open the Air Fryer and stir in the capers. Cook for another 3 minutes. Remove to a plate and serve hot.

Coconut Cheddar Sticks

Total Time: 20 min + chilling time | **Serves**: 4 | **Per serving**: Cal 288; Net Carbs 2.9g; Fat 11g; Protein 39g

Ingredients

7.5 oz cheddar cheese sticks
2 cups ground pork rinds

3 eggs
4 tbsp coconut milk

Directions

Place the pork rinds in a bowl. In a second bowl, crack the eggs and whisk with the coconut milk. Dip the cheese sticks in the egg mixture, then in the pork rinds, again in the eggs, and finally in the pork rinds. Transfer to a baking sheet and place in the freezer for 2 hours.

Preheat your Air Fryer to 380°F. Place the cheese sticks in the basket. Cook for 5 minutes, turn them halfway to get brown. Transfer to a plate and serve.

Cayenne Peppered Parsnip Fries

Total Time: 25 min | **Serves**: 4 | **Per serving**: Cal 104; Net Carbs 9.7g; Fat 3.1g; Protein 1.8g

Ingredients

3 parsnips, sliced
2 tsp olive oil

2 tsp cayenne pepper
Salt and black pepper to taste

Directions

Place the slices into a bowl and sprinkle with oil, cayenne, salt and black pepper. Toss and arrange the fries in the basket. Cook for 14 minutes at 360°F, giving it a toss halfway through cooking.

Crispy Paprika Squid

Total Time: 25 min | **Serves**: 2 | **Per serving**: Cal 233; Net Carbs 6.1g; Fat 16.5; Protein 15.2g

Ingredients

½ squid rings
¾ cup Parmesan cheese, shredded
2 eggs, beaten

1 tsp garlic powder
A pinch of salt
1 cup almond flour

1 tsp paprika powder
1 cup tomato dip, sugar-free

Directions

Preheat your Air Fryer to 350°F. In a bowl, put the eggs and set aside. Combine the cheese, garlic powder, salt, almond flour, and paprika powder in another bowl. Dip each squid in the eggs, then in the cheese mixture, again in the eggs, and finally in the cheese mixture. AirFry for 12-14 minutes, flipping once. Serve with tomato dip.

Crispy Italian Swiss Chard Chips

Total Time: 15 min | **Serves:** 2 | **Per serving:** Cal 167; Net Carbs 2.9g; Fat 15g; Protein 5g

Ingredients

2 tbsp olive oil
4 cups Swiss chard, stemmed

1 tsp Italian seasoning
1 tbsp yeast flakes

Sea salt to taste

Directions

Preheat your Air Fryer to 370°F. Combine the oil, Swiss chard, and Italian seasoning in a bowl. Mix in the yeast flakes, and stir. Throw the coated Swiss chard into the Air Fryer and cook for 8 minutes, tossing once after the 3-minute mark. Remove and season with sea salt to serve.

Hot Tabasco Wings

Total Time: 20 min | **Serves:** 3 | **Per serving:** Cal 295; Net Carbs 1.8g; Fat 21g; Protein 35g

Ingredients

⅓ cup butter
15 chicken wings

Salt and black pepper to taste
⅓ cup Tabasco sauce

½ tbsp white vinegar

Directions

Preheat Air Fryer to 360°F. Sprinkle the wings with salt and pepper. Cook in the Air Fryer for 15 minutes, shaking once. Melt butter in a saucepan over medium heat and stir in the vinegar and Tabasco sauce. Cook for 5 minutes. Remove the wings from the fryer and pour the sauce over; toss to coat. Serve and enjoy!

Turkey Bacon & Cheese Burritos

Total Time: 15 min | **Serves:** 4 | **Per serving:** Cal 392; Net Carbs 3.2g; Fat 35g; Protein 15g

Ingredients

2 lb dill pickles
1 lb cream cheese, softened

3 oz turkey bacon, sliced
2 almond tortillas

Directions

Smear half of the cream cheese on the almond tortillas. Top with turkey bacon slices and lay the remaining cheese on top. Add the pickles and roll-up. Preheat your Air Fryer to 340°F. Place the rolls in the air fryer basket and AirFry for 6 minutes until they are golden brown and crisp. Serve with salsa if desired.

All Spice Nut Mix

Total Time: 25 min | **Serves:** 6 | **Per serving:** Cal 170; Net Carbs 3g; Fat 15g; Protein 6g

Ingredients

½ cup macadamia
½ cup pecans
½ cup walnuts

A pinch of chili pepper
2 tbsp stevia sweetener
2 tbsp egg whites

2 tsp allspice

Directions

Preheat your Air Fryer to 300°F. In a bowl, mix the chili pepper, stevia, and allspice. Set aside. In a second bowl, combine the pecans, walnuts, macadamia, and egg whites. Add the spice mixture to the nuts and stir well.

Grease the basket with cooking spray. Add the nut mixture to the basket and cook for 10 minutes. Open the Air Fryer and shake. Cook for 10 more minutes. When ready, transfer the nuts to a bowl and let cool before serving.

Italian Sausage Meatballs

Total Time: 25 min | **Serves:** 4 | **Per serving:** Cal 221; Net Carbs 2.4g; Fat 13g; Protein 23g

Ingredients

16 oz ground Italian sausage meat
1 small finger ginger, crushed
1 tbsp hot sauce

3 tbsp vinegar
1 ½ tsp lemon juice
½ cup tomato ketchup, sugar-free

2 tbsp erythritol
¼ tsp dry mustard
Salt and black pepper to taste

Directions

Preheat your Air Fryer to 370°F. Mix the meat, ginger, hot sauce, vinegar, lemon juice, tomato ketchup, erythritol, dry mustard, pepper, and salt in a bowl. Shape the mixture into balls. Place in the fryer basket and cook for 15 minutes. Remove and serve warm.

Buttery Cheddar Cheese Bars

Total Time: 15 min | **Serves:** 3 | **Per serving:** Cal 112; Net Carbs 1g; Fat 10g; Protein 6g

Ingredients

6 (6 oz) cheddar cheese

2 tbsp butter

Directions

Preheat your Air Fryer to 390°F. Microwave the butter for 2 minutes until it is melted. Set aside. Slice the cheddar cheese into equal-sized sticks and spray each stick with butter. Align the coated sticks in the fryer basket and cook for 10 minutes. Turn once during cooking time to get brown. Serve with a tomato dip.

Almond Tortilla Chips

Total Time: 55 min | **Serves:** 3 | **Per serving:** Cal 165; Net Carbs 3g; Fat 14.4g; Protein 4.7g

Ingredients

2 cups mozzarella cheese, shredded
1 cup almond flour

Salt and black pepper to taste
1 tbsp golden flaxseed meal

Directions

Preheat your Air Fryer to 350°F. Microwave the mozzarella cheese for about 1 minute. Stir every 15 seconds. Once ready, add in the almond flour, salt, flaxseed meal, and pepper. Mix well with a fork.

Place the dough on a flat surface and knead it while is warm until the ingredients are well combined. Divide the dough in half and shape it into two rectangles. With a pastry cutter, cut out triangle-shaped and line them on a baking dish. Open the Air Fryer and grease the basket with cooking spray. Place the triangle chips in the basket. Do not overlap. Sprinkle with cooking spray, close and AirFry for 8 minutes. Serve and enjoy!

Cayenne Meat Bites

Total Time: 25 min + chilling time | **Serves:** 2 | **Per serving:** Cal 418; Net Carbs 0.5g; Fat 32.5g; Protein 29.2g

Ingredients

½ tsp onion powder
½ tsp cayenne pepper

1 lb ground beef
3 tbsp erythritol

Salt to taste
1 tsp liquid smoke

Directions

Combine the meat, erythritol, onion powder, cayenne pepper, salt, and liquid smoke in a bowl. Shape 4 sticks with the mixture and transfer to a plate. Let sit in the fridge for 2 hours. Preheat your Air Fryer to 350°F. Place the sticks in the air fryer basket and AirFry for 10-14 minutes. Serve with your favorite dipping sauce.

Parmesan Eggplant Chips

Total Time: 70 min | **Serves:** 4 | **Per serving:** Cal 140; Net Carbs 1g; Fat 9g; Protein 4g

Ingredients

2 pounds eggplants
1 cup pork rinds, crushed

2 eggs, beaten
1 cup grated Parmesan cheese

Salt and black pepper to taste
1 tsp smoked paprika

Directions

Slice the eggplants into tiny pieces. Combine the pork rinds, salt, pepper, cheese, and smoked paprika in a bowl. Dip each eggplant slice in egg, then in the cheese mixture. Arrange the slices on the wire rack.

Preheat your Air Fryer to 350°F and grease the slices with cooking spray. Open the Air Fryer and put the slices in the basket. Do not overlap. Close and AirFry for 14-16 minutes. Shake halfway through the cooking time. Transfer to a plate. Repeat the process if it is necessary. Sprinkle with salt and serve.

Crunchy Daikon Radish Chips

Total Time: 30 min | **Serves:** 4 | **Per serving:** Cal 48; Net Carbs 0.2g; Fat 2.7g; Protein 0.8g

Ingredients

1 pound white daikon radish, cleaned   Salt to taste

Directions

Cut the daikon radish into tiny slices. Put the radish slices in a casserole over medium heat with water. Bring to a boil and cook for about 4 minutes until turn translucent. Drain the slices and set aside.

Preheat your Air Fryer to 390°F and grease the basket with cooking spray. Open the Air Fryer and place in the radish slices. Close and cook for 8-10 minutes until they are golden brown. When ready, remove the radish chips to a paper towel-lined plate. Season with salt and serve. Serve and enjoy!

Almond Onion Rings

Total Time: 15 min | **Serves:** 3 | **Per serving:** Cal 165; Net Carbs 4.7g; Fat 8g; Protein 6g

Ingredients

1 cup buttermilk
3 onions

1 ½ cups almond flour
1 tbsp baking powder

1 egg
¾ cup pork rinds, crushed

Directions

Preheat your Air Fryer to 360°F. Cut the onion into rings. In a bowl, combine flour and baking powder. Beat the eggs with the buttermilk and pour in the flour mixture. Dip each floured onion ring into the egg mixture and coat. Place the pork rinds on a plate and dip each ring in it. Place the rings in the fryer and cook for 10 minutes.

Parsnip Sticks

Total Time: 20 min | **Serves:** 2 | **Per serving:** Cal 35; Net Carbs 6g; Fat 0g; Protein 1g

Ingredients

3 large parsnips, peeled   Salt to taste

Directions

Preheat your Air Fryer to 350°F. Slice the parsnips heightwise, very thinly. Place the strips in a bowl and season with salt. Grease the Air Fryer basket with cooking spray. Place in the parsnips and cook for 6 minutes. Stir the sticks and cook for another 4 minutes until crispy. Serve with dipping sauce.

Cheddar & Bresaola Croquettes

Total Time: 45 min | **Serves:** 6 | **Per serving:** Cal 346; Net Carbs 5.2g; Fat 25g; Protein 23g

Ingredients

12 slices bresaola
1 lb cheddar cheese, sliced

1 cup almond flour
2 eggs, beaten

4 tbsp olive oil
1 cup pork rinds, crushed

Directions

Wrap the cheddar cheese with 2 bresaola slices. Transfer to the freezer and let sit. Preheat your Air Fryer to 380°F. Grease the fryer basket with olive oil. Dip the bites in the flour, then in the eggs, and finally in the pork rinds. Place the bites in the fryer and cook for 7 minutes until golden. Serve and enjoy!

Onion & Pesto Zucchini Tortillas

Total Time: 25 min | **Serves:** 2 | **Per serving:** Cal 243; Net Carbs 2g; Fat 16g; Protein 13g

Ingredients

1 tbsp olive oil
1 tsp balsamic vinegar
1 oz zucchini, sliced
¼ large red onion, sliced

Salt and black pepper
3 flaxseed tortillas
2 oz cream cheese
2 tbsp pesto sauce

½ tomato
2 oz mozzarella cheese

Directions

Preheat your Air Fryer to 390°F. Combine the olive oil and balsamic vinegar. Put in the zucchini and onions. Sprinkle with salt and pepper. Cook for 5 minutes and remove to a plate. Lower the Air Fryer to 330°F. Brush each tortilla side with olive oil. Divide the cream cheese, zucchini, and onions between the tortillas. Pour the pesto sauce over and top with tomato and cheese. Cook for another 7 minutes. Serve and enjoy!

Dill Mackerel Balls

Total Time: 15 min | **Serves:** 2 | **Per serving:** Cal 389; Net Carbs 1.6g; Fat 32g; Protein 25g

Ingredients

6 oz tinned mackerel
1 large egg
4 tbsp celery, chopped

4 tbsp spring onion, sliced
1 tbsp fresh dill, chopped
½ tbsp garlic powder

5 tbsp pork rinds, crushed
3 tbsp olive oil

Directions

Preheat your Air Fryer to 370°F. Combine the mackerel, egg, celery, onion, dill, and garlic powder in a bowl. Mold small balls with the mixture and dip them in pork rinds. Warm the oil in a skillet over medium heat and cook the balls to flatten. Transfer the balls to the fryer and cook for 10 minutes. Serve and enjoy!

Basil Tomato Fries

Total Time: 20 min | **Serves:** 2 | **Per serving:** Cal 135; Net Carbs 6.7g; Fat 5g; Protein 1g

Ingredients

4 tomatoes, sliced
1 tbsp olive oil

Salt and black pepper to taste
1 clove garlic, minced

½ tbsp dried basil
3 tbsp Parmesan cheese, shredded

Directions

Preheat your Air Fryer to 390°F. Place tomatoes in a bowl and sprinkle with olive oil, salt, pepper, garlic, and basil. Place in the fryer and cook for 15 minutes. Sprinkle with Parmesan cheese to serve.

Shallot & Zucchini Spread

Total Time: 20 min | **Serves:** 2 | **Per serving:** Cal 287; Net Carbs 5.2g; Fat 7g; Protein 4g

Ingredients

2 zucchinis
2 tbsp pecans, chopped

2 shallots
1½ tbsp balsamic vinegar

1 tbsp olive oil

Directions

Preheat your Air Fryer to 360°F. Place the zucchinis in the air fryer basket and cook for 15 minutes, shaking once during cooking. Remove from the air fryer and allow to cool.

In a food processor, blend the shallots and pecans. Cut the zucchinis by half lengthwise and empty their insides with a spoon. Combine the insides zucchinis with the shallot mix and blitz. Add in vinegar, olive oil, and a pinch of salt and blend again. Serve cool with tomato sauce or ketchup if desired.

Shrimp in Capicola Wrap

Total Time: 10 min + chilling time | **Serves:** 4 | **Per serving:** Cal 125; Net Carbs 1.2g; Fat 10g; Protein 11g

Ingredients

1 lb capicola (cooked ham), sliced

2 lb shrimp, peeled

Juice from 1 lemon

Directions

Lay the capicola slices on a flat surface and wrap them around the shrimp. Put the wrapped shrimp in the fridge for 25 minutes. Preheat your Air Fryer to 390°F. Cook the shrimp for 6-8 minutes. Drizzle with lemon juice.

Atlantic Salmon Croquettes

Total Time: 25 min | **Serves:** 6 | **Per serving:** Cal 158; Net Carbs 3.1g; Fat 9.1g; Protein 16.8g

Ingredients

1 cup smoked Atlantic salmon, flaked
2 cups cauli rice
2 eggs, lightly beaten

1 cup Grana Padano cheese, grated
¼ cup dill, chopped
Salt and pepper to taste

1 cup pork rinds, crushed

Directions

Preheat your Air Fryer to 400°F. In a bowl, stir the salmon, cauli rice, eggs, Grana Padano cheese, dill, salt, and pepper. Form 12 balls with the mixture. Dip in the pork rinds and sprinkle with oil. Lay the balls in the air fryer basket and cook for 14-16 minutes, turning once until nice and crispy. Serve and enjoy!

Crispy Asparagus with Grana Padano Cheese

Total Time: 35 min | **Serves:** 4 | **Per serving:** Cal 213; Net Carbs 4.1g; Fat 12g; Protein 19g

Ingredients

½ cup Grana Padano cheese, grated
1 lb asparagus spears

¼ cup almond flour
1 cup pork rinds, crushed

2 eggs, beaten
Salt and black pepper to taste

Directions

Preheat your Air Fryer to 380°F. In a bowl, mix the pork rinds with Grana Padano cheese. Season with salt and pepper. Line a baking sheet with parchment paper. Dip the asparagus in the flour, then in the eggs, and finally in the pork rinds. Arrange the asparagus on the baking sheet and AirFry for 9-10 minutes, turning once. Serve and enjoy!

Old Bay Shrimp Sauté

Total Time: 15 min | **Serves:** 4 | **Per serving:** Cal 73; Net Carbs 0.6g; Fat 4g; Protein 6g

Ingredients

¼ tbsp paprika

4 oz tiger shrimp, 16 to 20

¼ a tbsp chili pepper

½ a tbsp old bay seasoning

A pinch of sea salt

1 tbsp olive oil

Directions

Preheat your Air Fryer to 390°F. Combine all the ingredients, except the shrimps, in a bowl. Dip the shrimps in the mixture to coat. Place in the basket and cook for 5 minutes. Serve and enjoy!

Crispy Kashkaval Chips

Total Time: 15 min | **Serves:** 4 | **Per serving:** Cal 173; Net Carbs 2.5g; Fat 14g; Protein 6g

Ingredients

1 tsp butter

1 cup almond flour

1 tsp baking powder

¼ tsp chili powder

3 tbsp kashkaval cheese, grated

Hot sauce, to serve

Directions

Preheat Air Fryer to 370°F. Combine the almond flour and baking powder. Add chili powder, butter, grated cheese, and a few drops of water. Mix to form a stiff dough. Knead the dough for a while. Spread some flour on the table and roll the dough. Cut it into chip shapes. AirFry them for 4 minutes. Serve with hot sauce.

Fontina & Soppressata Mushrooms

Total Time: 15 min | **Serves:** 3 | **Per serving:** Cal 340; Net Carbs 3.8g; Fat 19g; Protein 37g

Ingredients

3 portobello mushrooms, stems removed

12 slices soppressata

3 tbsp olive oil

3 tbsp tomato sauce

3 tbsp fontina cheese, shredded

A pinch of salt

A pinch of dried Italian seasonings

1 tsp red pepper flakes

Parmesan cheese, for garnish

Directions

Preheat your Air Fryer to 330°F. Spray each mushroom side with olive oil and season with salt and Italian seasoning. Pour the tomato sauce over the mushrooms and top with the cheese. Place the mushrooms in the fryer and cook for 5 minutes. After 1 minute, remove the basket and add the soppressata on top of the mushrooms. Put back in the Fryer and cook for another 5 minutes. Top with grated Parmesan cheese and red pepper flakes.

Monterey Jack Sticks

Total Time: 25 min | **Serves:** 3 | **Per serving:** Cal 314; Net Carbs 1.5g; Fat 16g; Protein 36g

Ingredients

8 oz Monterrey Jack cheese

1 egg

1 cup pork rinds, crushed

Salt to taste

2 tbsp olive oil

Directions

Slice the Monterey jack cheese into 6 strips. Beat the eggs with salt. Dip the strips in the egg, then in the pork rinds. Transfer to a plate and put in the freezer for 30 minutes. Preheat your Air Fryer to 360°F. Grease the fryer basket with olive oil. Place the strips in the basket and cook for 5 minutes, turning at least twice. Serve and enjoy!

Creole Fried Tomatoes

Total Time: 15 min | **Serves:** 3 | **Per serving:** Cal 123; Net Carbs 3.1g; Fat 18g; Protein 5.3g

Ingredients

1 green tomato, sliced
¼ tbsp Creole seasoning

Salt and black pepper to taste
¼ cup almond flour

½ cup buttermilk
1 cup pork rinds, crushed

Directions

Preheat Air Fryer to 400°F. Add almond flour to a bowl and buttermilk to another. Season the tomatoes with salt and pepper. Make a mix of creole seasoning and pork rinds. Cover tomato slices with almond flour, dip in buttermilk, and then into the pork rinds. Place the tomato slices in the air fryer basket and cook for 5 minutes.

Jamón Serrano Wrapped Avocados

Total Time: 15 min | **Serves:** 6 | **Per serving:** Cal 193; Net Carbs 2.3g; Fat 18g; Protein 3.4g

Ingredients

12 strips jamón serrano
3 avocados, sliced

⅓ tsp salt
⅓ tsp chili powder

⅓ tsp cumin powder

Directions

Wrap each avocado slice with a piece of serrano, tucking one the serrano end into the wrap. Lay on a flat surface and sprinkle them with salt, chili powder, and cumin powder on both sides.

Preheat your Air Fryer to 350°F. Place in the wrapped pieces and cook for 8-10 minutes, turning halfway through cooking, until the serrano is browned and crunchy. Transfer to a wire rack. Serve and enjoy!

Coconut Fried Prawns

Total Time: 25 min | **Serves:** 5 | **Per serving:** Cal 260; Net Carbs 2g; Fat 14g; Protein 8g

Ingredients

1 lb jumbo prawns, peeled and deveined
¾ cup unsweetened coconut, shredded

1 tbsp erythritol
½ cup pork rinds, crushed

⅓ cup arrowroot starch
½ cup coconut milk

Directions

Preheat your Air Fryer to 350°F.

In a sealable bag, add the arrowroot starch and prawns. Seal and shake well to coat. In a bowl, combine the erythritol and coconut milk. Set aside. In a second bowl, mix the pork rinds and shredded coconut. Remove the prawns and drain the starch excess. Dip each prawn in the coconut milk mixture, then in the pork rinds.

Transfer to the Air Fryer without overcrowding and cook for 6-8 minutes. Open the Air Fryer, turn the prawns and cook for another 3-4 minutes until golden brown. Serve with a coconut-based dip if desired. Serve and enjoy!

Savory Tuna Patties

Total Time: 20 min + chilling time| **Serves:** 6 | **Per serving:** Cal 433; Net Carbs 4.1g; Fat 25g; Protein 48.2g

Ingredients

15 oz tinned tuna, flaked
1 cup grated onion
1 ½ cups grated carrots
3 large eggs

1 ½ tbsp chives, chopped
4 tbsp mayonnaise
4 tbsp pork rinds, crushed
2 ½ tsp Italian seasoning

Salt and black pepper to taste
2 ½ tsp lemon juice

Directions

In a bowl, mix tuna, onion, carrots, eggs, chives, mayonnaise, pork rinds, Italian seasoning, pepper, salt, and lemon juice. Shape the mixture into 2-inch balls. Leave in the fridge for 45 minutes.

Preheat your Air Fryer to 390°F. Grease the fryer basket with cooking spray. Remove the balls from the fridge and put them in the air fryer basket. Grease with cooking spray and cook for 6 minutes until crispy. Turn the balls, grease again, and cook for another 4 minutes. Serve with a dill dip if desired.

Tasty Kale Croquettes

Total Time: 25 min + chilling time | **Serves:** 4 | **Per serving:** Cal 224; Net Carbs 8.6g; Fat 14.2g; Protein 10.3g

Ingredients

½ cup kale chopped	2 tsp + 3 tsp butter	½ red onion, chopped
1 ½ cups pork rinds, crushed	2 tsp olive oil	2 cloves garlic, minced
1 lb turnips	2 red peppers, chopped	1 medium carrot, grated
2 cups water	3 mushrooms, chopped	⅓ cup almond flour
¼ cup coconut milk	¼ cup broccoli florets, chopped	1 cup unsweetened almond milk
Salt to taste	1/6 cup sliced green onions	2 tbsp arrowroot starch

Directions

Preheat your Air Fryer to 390°F. Warm the water in a casserole over medium heat and boil the turnips. Cook until tender and mashable. Strain and transfer to a bowl. Add 2 tbsp of butter, coconut milk, and salt; mash well.

Melt the remaining butter in a skillet over medium heat. Add the onion, garlic, red peppers, broccoli, and mushrooms. Cook for 2 minutes, stirring constantly. Add in green onions and grated carrot. Season with a bit of salt and stir in the kale until it wilts. Transfer to the turnip mash bowl and mash together; let cool. Shape balls out of the mixture and place them on a baking sheet. Let chill in the fridge for 30 minutes.

Meanwhile, place the pork rinds in a bowl and the almond flour in another bowl. Combine the arrowroot starch, almond milk, and salt in a third bowl. Set aside. Remove the patties from the fridge and dip in the almond flour, then in the arrowroot starch mixture, and finally in the pork rinds.

Working in batches, place the patties in the Air fryer basket. Do not overlap. Drizzle with olive oil and cook for 2 minutes. Toss and drizzle again. Cook for another 3 minutes. Remove to a wire rack. Serve with tomato sauce.

Cauli Rice Arancini

Total Time: 25 min + chilling time | **Serves:** 6 | **Per serving:** Cal 95; Net Carbs 3g; Fat 5.8g; Protein 5.6g

Ingredients

½ lb bell peppers, diced	3 cups cauli rice	¼ cup coconut oil
3 tbsp olive oil	2 tbsp vegetable stock	2 sprigs fresh thyme, chopped
1 onion, chopped	1 cup pork rinds, crushed	Salt and black pepper to taste
3 cloves garlic, minced	1 cup Grana Padano cheese	

Directions

In a skillet over medium heat, warm the olive oil and sauté garlic and onion until tender. Stir in the bell pepper and cook for 4 minutes. Add in the cauli rice and stir-fry for 5 minutes. Pour in the vegetable stock and thyme. Cook until the rice has absorbed the stock. Stir in the Grana Padano cheese, pepper, and salt. Turn off the heat. Let cool. Shape bite-sized balls with the mixture and place them on a plate. Transfer to the fridge for 30 minutes.

Preheat your Air Fryer to 350°F. Mix the pork rinds and the coconut oil in a bowl. Remove the balls from the fridge and dip them into the rinds mixture. Place them in the fryer basket without overcrowding and cook for 15 minutes. Turn every 5 minutes. Repeat the process with the remaining balls. Serve and enjoy!

Kohlrabi & Cheese Balls

Total Time: 50 min | **Serves:** 6 | **Per serving:** Cal 176; Net Carbs 5g; Fat 15g; Protein 5g

Ingredients

2 cups crumbled feta cheese
2 cups Parmesan cheese, grated
2 kohlrabi, peeled and chopped
1 onion, chopped

1 ½ tsp red chili flakes
1 green chili, finely chopped
Salt to taste
4 tbsp cilantro, chopped

1 cup almond flour
1 cup pork rinds, crushed

Directions

Boil the kohlrabi in salted water over medium heat for about 25-30 minutes until tender. Drain and place in a bowl. Mash the kohlrabi and let chill. Add the feta cheese, Parmesan cheese, onion, red chili flakes, green chili, salt, cilantro, and almond flour to the kohlrabi mash. Mix thoroughly and shape into balls. Dip in the pork rinds. Transfer to a baking tray.

Preheat your Air Fryer to 350°F. Put the cheese balls in the Air Fryer, close it, and cook for 15 minutes. When ready, transfer to a plate to serve.

Bell Pepper Bites with Cheese

Total Time: 25 min | **Serves:** 4 | **Per serving:** Cal 378; Net Carbs 7.3g; Fat 20.4g; Protein 38g

Ingredients

2 cups Parmigiano Reggiano cheese, grated
2 eggs, beaten
1 lb bell peppers, sliced

2 cups pork rinds, crushed
Salt and black pepper to taste

Directions

Preheat your Air Fryer to 360°F. In a bowl, mix the pork rinds, salt, and pepper. In another bowl, place the cheese and set aside. After that, dip bell peppers in the eggs in the pork rinds, and finally in the cheese. Transfer the bell peppers to your air fryer basket and AirFry them for 14-16 minutes.

Sunday Eggplant Fries

Total Time: 25 min | **Serves:** 4 | **Per serving:** Cal 367; Net Carbs 5g; Fat 28g; Protein 11g

Ingredients

3 medium eggplants, sliced
2 egg whites

½ cup seasoned pork rinds, crushed
2 tbsp Parmesan cheese, grated

¼ tsp garlic powder
Salt and black pepper to taste

Directions

Preheat your Air Fryer to 425°F. Grease a rack with cooking spray. In a bowl, whisk the egg whites with salt and pepper. In a second bowl, combine the garlic powder, Parmesan cheese, and pork rinds. Dip the eggplant slices in the egg, then in the rinds. Place the slices in the rack and sprinkle with spray. Cook for 20 minutes. Serve.

Chicken Habanero Poppers

Total Time: 35 min | **Serves:** 6 | **Per serving:** Cal 523; Net Carbs 8.7g; Fat 42.8g; Protein 49.6g

Ingredients

8 habanero peppers, halved
4 chicken breasts, butterflied
6 oz cream cheese

6 oz mozzarella cheese, shredded
16 slices bacon
1 cup pork rinds, crushed

Salt and black pepper to taste
2 eggs

Directions

Preheat your Air Fryer to 350°F. Flatten the chicken breasts with a meat tenderizer. Then, season thoroughly with salt and pepper. Combine the cream cheese, mozzarella cheese, and a pinch of salt and pepper in a bowl. Stir well.

Fill habanero peppers with the cheese mixture. Transfer the chicken to a chopping board and lay 2 bacon slices on top of each half. Wrap each stuffed habanero pepper with a chicken half. In a bowl, beat the eggs.

In another bowl, place the pork rinds. Grease Air Fryer with cooking spray. Set habaneros inside and cook for 7 minutes. Toss the peppers and cook for another 4 minutes. Transfer to a paper towel-lined plate. Serve and enjoy!

Paprika Colby Snacks

Total Time: 25 min | **Serves:** 4 | **Per serving:** Cal 112; Net Carbs 3.1g; Fat 5.6g; Protein 2.8g

Ingredients

4 tbsp grated Colby cheese + extra for rolling
1 cup almond flour + extra for kneading
¼ tsp smoked paprika   3 tsp butter
½ tsp baking powder   A pinch of salt

Directions

Preheat your Air Fryer to 350°F. Mix the cheese, almond flour, baking powder, smoked paprika powder, butter, and salt in a bowl. Pour the water and mix to get a dough. Transfer onto a flat surface. Knead the dough for a while with your hands. Place some flour on the flat surface and roll the dough into a tiny layer.

With a pastry cutter, slice the dough into your desired shapes. Place them in the fryer basket and cook for 2 minutes. Open the Air Fryer and stir the cheese lings. Cook for another 3 minutes. Serve and enjoy!

Herby Tomato Galette

Total Time: 15 min | **Serves:** 3 | **Per serving:** Cal 131; Net Carbs 2g; Fat 5g; Protein 13g

Ingredients

3 large tomatoes   A pinch of black pepper   1 cup mozzarella cheese, shredded
A pinch of salt   2 tbsp mixed herbs

Directions

Preheat your Air Fryer to 340°F. Cut the tomatoes into slices and arranges them on the greased air fryer basket. Sprinkle with herbs, pepper, and salt. Top with mozzarella cheese. Bake for 8-10 minutes. Serve warm and enjoy!

Parmesan Caperberries

Total Time: 20 min | **Serves:** 4 | **Per serving:** Cal 255; Net Carbs 4.2g; Fat 15.5g; Protein 24.7g

Ingredients

2 eggs   2 tsp water   1 ½ cups pork rinds, crushed
3 cups caperberries   1 cup Parmesan cheese, grated   Black pepper to taste

Directions

In a bowl, combine the pork rinds and black pepper. In a separate bowl, beat the eggs with the water. In a third bowl, place the cheese. Pat dry the caperberries with a paper towel.

Preheat your Air Fryer to 400°F. Dip the caperberries in the egg mixture, then in the pork rinds, and finally in the cheese. Transfer to the Air Fryer. Cook for 9 minutes, tossing halfway through cooking until crispy. Enjoy!

Parmesan Zucchini Fries

Total Time: 15 min | **Serves:** 3 | **Per serving:** Cal 193; Net Carbs 0.3g; Fat 21g; Protein 1g

Ingredients

¼ cup Parmesan cheese, grated
4 large zucchinis, cut into strips

½ tsp paprika
½ tsp dry dill

¼ cup olive oil
A pinch of salt

Directions

Preheat your Air Fryer to 390°F. Combine the Parmesan cheese, olive oil, salt, paprika, dill, and zucchini strips in a bowl. Toss to coat. Lay on the fryer basket and AirFry for 15 minutes, shaking once. Serve and enjoy!

Vegetable Caviar with Dill Pickles

Total Time: 15 min | **Serves:** 4 | **Per serving:** Cal 212; Net Carbs 7.8g; Fat 13g; Protein 10g

Ingredients

1 red bell pepper
1 lb tomatoes
1 onion

1 garlic clove
Salt and black pepper to taste
1 tbsp olive oil

10 black olives, sliced
2 dill pickles, chopped

Directions

Preheat your Air Fryer to 300°F. Lay the red bell pepper, tomatoes, and onion in the basket and cook for 5 minutes. Turn them and cook for another 5 minutes. Transfer to a plate and peel. Put the vegetables, garlic, and olive oil in a blender, season with salt and pepper, and blitz until smooth. Serve topped with olives and dill pickles.

Jalapeño Rellenos with Cheese

Total Time: 35 min | **Serves:** 4 | **Per serving:** Cal 258; Net Carbs 2g; Fat 20g; Protein 15g

Ingredients

2 jalapeño peppers, halved and seeded
1 cup mozzarella cheese, shredded

1 cup cheddar cheese, shredded
2 large eggs, beaten
½ cup water

2 tbsp almond flour
½ cup almond milk
1 can sugar-free tomato sauce

Directions

Preheat your Air Fryer to 350°F. Grease a baking dish with cooking spray. Mix the eggs, water, flour, and milk in a bowl. Fill the jalapeño halves with the mixture and top with cheddar cheese. Arrange them on a greased baking dish. Bake in the air fryer for 25 minutes. Take out the basket and cover with the tomato sauce. Bake for another 10 minutes. Serve sprinkled with mozzarella cheese. Enjoy!

Cheesy Broccoli Balls

Total Time: 25 min | **Serves:** 4 | **Per serving:** Cal 167; Net Carbs 5.2g; Fat 10g; Protein 12g

Ingredients

10 oz riced broccoli
1 onion, chopped
2 garlic cloves, chopped

2 eggs, beaten
½ cup Manchego cheese, grated
Salt and black pepper to taste

½ cup pork rinds, crushed

Directions

Preheat your Air Fryer to 380°F. Mix the broccoli rice, onion, garlic, eggs, manchego cheese, salt, and pepper. Mould 10 balls. Place the pork rinds on a plate and dip in the balls. Sprinkle with oil. Place the balls in the fryer and cook for 16 minutes until golden and crispy. Turn over halfway through the cooking time. Serve and enjoy!

Roasted Trout with Yogurt Sauce

Total Time: 15 min | **Serves:** 2 | **Per serving:** Cal 291; Net Carbs 5.6g; Fat 23g; Protein 15g

Ingredients

2 trout fillets
2 tbsp olive oil

½ cup yogurt
½ cup buttermilk

A pinch of salt
2 tbsp fresh dill, finely chopped

Directions

Preheat your Air Fryer to 370°F. In a bowl, mix yogurt, buttermilk, salt, and dill and set aside. Brush the trout with olive oil and season with salt. Place in the fryer basket and cook for 10 minutes. Flip the fillets over at half-time. Top the trout with the sauce and serve. Enjoy!

Cheesy Mushrooms with Red Onion

Total Time: 20 min | **Serves:** 4 | **Per serving:** Cal 240; Net Carbs 7.2g; Fat 19g; Protein 10g

Ingredients

1 red onion, chopped
6 portobello mushrooms

2 tbsp olive oil
2 cloves garlic, minced

1 tbsp fresh parsley, chopped
1 cup cream cheese, grated

Directions

Preheat your Air Fryer to 390°F. Remove the stems of the mushrooms. In a food processor, blend the mushroom stems, garlic, red onion, parsley, and olive oil until smooth. Place the caps of the mushrooms in the air fryer basket. Stuff the caps with the mixture and top with cream cheese. Cook for 20 minutes. Serve and enjoy!

Gorgonzola Filled Mushrooms

Total Time: 30 min | **Serves:** 5 | **Per serving:** Cal 65; Net Carbs 3.2g; Fat 4.5g; Protein 3.4g

Ingredients

½ cup gorgonzola cheese, crumbled
10 mushrooms, stems removed

3 tbsp olive oil
1 cup cream cheese

1 green onion, chopped
Salt and black pepper to taste

Directions

Preheat your Air Fryer to 360°F. Drizzle the mushrooms with olive oil and set aside. Combine the gorgonzola cheese, cream cheese, green onion, salt, and pepper in a bowl. Stuff the mushrooms with the mixture. Place the mushrooms in the fryer. Cook for 14 minutes until the mushrooms are golden brown and the cheese has melted.

Herby Chicken Meatballs

Total Time: 30 min | **Serves:** 3 | **Per serving:** Cal 483; Net Carbs 8.2g; Fat 23g; Protein 54g

Ingredients

1 lb ground chicken
3 green onions, chopped
1 garlic clove, finely chopped

2 eggs
1 cup pork rinds, crushed
1 tbsp fresh mint, chopped

1 tbsp flat-leaf parsley, chopped
Salt and black pepper to taste

Directions

Preheat your Air Fryer to 380°F. Combine the ground chicken, green onions, garlic, pork rinds, eggs, mint, parsley, salt, and pepper in a bowl and shape well-sized balls. Place in the air fryer basket and AirFry them for 14-16 minutes, turning them halfway through the cook time. Serve and enjoy!

Rosemary Turnip Strips

Total Time: 25 min | **Serves:** 2 | **Per serving:** Cal 162; Net Carbs 6.2g; Fat 14g; Protein 1.4g

Ingredients

½ tsp paprika

3 turnips, cut into strips

2 tbsp olive oil

2 garlic cloves, crushed

1 tsp fresh rosemary, chopped

Salt and black pepper to taste

Directions

Preheat your Air Fryer to 360°F. In a bowl, combine the olive oil, paprika, garlic, rosemary, salt, and pepper. Dip the turnips in the mixture to coat. Place the slices in the basket and cook for 14 minutes, flipping twice. Serve.

Coconut Calamari Rings

Total Time: 15 min + cooling time | **Serves:** 4 | **Per serving:** Cal 233; Net Carbs 0.7g; Fat 11g; Protein 32g

Ingredients

¼ cup coconut flour

1 lb calamari (squid), cut in rings

2 large eggs, beaten

1 cup pork rinds, crushed

Directions

Coat the calamari rings in the flour, then in the eggs, and finally in the pork rinds. Put in the fridge for 2 hours. Preheat Air Fryer to 380°F. Lay the rings in the fryer basket. Spray with cooking oil. AirFry for 10 minutes. Serve.

Prosciutto Wrapped Goat Cheese Balls

Total Time: 25 min | **Serves:** 15 | **Per serving:** Cal 151; Net Carbs 8.2g; Fat 10.5g; Protein 9g

Ingredients

1 cup unsweetened dried blueberries

16 oz soft goat cheese

2 tbsp fresh rosemary, finely chopped

1 cup almonds, chopped into small pieces

Salt and black pepper to taste

15 prosciutto slices

Directions

Preheat your Air Fryer to 400°F and line with baking paper. In a bowl, stir the goat cheese, rosemary, almonds, salt, pepper, and dried blueberries. Shape well-sized balls and wrap them with prosciutto slices. Place in the fryer and cook for 10 minutes. Be careful not to overcook. Allow cooling before removing. Serve with toothpicks.

Fried Green Tomatoes

Total Time: 15 min | **Serves:** 3 | **Per serving:** Cal 123; Net Carbs 3.1g; Fat 18g; Protein 5.3g

Ingredients

¼ tbsp Italian seasoning

3 green tomatoes, sliced

Salt and black pepper to taste

¼ cup hazelnut flour

½ cup buttermilk

1 cup pork rinds, crushed

Directions

Preheat your Air Fryer to 400°F. Place in a bowl the flour and in a second bowl the buttermilk. Sprinkle the tomatoes with salt and pepper. In another bowl, combine the Italian seasoning with the pork rinds.

Dip tomatoes in the flour, then in the buttermilk, and finally in the rinds mix. Repeat the process with each tomato slice. Place the tomatoes in the fryer and cook for 5 minutes. Remove to a plate and serve.

Sesame Fried Tofu

Total Time: 25 min | **Serves:** 4 | **Per serving:** Cal 427; Net Carbs 5.1g; Fat 31g; Protein 38g

Ingredients

½ cup sesame flour
3 blocks of firm tofu, cubed

2 tbsp olive oil
½ cup pork rinds, crushed

Salt and black pepper to taste

Directions

Preheat your Air Fryer to 360°F. Brush the tofu with olive oil. Combine the sesame flour, pork rinds, salt, and pepper on a plate. Dip the tofu in the flour mixture. Sprinkle with olive oil and place the tofu in the lined air fryer basket. Cook for 14 minutes, turning once. Serve and enjoy!

Rib Steak with Chili-Garlic Sauce

Total Time: 35 min | **Serves:** 2 | **Per serving:** Cal 616; Net Carbs 2.4g; Fat 53g; Protein 41.7g

Ingredients

1 tsp ground nutmeg
½ cup chili-garlic sauce

1 rack rib steak
Salt and white pepper to taste

½ tsp red pepper flakes

Directions

Preheat Air Fryer to 360°F. Rub the rib rack with salt, nutmeg, white pepper, and red pepper flakes. Place in the basket and cook for 15 minutes. Flip the ribs over and cook for another 15 minutes. Transfer the ribs onto a chopping board and let sit for 3 minutes before slicing. Top with chili-garlic sauce to serve.

Fontina & Soppressata Mushrooms

Total Time: 25 min | **Serves:** 3 | **Per serving:** Cal 340; Net Carbs 3.8g; Fat 19g; Protein 37g

Ingredients

3 portobello mushrooms, stems removed
12 slices soppressata
3 tbsp olive oil
3 tbsp tomato sauce

3 tbsp fontina cheese, shredded
A pinch of salt
A pinch of dried Italian seasonings

Flakes red pepper, crushed for garnish
Parmesan cheese, for garnish

Directions

Preheat your Air Fryer to 330°F. Spray each mushroom side with olive oil and season with salt and Italian seasoning. Pour the tomato sauce over the mushrooms and top with the cheese. Place the mushrooms in the fryer and cook for 5 minutes. After 1 minute, remove the basket and add the soppressata on top of the mushrooms. Put back in the Fryer and cook for another 5 minutes. Top with Parmesan cheese and red pepper flakes to serve.

Monterey Jack Sticks

Total Time: 20 min + cooling time | **Serves:** 3 | **Per serving:** Cal 314; Net Carbs 1.5g; Fat 16g; Protein 36g

Ingredients

8 oz Monterrey Jack cheese
1 egg

1 cup pork rinds, crushed
Salt to taste

1 tbsp olive oil

Directions

Slice the Monterey jack cheese into 6 strips. Beat the eggs with salt. Dip the strips in the egg, then in the pork rinds. Put in the refrigerator for at least 30 minutes. Preheat your Air Fryer to 360°F. Grease the fryer basket with olive oil. Arrange the strips on the air fryer basket and AirFry for 10 minutes, turning once. Serve and enjoy!

Ricotta & Broccoli Cups

Total Time: 20 min | **Serves:** 3 | **Per serving:** Cal 432; Net Carbs 3.2g; Fat 37g; Protein 24g

Ingredients

1 cup ricotta cheese
1 head broccoli, cut into florets
1 egg, beaten

A pinch of nutmeg
1 tbsp ginger powder
1 cup cheddar cheese, shredded

Salt and black pepper to taste

Directions

Steam the broccoli for 4 minutes. Drain and transfer to a bowl. Leave to cool for a few minutes. Combine with the egg and ricotta cheese. Stir in the nutmeg, ginger, salt, and pepper.

Preheat your Air Fryer to 320°F. Grease the small ramekins with butter. Spoon the mixture into the ramekins and sprinkle with cheddar cheese. Bake for 10-12 minutes until golden on top. Serve and enjoy!

Chili Cuttlefish Bites

Total Time: 25 min | **Serves:** 3 | **Per serving:** Cal 128; Net Carbs 0g; Fat 3g; Protein 22g

Ingredients

1 head cuttlefish, cut in bite-sized pieces
1 cup pimiento-stuffed green olives, sliced
½ piece coriander, chopped
2 strips chili pepper, chopped

1 tbsp olive oil
Salt and black pepper to taste

Directions

Preheat your Air Fryer to 400°F. Combine the cuttlefish, chili pepper, salt, black pepper, olive oil, and coriander in a bowl. Marinate for 10 minutes. Transfer the pieces to an oven-safe bowl. Place in the air fryer basket and cook for 15 minutes. Stir every 5 minutes. After 15 minutes, stir in the green olives and cook for another 3 minutes. When ready, remove it to a serving platter. Serve hot with bread slices and mayonnaise.

Neapolitan-Style Stuffed Tomatoes

Total Time: 15 min | **Serves:** 2 | **Per serving:** Cal 302; Net Carbs 4.2g; Fat 16g; Protein 30g

Ingredients

1 cup Buffalo mozzarella cheese, crumbled
2 tomatoes
4 eggs

2 tbsp parsley
1 tbsp olive oil

Salt and black pepper to taste

Directions

Preheat Air Fryer to 360°F. Chop the tomatoes into two halves and scoop out seeds and pulp. Sprinkle with salt and pepper and transfer to air fryer basket. Fill the tomatoes with half of the cheese and parsley. Crack 1 egg in each tomato half and top with the remaining cheese. Spray with olive oil. Cook for 8 minutes at 370°F.

Veggie Stuffed Cabbage Rolls

Total Time: 30 min | **Serves:** 4 | **Per serving:** Cal 88; Net Carbs 7.2g; Fat 3.1g; Protein 2g

Ingredients

8 cabbage leaves
2 garlic cloves, chopped
1 tbsp fresh ginger, minced

2 tbsp soy sauce, sugar-free
1 tsp sesame oil
1 red bell pepper, chopped

1 cup mushrooms, chopped
1 carrot, chopped
½ cup scallions, chopped

Directions

Preheat your Air Fryer to 340°F. Warm the sesame oil in a saucepan over medium heat. Stir-fry the garlic, ginger, soy sauce, bell pepper, mushroom, carrot, and scallions for 3-5 minutes until soft. Spoon the veggie mixture into the center of the cabbage leaves. Roll and secure the rolls with toothpicks. Place the cabbage rolls in the greased basket and cook for 12-14 minutes until golden and crispy. Serve with chili sauce if desired.

Chili Parsnip Chips

Total Time: 25 min | **Serves:** 4 | **Per serving:** Cal 104; Net Carbs 9.7g; Fat 3.1g; Protein 1.8g

Ingredients

1 tsp chili powder

3 parsnips, sliced

2 tsp olive oil

Garlic salt and black pepper to taste

Directions

Preheat your Air Fryer to 360°F. Put the parsnip and drizzle with olive oil, chili powder, garlic salt, and black pepper in a bowl. Place in the fryer and cook for 14 minutes until golden and crispy. Turn them at least once.

Buttery Beets Slices

Total Time: 20 min | **Serves:** 4 | **Per serving:** Cal 54; Net Carbs 5g; Fat 5.8g; Protein 2.4g

Ingredients

1 pound beets, sliced

1 tsp dried dill

1 tbsp butter, melted

1 tbsp erythritol

Salt and black pepper to taste

Directions

Preheat your Air Fryer to 350°F. Combine the butter, beets, and erythritol in a bowl. Toss to coat. Season with dill, salt, and pepper. Place in the air fryer and cook for 12 minutes.

Roasted Eggplants with Parsley

Total Time: 15 min | **Serves:** 6 | **Per serving:** Cal 95; Net Carbs 8.7 g; Fat 5.3g; Protein 2g

Ingredients

1 tsp caraway seeds

20 oz eggplants, sliced

1 tbsp olive oil

A handful of fresh parsley

Directions

Preheat your Air Fryer to 350°F. In a bowl, stir the olive oil, eggplants, and caraway, mix to coat. Place the slices in the fryer and cook for 12 minutes. Top with fresh parsley to serve.

Zucchini Chips

Total Time: 20 min | **Serves:** 2 | **Per serving:** Cal 265; Net Carbs 4,2g; Fat 21g; Protein 4g

Ingredients

2 zucchinis

¼ cup almond flour

¼ cup olive oil

½ cup water

Directions

Preheat your Air Fryer to 390°F. Slice the zucchinis in half-inch size. Combine the almond flour, olive oil, and water in a bowl. Dip the zucchinis slices to coat. Cook for 12 minutes until browned. Repeat the process with the remaining slices. Serve with tomato sauce.

FISH & SEAFOOD

Buttered Cod with Lemon & Olives

Total Time: 20 min | **Serves:** 4 | **Per serving:** Cal 180; Net Carbs 0.2g; Fat 10.9g; Protein 17.5g

Ingredients

4 cod fillets
3 tbsp salted butter, melted

1 tsp Old Bay seasoning
1 medium lemon, sliced

1 cup jalapeño-stuffed olives, sliced
Salt and black pepper to taste

Directions

Preheat the Air Fryer to 360°F. Coat the cod fillets with melted butter and season with Old Bay seasoning, salt, and black pepper. Transfer them to a baking dish; place the dish in the air fryer basket. Cook for 8-10 minutes until the cod flakes easily with a fork. Top with lemon slices and olives. Serve and enjoy!

Gingery Salmon

Total Time: 25 min + marinating time | **Serves:** 4 | **Per serving:** Cal 109; Net Carbs 0.2g; Fat 4g; Protein 14.9g

Ingredients

1 lb salmon, skinless and boneless
¼ cup soy sauce
½ tsp liquid smoke

Salt and black pepper to taste
½ medium lime, juiced
½ tsp ground ginger

¼ tsp red pepper flakes
¼ tsp cayenne pepper
¼ tsp powdered erythritol

Directions

In a mixing bowl, thoroughly combine all ingredients, except for the salmon, and stir well. Slice the salmon lengthwise into strips, about ½-inch thick. Add the strips to the marinade and toss to coat. Cover the bowl with plastic foil and place it in the refrigerator for 1 hour.

Preheat the Air Fryer to 350°F. Working in batches, arrange the salmon slices on the air fryer basket. Cook for 14-16 minutes. Serve and enjoy!

Pesto & Almond Crusted Cod Fillets

Total Time: 20 min | **Serves:** 4 | **Per serving:** Cal 432; Net Carbs 0.8g; Fat 34g; Protein 23.4g

Ingredients

1 lemon, zested and juiced
½ cup pesto

½ cup almonds, roughly chopped
4 cod fillets

3 tbsp butter, melted
Salt and black pepper to taste

Directions

Preheat the Air Fryer to 395°F. Place the almonds in a bowl and stir in the lemon zest, half of the lemon juice, and pesto. Season with salt and pepper. Spread the mixture on top of the fish. Arrange the fillets on the air fryer basket and drizzle with butter. Cook for 10-12 minutes until the cod flakes easily with a fork. Drizzle with the remaining lemon juice. Serve warm and enjoy!

Mediterranean Salmon Parcels

Total Time: 25 min | **Serves:** 4 | **Per serving:** Cal 250; Net Carbs 0.2g; Fat 17g; Protein 22g

Ingredients

4 salmon fillets, skin removed
4 tbsp unsalted butter, melted

2 garlic cloves, sliced
1 fennel bulb, finely sliced

1 medium lemon, zested
½ tsp dried dill

Directions

Preheat the Air Fryer to 390°F. Cut a sheet of aluminum foil into 4 squares, approximately 5x5 inches. Divide the salmon fillets between the foil pieces and brush them with butter. Arrange the garlic and fennel slices on top of the fillets and sprinkle with lemon zest and dill. Wrap and secure the parcels tightly to enclose the ingredients perfectly. Transfer the parcels to the air fryer basket and cook for 12-14 minutes. Once the time is done, the salmon should be cooked through. Serve and enjoy!

Cajun-Spiced Fish Taco Bowls

Total Time: 20 min | **Serves**: 2 | **Per serving**: Cal 340; Net Carbs 2.7g; Fat 25g; Protein 16g

Ingredients

1 cup Savoy cabbage, shredded
¼ cup sour cream
2 tbsp mayonnaise
¼ cup chopped pickled jalapeños
¼ cup red onions, sliced

2 haddock fillets
1 tsp chili powder
½ tsp Cajun seasoning
1 tsp cumin
½ tsp paprika

¼ tsp garlic powder
1 medium avocado, sliced
½ lime, juiced
1 tbsp cilantro, chopped

Directions

Preheat the Air Fryer to 375°F. In a mixing bowl, thoroughly combine Savoy cabbage, sour cream, mayonnaise, jalapeños, and red onions and toss until well coated. Place in the refrigerator for 20 minutes.

Mix the chili powder, Cajun seasoning, cumin, paprika, and garlic powder in a small bowl. Rub the mixture onto the haddock fillets. Transfer them to the greased air fryer basket; spritz them with cooking spray. Cook for 8-10 minutes, turning them over halfway through cooking until crispy.

When ready, cut the fish into pieces. Assemble the bowls with the previously prepared slaw and fish pieces. Drizzle with lime juice and sprinkle with cilantro. Serve topped with avocado and enjoy!

Crispy Tilapia Sticks

Total Time: 25 min | **Serves**: 4 | **Per serving**: Cal 208; Net Carbs 0.4g; Fat 11g; Protein 25g

Ingredients

1 oz pork rinds, finely ground
¼ cup almond flour

½ tsp seafood seasoning
2 tbsp coconut oil

1 large egg
1 lb tilapia fillets, cut into strips

Directions

Preheat the Air Fryer to 390°F. Beat the egg in a bowl. Mix the pork rinds, almond flour, seafood seasoning, and coconut oil in another bowl. Dredge the tilapia strips in the egg, then in the pork rind mixture. Transfer the fish to the air fryer basket and AirFry for 10 minutes, flipping once. Serve hot.

Spicy Salmon Cakes

Total Time: 20 min | **Serves**: 4 | **Per serving**: Cal 320; Net Carbs 1.4g; Fat 19g; Protein 34g

Ingredients

1 (14.75-oz) can pink salmon
2 medium eggs
2 green onions, chopped

1 tsp dried dill
½ cup pork rinds, ground
2 tbsp mayonnaise

3 tsp sriracha
1 tsp chili powder
Salt and black pepper to taste

Directions

Preheat the Air Fryer to 390°F. Place all ingredients in a large bowl and mix with your hands until everything is well incorporated. Shape the mixture into 4 cakes. Transfer them to the air fryer basket. Cook for 8-10 minutes, turning them over halfway through cooking until crispy. Serve and enjoy!

Baked Salmon with Peppers

Total Time: 25 min | **Serves:** 4 | **Per serving:** Cal 165; Net Carbs 0.3g; Fat 10g; Protein 15.9g

Ingredients

2 bell peppers, deveined and sliced
2 jalapeños, sliced
4 salmon fillets, skin removed

1 tbsp butter, melted
1 tsp Ancho chili powder
2 garlic cloves, finely minced

1 lime, juiced
2 tbsp cilantro, chopped
Salt and black pepper to taste

Directions

Preheat the Air Fryer to 375°F. Rub the salmon with butter, chili powder, and garlic. Arrange the fillets on the air fryer basket and add the jalapeños and bell peppers. Drizzle with lime juice and sprinkle with salt and pepper. Cook for 10-12 minutes until the salmon flakes easily with a fork and the peppers are tender. Garnish with cilantro and serve warm.

Tuna-Avocado Bites

Total Time: 20 min | **Serves:** 4 | **Per serving:** Cal 321; Net Carbs 0.7g; Fat 25g; Protein 17.3g

Ingredients

½ tsp garlic powder
¼ tsp onion powder
Salt and black pepper to taste

2 (5-oz) cans tuna, drained
¼ cup mayonnaise
1 celery stalk, chopped

1 medium avocado, mashed
½ cup almond flour
2 tsp coconut oil, melted

Directions

Preheat the Air Fryer to 390°F. Place the garlic powder, onion powder, salt, pepper, tuna, mayonnaise, celery, and mashed avocado and mix everything until well incorporated. Shape the mixture into small balls and roll them in the almond flour. Coat with coconut oil and transfer the balls to the air fryer basket. Cook for 8 minutes, turning them over halfway through cooking. Serve warm.

Asian-Style Tuna Steaks

Total Time: 15 min | **Serves:** 3 | **Per serving:** Cal 281; Net Carbs 0g; Fat 10g; Protein 42.9g

Ingredients

3 tuna steaks
2 tsp coconut oil, melted
½ tsp garlic powder

½ tsp ginger powder
½ tbsp fish sauce
1 tbsp soy sauce

1 tbsp white sesame seeds
1 tbsp black sesame seeds
1 lemon, sliced

Directions

Preheat the Air Fryer to 395°F. In a small bowl, whisk the coconut oil, garlic powder, ginger powder, fish sauce, and soy sauce. Brush the tuna steaks with the mixture and arrange them on the air fryer basket. Top with sesame seeds and press to coat well. Cook for 8-10 minutes until the tuna flakes easily with a fork. Garnish with lemon.

Norwegian Tuna Zoodle Bake

Total Time: 30 min | **Serves:** 4 | **Per serving:** Cal 340; Net Carbs 4.2g; Fat 25g; Protein 14.8g

Ingredients

2 tbsp butter
1 shallot, chopped
¼ cup white mushrooms, chopped
2 celery stalks, finely chopped
½ cup heavy cream

½ cup vegetable broth
2 tbsp mayonnaise
¼ tsp xanthan gum
½ tsp red pepper flakes
2 medium zucchini, spiralized

2 (5-oz) cans albacore tuna
6 anchovy fillets, cut in half lengthways
1 oz pork rinds, finely ground
Salt and black pepper to taste

Directions

Preheat the Air Fryer to 390°F. Melt the butter in a skillet over medium heat. Add the shallot, mushrooms, and celery and stir-fry for 4-5 minutes until tender. Stir in heavy cream, broth, mayonnaise, and xanthan gum. Reduce the heat to low and cook for an additional 3 minutes or until the mixture has thickened. Sprinkle with red pepper flakes, salt, and pepper and add the zoodles and tuna. Remove and stir to coat.

Transfer the mixture to a baking dish and place the dish in the air fryer basket. Sprinkle over the pork rinds and lay the anchovies on top. Cover with a piece of aluminum foil and cook for 12 minutes. Remove the foil and cook for 3-4 more minutes until the top is crisp and golden brown. Serve warm.

Harissa-Spiced Salmon

Total Time: 15 min | **Serves**: 3 | **Per serving**: Cal 250; Net Carbs 0.2g; Fat 17g; Protein 21g

Ingredients

1 tbsp harissa seasoning	½ tsp garlic powder	3 salmon fillets, skin removed
2 tbsp butter, melted	1 tsp paprika	2 tsp cilantro, chopped
⅛ tsp ground cayenne pepper	Sea salt and black pepper to taste	1 lemon, sliced

Directions

Preheat the Air Fryer to 390°F. In a mixing bowl, whisk the harissa seasoning, butter, cayenne pepper, garlic powder, paprika, sea salt, and black pepper. Add in the salmon and toss to coat. Arrange the salmon fillets on the air fryer basket. Cook for 6-8 minutes, turning the salmon halfway through cooking until it flakes easily with a fork. Sprinkle with cilantro and top with lemon slices. Serve and enjoy!

Awesome Cod Fish Nuggets

Total Time: 20 min | **Serves**: 4 | **Per serving**: Cal 168; Net Carbs 0.4g; Fat 7.5g; Protein 16.8g

Ingredients

4 cod fillets	2 eggs, beaten	A pinch of salt
2 tbsp olive oil	1 cup pork rinds, crushed	1 cup almond flour

Directions

Preheat the Air Fryer to 390°F. Place the pork rinds, olive oil, and salt in a bowl and mix until combined. Pour the eggs into another bowl and the almond flour into a third bowl.

Toss cod fillets in the almond flour, then in the eggs, and then in the pork rind mixture. Place them in the fryer basket, close the Air Fryer, and cook for 9 minutes. At the 5-minute mark, quickly turn the chicken nuggets over. Once golden brown, remove onto a serving plate and serve with vegetable fries.

Dilled Salmon

Total Time: 25 min | **Serves**: 4 | **Per serving**: Cal 240; Net Carbs 0g; Fat 6g; Protein 16g

Ingredients

4 (6-oz) salmon pieces	2 tsp olive oil	1 cup sour cream
Salt and black pepper to taste	3 tbsp chopped dill + for garnishing	1 cup Greek yogurt

Directions

Preheat the Air Fryer to 370°F. In a bowl, add the sour cream, Greek yogurt, dill, and salt. Mix well and set aside until ready to serve. Drizzle the olive oil over the salmon. Season with salt and pepper. Rub lightly with your hands. Arrange the salmon pieces on the fryer basket and AirFry them for 15 minutes. Remove the salmon to a serving platter and top with previously prepared dill sauce. Serve and enjoy!

Fennel Trout en Papillote with Herbs

Total Time: 30 min | **Serves:** 2 | **Per serving:** Cal 305; Net Carbs 8.9g; Fat 21.1g; Protein 9.6g

Ingredients

¾ lb whole trout, scaled and cleaned
¼ bulb fennel, sliced
½ brown onion, sliced

3 tbsp chopped parsley
3 tbsp chopped dill
2 tbsp olive oil

1 lemon, sliced
Salt and black pepper to taste

Directions

In a bowl, add the onion, parsley, dill, fennel, salt, and pepper. Mix and drizzle the olive oil over it. Preheat the Air Fryer to 350°F. Open the cavity of the fish and fill with the fennel mixture. Wrap the fish thoroughly in parchment paper and then in foil. Place the fish in the fryer basket and cook for 10 minutes. Remove the paper and foil and top with lemon slices. Serve with a side of cooked mushrooms.

Lemon-Zest Salmon

Total Time: 20 min | **Serves:** 2 | **Per serving:** Cal 421; Net Carbs 1.3g; Fat 17g; Protein 64g

Ingredients

2 salmon fillets

Pink salt to taste

Zest of 1 lemon

Directions

Spray the fillets with cooking spray. Rub them with salt and lemon zest. Line baking paper in your air fryer basket to avoid sticking. Cook the fillets for 10 minutes at 360°F, turning once halfway through cooking. Serve with steamed asparagus and a drizzle of lemon juice.

Perfect Salmon Quiche

Total Time: 35 min | **Serves:** 4 | **Per serving:** Cal 515; Net Carbs 2.6g; Fat 54g; Protein 11g

Ingredients

5 oz salmon fillets, cubed
2 cups almond flour
1 cup cold butter, cubed

4 tbsp whipping cream
2 large eggs and 1 yolk
1 large green onion, finely sliced

1 tbsp lemon juice
Salt and black pepper to taste

Directions

Preheat the Air Fryer to 360°F. Season salmon fillets with salt, pepper and lemon juice. Set it aside. In a large bowl, stir the butter and almond flour. Add the egg yolk, 1 tbsp of water and knead the entire mixture into a ball. Roll the dough onto a floured surface. Put the round dough into the quiche pan and seal on the edges.

Trim the dough to fit the edges of the pan you intend to use, or just let it stick out. Beat eggs with cream, then add a pinch of salt and pepper. Spoon the mixture into a quiche pan and sprinkle with green onions. Place the pan in the Air fryer and Bake for 20 minutes until golden brown. Serve warm or cold with a green salad if desired.

Saucy Lemon Barramundi

Total Time: 25 min | **Serves:** 3 | **Per serving:** Cal 512; Net Carbs 8.1g; Fat 53g; Protein 25.3g

Ingredients

3 barramundi fillets
2 lemons, juiced
Salt and black pepper to taste
3 tbsp butter

¾ cup heavy cream
½ cup white wine
2 bay leaves
15 black peppercorns

2 cloves garlic, minced
2 shallots, chopped

Directions

Preheat the Air Fryer to 390°F. Place the barramundi fillets in the greased air fryer basket. Grill for 15 minutes. Melt the butter in a small pan over medium heat. Add the garlic and shallots and stir-fry for 1-2 minutes. Pour in the wine, bay leaves, and peppercorns. Stir and allow the liquid to reduce by three quarters. Stir in heavy cream and let the sauce thicken. Add the lemon juice, pepper, and salt. Turn the heat off. Strain the sauce into a serving bowl. Pour the sauce over the fish. Serve and enjoy!

Crispy Fish Strips

Total Time: 20 min | **Serves:** 4 | **Per serving:** Cal 183; Net Carbs 2.6g; Fat 6.7g; Protein 24g

Ingredients

2 fresh white fish fillets, cut into 4 fingers each

1 egg, beaten
½ cup buttermilk

1 cup pork rinds, crushed
Salt and black pepper to taste

Directions

In a bowl, mix egg and buttermilk. On a plate, mix pork rinds, salt and black pepper. Dip each finger into the egg mixture, then roll it up in the pork rinds, and grease with cooking spray. Arrange them in the air fryer and cook for 10 minutes at 340°F, turning once halfway through cooking. Serve with garlic mayo and lemon wedges.

Hot Catfish

Total Time: 20 min + marinating time | **Serves:** 2 | **Per serving:** Cal 365; Net Carbs 5.2g; Fat 21g; Protein 33g

Ingredients

2 catfish fillets
Salt and pepper to taste
1 cup buttermilk

2 tbsp hot sauce
2 tbsp oil
1 cup almond flour

1 tbsp crab seasoning
1 tbsp garlic powder

Directions

Season the catfish fillets with salt and pepper. In a dish, combine the buttermilk with the hot sauce. Add the catfish fillets and toss to coat. Cover with plastic wrap and let marinate for 30 minutes. Whisk the almond flour, crab seasoning, and garlic powder in a bowl. Remove the catfish from the buttermilk and let the excess oil drip off.

Preheat the Air Fryer to 390°F. Coat the catfish with the almond mixture. Place the fillets in the greased air fryer basket and drizzle with olive oil. AirFry for 15 minutes. When the cooking time is complete, slide out the basket, gently turn the fillets, spray them with oil, and cook for 5 more minutes. Serve and enjoy!

Herb & Lemon Crusted Haddock

Total Time: 20 min | **Serves:** 4 | **Per serving:** Cal 173; Net Carbs 0.5g; Fat 18g; Protein 4g

Ingredients

1 tbsp chopped dill
2 tbsp chopped parsley
2 tbsp chopped scallions
½ cup almond flour

1 lemon, zested
¼ cup olive oil
4 haddock fillets, skinless and boneless

1 lemon, cut into wedges
Salt and black pepper to taste

Directions

Preheat the Air Fryer to 390°F. Place the dill, parsley, scallions, almond flour, lemon zest, half of the olive oil, and a little salt and pepper in a bowl. Arrange the haddock fillets on a baking dish and top them with the almond mixture evenly. Using your fingers, gently press down to make a tightly packed crust. Drizzle with the remaining olive oil and Bake in the air fryer for 12-14 minutes until the crust is golden brown and the fish is cooked through.

Quick Tuna Sandwich with Mozzarella

Total Time: 20 min | **Serves:** 2 | **Per serving:** Cal 451; Net Carbs 7.2g; Fat 17g; Protein 61g

Ingredients

4 slices zero-carb bread
2 small tins of tuna, drained

½ onion, finely chopped
2 tbsp mayonnaise

1 cup mozzarella cheese, shredded

Directions

Lay your zero-carb bread out onto a board. In a small bowl, mix tuna, onion, mayonnaise. Spoon the mixture over 2 bread slices. Top with cheese and put the other piece of bread on top. Spray with cooking spray and arrange the sandwiches on the air fryer basket. Cook at 360°F for 6 minutes, turning once halfway through cooking. Serve.

Mediterranean Halibut

Total Time: 25 min | **Serves:** 6 | **Per serving:** Cal 432; Net Carbs 7.1g; Fat 32g; Protein 27g

Ingredients

2 lb halibut fillets, cut in 6 pieces
Salt and black pepper

3-4 chopped green onions
½ cup mayonnaise

½ cup sour cream
1 tbsp dried dill weed

Directions

Preheat the Air Fryer to 390°F. Season the halibut with salt and pepper. In a bowl, mix onions, mayonnaise, sour cream, and dill. Spread this mixture over the fish. Bake for 14-16 minutes. Serve and enjoy!

Ultra Crispy Pomfret Fish

Total Time: 15 min | **Serves:** 3 | **Per serving:** Cal 463; Net Carbs 3.4g; Fat 23g; Protein 55g

Ingredients

1 lb silver pomfret fish, washed
1 tsp red chili powder

1 tbsp garlic paste
1 tbsp lemon zest

1 tbsp olive oil
Salt and black pepper to taste

Directions

Preheat the Air Fryer to 390°F. Using a sharp knife, make diagonal-shaped slits on the pomfret fish. Combine salt, pepper, garlic paste, lemon zest, and red chili powder in a bowl. Rub the mixture above and inside the fish. Put it in the greased air fryer basket and drizzle with olive oil. AirFry for 14-16 minutes, flipping once. Serve and enjoy!

Southern-Style Catfish

Total Time: 25 min + marinating time | **Serves:** 2 | **Per serving:** Cal 365; Net Carbs 5.2g; Fat 21g; Protein 33g

Ingredients

1 cup sour cream
2 catfish fillets
Salt and black pepper to taste

2 tbsp hot sauce
1 cup almond flour
1 tbsp fish seasoning

1 tbsp garlic powder

Directions

Season the catfish with salt and pepper on all sides. Combine the sour cream and hot sauce in a bowl. Add in the catfish and toss to coat. Let it sit for 30 minutes. In another bowl, mix the almond flour, fish seasoning, and garlic powder. Remove the catfish and shake the excess liquid.

Preheat your Air Fryer to 390°F. Dip the catfish in the flour mixture and place in the air fryer basket. Blitz with cooking spray and AirFry for 14-16 minutes, flipping the fish halfway through the cooking time. Serve and enjoy!

Herb-Crusted Halibut

Total Time: 25 min | **Serves:** 4 | **Per serving:** Cal 287; Net Carbs 1.3g; Fat 18g; Protein 22g

Ingredients

¾ cup pork rinds, crushed
4 halibut fillets
½ cup fresh parsley, chopped

¼ cup fresh dill, chopped
¼ cup fresh chives, chopped
1 tbsp extra virgin olive oil

1 tbsp finely grated lemon zest
Sea salt and black pepper to taste

Directions

Preheat the Air Fryer to 390°F. In a large bowl, mix the pork rinds, the parsley, the dill, the chives, the olive oil, the lemon zest, the sea salt, and black pepper. Rinse the halibut fillets and dry them on a paper towel. Arrange the halibut fillets on a baking sheet. Spoon the rinds on the fish. Lightly press the crumb mixture on the fillet. Cook the fillets in a preheated air fryer basket for 14-16 minutes. Serve and enjoy!

Chinese Fish with Mushrooms

Total Time: 20 min | **Serves:** 4 | **Per serving:** Cal 267; Net Carbs 3.5g; Fat 8g; Protein 39g

Ingredients

1 lb white fish fillets
Salt to taste
4 mushrooms, sliced

1 tbsp liquid stevia
2 onions, sliced
4 tbsp soy sauce

2 tbsp red chili powder
2 tbsp vinegar
2 Chinese winter pickles, sliced

Directions

Preheat the Air Fryer to 350°F. Fill the fish with the pickle, onion, and mushroom slices. In a bowl, mix the remaining ingredients. Spread over the fish. AirFry the fish for 10-14 minutes. Serve and enjoy!

Ginger Cedar Planked Salmon

Total Time: 25 min + marinating time | **Serves:** 6 | **Per serving:** Cal 476; Net Carbs 4.1g; Fat 38g; Protein 33g

Ingredients

4 untreated cedar planks, soaked
½ cup vegetable oil
1½ tbsp rice vinegar

1 tbsp sesame oil
½ cup soy sauce
¼ cup green onions, chopped

1 tbsp fresh ginger root, grated
1 tbsp garlic, grated
2 lb salmon fillets, skin removed

Directions

Start soaking the cedar planks for 2 hours. Take a shallow dish and stir in the vegetable oil, rice vinegar, sesame oil, soy sauce, green onions, garlic, and ginger. Put the salmon fillets in the prepared marinade for at least 20 minutes. Place the planks and fillets in the air fryer basket. Cook for 15 minutes at 360°F. Serve and enjoy!

Saucy Salmon

Total Time: 25 min | **Serves:** 4 | **Per serving:** Cal 240; Net Carbs 0g; Fat 6g; Protein 16g

Ingredients

2 tsp olive oil
4 (6-oz) salmon pieces

Salt and black pepper to taste
3 tbsp chopped tarragon

1 cup sour cream
1 cup Greek yogurt

Directions

Combine the sour cream, yogurt, tarragon, and salt in a bowl. Preheat your Air Fryer to 270°F. Grease the salmon with olive oil and sprinkle with salt and pepper. Place in the fryer basket and cook for 15 minutes. Transfer to a plate and pour the tarragon sauce on top. Serve with steamed asparagus.

Crispy Fish & Turnip Chips

Total Time: 25 min | **Serves:** 4 | **Per serving:** Cal 265; Net Carbs 3.3g; Fat 10.3g; Protein 34g

Ingredients

2 turnips, cut into thin slices chips
Salt and black pepper to taste

4 white fish fillets
2 tbsp almond flour

1 egg, beaten
1 cup pork rinds, crushed

Directions

Grease the turnip chips with cooking spray and season with salt and black pepper. Places them in the air fryer, and cook for 20 minutes at 400°F. Spread almond flour on a plate and coat the fish. Dip them in the egg, then into the pork rinds and season with salt and black pepper. At the 10 minutes' mark, add the fish to the fryer and cook with the chips. Cook until crispy. Serve with lemon slices.

Lime Salmon with Broccoli

Total Time: 25 min | **Serves:** 2 | **Per serving:** Cal 511; Net Carbs 7.2g; Fat 21g; Protein 64g

Ingredients

2 salmon fillets
1 tsp olive oil
Juice of 1 lime

1 tsp chili flakes
Salt and black pepper to taste
1 head of broccoli, cut into florets

1 tbsp soy sauce, sugar-free

Directions

In a bowl, add oil, lime juice, flakes, salt and black pepper. Rub the mixture onto fillets. Lay the florets into your air fryer and drizzle with oil. Arrange the fillets around or on top and cook for 10 minutes at 340°F. Drizzle the florets with soy sauce to serve. Serve and enjoy!

Easy Mackerel Cheese Pie

Total Time: 30 min | **Serves:** 4 | **Per serving:** Cal 515; Net Carbs 2.6g; Fat 54g; Protein 11g

Ingredients

½ lb smoked mackerel, flaked
6 eggs

¼ cup heavy whipping cream
1 cup baby spinach

1 cup shredded cheddar cheese
1 shallot, diced

Directions

Preheat your Air Fryer to 320°F. Whisk the eggs in a bowl and add the remaining ingredients. Mix well. Pour the mixture into a greased baking dish and place it into the air fryer basket. Bake for about 20 minutes until the eggs are firm and slightly golden. Serve warm and enjoy!

Almond Pollack Nuggets

Total Time: 20 min | **Serves:** 4 | **Per serving:** Cal 168; Net Carbs 0.4g; Fat 7.5g; Protein 16.8g

Ingredients

4 Alaskan pollack fillets
2 tbsp olive oil

2 eggs, beaten
1 cup pork rinds, crushed

A pinch of salt
1 cup almond flour

Directions

Preheat your Air Fryer to 390°F. In a bowl, combine the pork rinds with salt and olive oil. In another bowl, place the beaten eggs, and in a third bowl, put the almond flour.

Dip the pollack in the flour, then in the eggs, and finally in the rinds. Place in the fryer basket and cook for 9 minutes, until golden brown. Turn after 5 minutes. Transfer to a plate and serve with veggie fries.

Tuna in Coconut Sauce

Total Time: 25 min | **Serves:** 4 | **Per serving:** Cal 512; Net Carbs 8.1g; Fat 53g; Protein 25.3g

Ingredients

4 tuna fillets
2 lemons, juiced
Salt and black pepper to taste

2 tbsp coconut oil
1 cup coconut cream
15 black peppercorns

2 cloves garlic, minced
2 shallots, chopped

Directions

Preheat your Air Fryer to 390°F. Place the tuna fillets on the greased air fryer basket. AirFry for 15 minutes, flipping once. Warm the coconut oil in a skillet over medium heat and sauté the garlic and shallots for 2-3 minutes. Add the peppercorns and coconut cream and stir until the sauce thickens. Stir in the lemon juice, salt, and pepper. Turn the heat off. Pour the sauce over the tuna fillets. Serve and enjoy!

Simple Fried Red Snapper

Total Time: 25 min | **Serves:** 4 | **Per serving:** Cal 463; Net Carbs 3.4g; Fat 23g; Protein 55g

Ingredients

4 red snappers, washed
1 tbsp curry powder

¾ tbsp ginger powder
1 tbsp ground coriander

2 tbsp lemon juice
Salt and black pepper to taste

Directions

Preheat your Air Fryer to 390°F. Place the fish on a cutting board and using a sharp knife, create deep slits on both sides of the snappers. Mix the ginger powder, lemon juice, ground coriander, curry powder, salt, and pepper. Rub the fish with the mixture. Place the fish in the fryer basket and spray it with cooking spray. Cook 12-14 minutes.

Cilantro Haddock

Total Time: 30 min | **Serves:** 2 | **Per serving:** Cal 182; Net Carbs 2.8g; Fat 12.8g; Protein 11.2g

Ingredients

2 haddock fillets
3 tbsp pork rinds, crushed

1 tsp cayenne pepper
1 tsp fish seasoning

2 sprigs cilantro, chopped
Salt to taste

Directions

Preheat Air Fryer to 400°F. Place all the dry ingredients in a sealable bag. Put one piece of the fish in the bag. Seal the bag and shake to coat. Repeat the process with the remaining pieces. Spay with olive oil. Place the pieces in the fryer basket and cook for 10 minutes. Turn them and cook for another 10 minutes. Garnish with cilantro.

Crunchy Flounder with Herbs

Total Time: 30 min | **Serves:** 4 | **Per serving:** Cal 287; Net Carbs 1.3g; Fat 18g; Protein 22g

Ingredients

4 flounder fillets
¾ cup pork rinds, crushed
½ cup fresh parsley, chopped

¼ cup fresh dill, chopped
¼ cup fresh chives, chopped
1 tbsp olive oil

1 tbsp grated lemon zest
Salt and black pepper to taste

Directions

Preheat your Air Fryer to 390°F. In a bowl, combine the pork rinds, parsley, dill, chives, olive oil, lemon zest, sea salt, and black pepper. Wash the flounder and pat dry. Place the fish on a baking sheet and scatter with the rinds mixture. Place in the fryer and cook for 30 minutes.

Fried Haddock with Carrots Chips

Total Time: 25 min | **Serves**: 4 | **Per serving**: Cal 265; Net Carbs 3.3g; Fat 10.3g; Protein 34g

Ingredients

2 carrots, cut into thin slices chips	2 tbsp almond flour	1 cup pork rinds, crushed
4 haddock fillets	1 egg, beaten	Salt and black pepper to taste

Directions

Preheat your Air Fryer to 400°F. Grease the chips with cooking spray and sprinkle with salt and pepper. Place in the fryer basket and cook for 20 minutes.

In the meantime, put the almond flour on a plate. Add in the fish and toss to coat. Dip each fish in the beaten egg, then in the rinds. Season with salt and pepper. After 10 minutes of cooking, add the fish to the fryer and continue cooking until crispy. Serve with lemon.

Lemon & Celery Stuffed Trout

Total Time: 30 min | **Serves**: 2 | **Per serving**: Cal 305; Net Carbs 8.9g; Fat 21.1g; Protein 9.6g

Ingredients

1 celery stick, sliced	3 tbsp chopped parsley	1 garlic clove, minced
2 shallots, sliced	2 tbsp olive oil	
1 whole trout, scaled and cleaned	1 lemon, sliced	

Directions

Preheat Air Fryer to 350°F. In a bowl, combine the shallots, parsley, celery, olive oil, and garlic and mix well. Stuff the trout cavities with the mixture and wrap in aluminium foil. Place in the air fryer basket and cook for 10 minutes. Remove the foil and put the lemon slices on top. Serve with cooked mushrooms if desired.

Easy Sesame Salmon

Total Time: 20 min + marinating time | **Serves**: 6 | **Per serving**: Cal 476; Net Carbs 4.1g; Fat 38g; Protein 33g

Ingredients

1 ½ tbsp rice wine vinegar	½ cup soy sauce	2 lb salmon fillets, skin removed
1 tbsp sriracha sauce	¼ cup chives, chopped	
½ cup sesame oil	1 tbsp minced ginger	

Directions

In a bowl, combine the rice vinegar, sriracha sauce, sesame oil, soy sauce, chives, and ginger. Dip the salmon and marinate for at least for 20 minutes. Preheat your Air Fryer to 360°F. Cook for 15 minutes. Serve and enjoy!

Lemon Rosemary Salmon

Total Time: 20 min | **Serves**: 2 | **Per serving**: Cal 421; Net Carbs 1.3g; Fat 17g; Protein 64g

Ingredients

Zest of 1 lemon	Salt to taste
2 salmon fillets	1 tbsp rosemary, chopped

Directions

Preheat your Air Fryer to 360°F. Grease the fillets with cooking spray. Sprinkle with salt, rosemary, and lemon zest. Line your basket with baking paper and place the fillets. Cook for 10 minutes, flipping once. Serve with steamed asparagus and pour the lemon juice on top.

Crunchy Halibut Fingers

Total Time: 20 min | **Serves:** 4 | **Per serving:** Cal 183; Net Carbs 2.6g; Fat 6.7g; Protein 24g

Ingredients

2 halibut fillets, cut into 4 fingers each | ½ cup sour cream | Salt and black pepper to taste
1 egg, beaten | 1 cup pork rinds, crushed

Directions

Preheat your Air Fryer to 340°F. In a bowl, combine the egg and sour cream. Mix the pork rinds with salt and pepper on a plate. Dip each finger in the egg, then in the pork rinds.

Grease the fryer basket with cooking spray. Place the fingers in the basket and cook for 10 minutes. Flip the fingers once during the cooking time. Plate with garlic mayo and lemon wedges.

Rich Catfish Fillets

Total Time: 35 min | **Serves**: 2 | **Per serving**: Cal 182; Net Carbs 2.8g; Fat 12.8g; Protein 11.2g

Ingredients

2 catfish fillets | 1 tsp cayenne pepper | 2 sprigs parsley, chopped
3 tbsp pork rinds, crushed | 1 tsp dry fish seasoning | Salt to taste

Directions

Preheat Air Fryer to 400°F. Pour all the dry ingredients except the parsley in a zipper bag. Pat dry and add the fish pieces. Close the bag and shake to coat the fish well. Do this with one fish piece at a time. Lightly spray the fish with olive oil. Arrange them in the fryer basket, one at a time, depending on the size of the fish. Close the Air Fryer and cook for 10 minutes. Flip the fish and cook further for 10 minutes. Garnish with parsley and serve.

Chili Mackerel with Asparagus

Total Time: 25 min | **Serves:** 2 | **Per serving:** Cal 511; Net Carbs 7.2g; Fat 21g; Protein 64g

Ingredients

2 mackerel fillets | 1 tsp chili flakes | 1 tbsp soy sauce, sugar-free
1 tsp olive oil | Salt and black pepper to taste
Juice of 1 lime | 1 asparagus, cut into 2-inch pieces

Directions

Preheat your Air Fryer to 340°F. Mix the olive oil, lime juice, flakes, salt, and black pepper in a bowl. Brush the mackerel with the mixture. Place the asparagus and the mackerel in the fryer basket. Pour in the oil and cook for 10 minutes. Serve and dress the asparagus with soy sauce.

Coconut-Crusted Tilapia

Total Time: 25 min | **Serves:** 4 | **Per serving:** Cal 173; Net Carbs 0.5g; Fat 18g; Protein 4g

Ingredients

2 tbsp olive oil | 2 tbsp desiccated coconut | 2 tbsp cilantro, chopped
1 tbsp curry powder | 4 tilapia fillets | 1 lemon, cut into wedges

Directions

Preheat your Air Fryer to 370°F. Mix the olive oil, curry powder, and desiccated coconut in a bowl. Place the tilapia fillets on a lightly greased baking dish. Spread the mix on the fish and Bake it in the air fryer for 14-16 minutes until the fish is cooked through. Sprinkle with cilantro. Serve with lemon wedges and enjoy!

Cottage & Tuna Sandwiches

Total Time: 10 min | **Serves:** 2 | **Per serving:** Cal 451; Net Carbs 7.2g; Fat 17g; Protein 61g

Ingredients

1 tbsp capers

4 slices zero-carb bread

2 small tins of tuna, drained

½ onion, finely chopped

2 tbsp mayonnaise

1 cup cottage cheese, crumbled

Directions

Preheat Air Fryer to 360°F. Combine tuna, onion, capers and mayonnaise in a bowl. Lay 2 bread slices on a flat surface and share the tuna mixture in equal parts. Add the cottage cheese and top with the remaining slices. Grease each sandwich with cooking spray and place in the fryer basket. Cook for 6 minutes, flipping once. Serve .

Greek-Style Cod Fillets

Total Time: 20 min | **Serves:** 6 | **Per serving:** Cal 432; Net Carbs 7.1g; Fat 32g; Protein 27g

Ingredients

6 cod fillets

Salt and black pepper

4 chopped spring onions

½ cup mayonnaise

½ cup sour cream

1 tbsp dried basil

Directions

Preheat Air Fryer to 390°F. Sprinkle the cod with salt and pepper. Combine onions, mayonnaise, sour cream, and basil in a bowl. Rub the halibut with the dill mixture. Cook for 12-14 minutes. Serve and enjoy!

Korean-Style Cod

Total Time: 20 min | **Serves:** 4 | **Per serving:** Cal 267; Net Carbs 3.5g; Fat 8g; Protein 39g

Ingredients

2 lb Atlantic cod fillets

Salt to taste

4 shiitake mushrooms, sliced

1 tbsp xylitol

2 onions, sliced

4 tbsp soy sauce

2 tbsp vinegar

2 tbsp Korean pickles

Directions

Preheat your Air Fryer to 350°F. Stuff the fish with the pickle and mushrooms. Add in the onion. In a bowl, combine the vinegar, soy sauce, xylitol, and salt. Pour over the fish. Cook for 10 minutes. Serve and enjoy!

Crunchy Firecracker Shrimp

Total Time: 20 min | **Serves:** 4 | **Per serving:** Cal 144; Net Carbs 1.4g; Fat 6.5g; Protein 16g

Ingredients

1 lb medium shrimp, deveined

2 tbsp chili oil

½ tsp seafood seasoning

¼ tsp garlic powder

2 tbsp sriracha sauce

¼ tsp powdered erythritol

¼ cup mayonnaise

Salt and black pepper to taste

1 jalapeño pepper, sliced

Directions

Preheat the Air Fryer to 390°F. Place the chili oil, seafood seasoning, and garlic powder in a large bowl. Add in the shrimp and toss well to coat. Put the shrimp in the air fryer basket and cook for 6-8 minutes until crispy. Shake the basket halfway through. Once ready, the shrimp should be crispy.

Meanwhile, in a bowl, thoroughly combine the sriracha sauce, powdered erythritol, mayonnaise, salt, and pepper. Coat the shrimp with the sauce and top with jalapeño pepper. Serve and enjoy!

Lemon Garlic Shrimp

Total Time: 15 min | **Serves:** 3 | **Per serving:** Cal 192; Net Carbs 0.5g; Fat 12g; Protein 16g

Ingredients

1 medium lemon, zested and juiced
1 lb shelled and deveined shrimp

2 tbsp butter, melted
½ tsp seafood seasoning

1 garlic clove, minced
½ tsp red pepper flakes

Directions

Preheat the Air Fryer to 390°F. In a mixing bowl, thoroughly combine lemon juice, lemon zest, butter, seafood seasoning, and garlic. Add in the shrimp and toss to coat.

Transfer the shrimp to a baking dish and place the dish in the air fryer basket. AirFry for 5-6 minutes, shaking the basket halfway through cooking until the shrimp are no longer pink. Sprinkle with red pepper flakes. Serve.

King Prawn Kebabs

Total Time: 20 min | **Serves:** 4 | **Per serving:** Cal 165; Net Carbs 4.3g; Fat 10.8g; Protein 9.4g

Ingredients

1 lb raw peeled king prawns
1 zucchini, cubed
½ red bell pepper, cut into chunks

½ lb cherry tomatoes
1 ½ tbsp coconut oil, melted
2 tsp chili powder

½ tsp paprika
Sea salt and black pepper to taste
4 bamboo skewers, soaked in water

Directions

Preheat the Air Fryer to 395°F. Toss all ingredients in a mixing bowl until everything is well coated. Thread the prawns and vegetables onto the soaked skewers. Add them to the greased air fryer basket. Cook for 6-8 minutes, turning once until the prawns are cooked through with no pink showing and the vegetables are tender. Serve.

Mojito Crab Dip

Total Time: 20 min | **Serves:** 4 | **Per serving:** Cal 440; Net Carbs 6.5g; Fat 34g; Protein 17.9g

Ingredients

1 tbsp fresh mint leaves, chopped
1 tsp white rum
1 cup cream cheese, softened
¼ cup mayonnaise

¼ cup sour cream
1 tbsp lemon juice
½ tsp hot sauce
¼ cup chopped pickled jalapeños

¼ cup green onions, sliced
2 (6-ounce) cans lump crab meat
½ cup cheddar cheese, shredded

Directions

Preheat the Air Fryer to 395°F. In a baking dish, thoroughly combine all ingredients and toss to coat. Fit the dish into the air fryer basket. Cook for 8-10 minutes or until bubbling. Serve and enjoy!

Cauli Rice & Crabmeat Cabbage Rolls

Total Time: 25 min | **Serves:** 4 | **Per serving:** Cal 178; Net Carbs 5.8g; Fat 15g; Protein 2.4g

Ingredients

½ lb crab meat
4 cabbage leaves

1 carrot, chopped
2 cups cauli rice

1 tbsp olive oil
1 cup almonds, ground

Directions

Preheat your Air Fryer to 360°F. In a bowl, mix cauli rice, carrot, crab meat, olive oil, and almonds. Place the cabbage leaves on a flat surface. Divide the mixture between the cabbage. Roll up and seal the edges. Place the rolls in the fryer basket and cook for 14-16 minutes, flipping once. Serve and enjoy!

Spicy Crab Croquettes

Total Time: 35 min | **Serves**: 6 | **Per serving**: Cal 306; Net Carbs 0.4g; Fat 15.3g; Protein 14g

Ingredients

Filling:

1 ½ lb lump crab meat	1 ½ tbsp olive oil	½ tsp tarragon, chopped
3 egg whites, beaten	1 red pepper, chopped finely	½ tsp chives, chopped
⅓ cup sour cream	⅓ cup red onion, chopped	1 tsp parsley, chopped
⅓ cup mayonnaise	2 ½ tbsp celery, chopped	1 tsp cayenne pepper

Breading:

1 ½ cup pork rinds, crushed	1 cup almond flour	Salt to taste
2 tsp olive oil	4 eggs, beaten	

Directions

Place a skillet over medium heat, add 1 ½ tbsp olive oil, red pepper, onion, and celery. Sauté for 5 minutes or until sweaty and translucent. Turn off heat. Add the pork rinds, remaining olive oil, and salt to a food processor. Blend to mix evenly. Set aside. In two separate bowls, add the almond flour and 4 eggs, respectively.

In a separate mixing bowl, add the crab meat, mayonnaise, egg whites, sour cream, tarragon, chives, parsley, cayenne pepper, and the celery sauté and mix evenly. Form bite-sized balls from the mixture; place into a plate.

Preheat the Air Fryer to 390°F. Dip croquettes in the egg mixture and press them in the pork rind mixture. Place in the fryer basket. Close the Air Fryer and cook for 10 minutes or until golden brown. Remove them and plate them. Serve the crab croquettes with tomato dipping sauce and a side of vegetable fries.

Buttered Shrimp Scampi

Total Time: 20 min | **Serves**: 4 | **Per serving**: Cal 239; Net Carbs 0.7g; Fat 17g; Protein 16.8g

Ingredients

4 tbsp butter	¼ tsp xanthan gum	1 lb medium shrimp, peeled and
1 tsp roasted garlic puree	¼ tsp red pepper flakes	deveined
¼ cup heavy cream	1 tsp hot paprika	2 tbsp fresh cilantro, chopped

Directions

Preheat the Air Fryer to 390°F. Melt the butter in a skillet over medium heat and add the garlic, heavy cream, xanthan gum, red pepper flakes, and hot paprika and stir-fry for 4-5 minutes until the mixture thickens.

Transfer the mixture to a baking dish and place the dish in the air fryer basket. Add the shrimp and toss to coat. Cook for 12 minutes, stirring once or twice. Sprinkle with cilantro and serve.

Calamari Rings with Poblano Sauce

Total Time: 15 min | **Serves**: 3 | **Per serving**: Cal 195; Net Carbs 4.2g; Fat 7g; Protein 25g

Ingredients

2 tbsp ground coriander seeds	A pinch of salt	1 tbsp olive oil
7 medium poblano peppers	2 drops liquid stevia	1 lb calamari rings
2 cloves garlic	2 small limes	1 tsp fish sauce

Directions

Preheat your Air Fryer to 370°F. Mash the coriander seeds. Add in the poblano peppers, 2 cloves of garlic, a pinch of salt, stevia, 1 tbsp of fish sauce, the juice of 2 limes, and 1 tbsp of olive oil. Remove to a bowl. Place the calamari rings in the fryer basket and cook for 4 minutes. Serve with the poblano sauce.

Cajun-Style Blackened Shrimp

Total Time: 15 min | **Serves:** 4 | **Per serving:** Cal 193; Net Carbs 0.3g; Fat 12g; Protein 17g

Ingredients

1 lb medium shrimp, shelled and deveined

3 tbsp salted butter, melted

1 tsp hot paprika

½ tsp ground cumin

½ tsp ground coriander

½ tsp garlic powder

¼ tsp onion powder

½ tsp Cajun seasoning

1 lime, cut into wedges

Directions

Preheat the Air Fryer to 390°F. In a bowl, mix well the butter, hot paprika, ground cumin, ground coriander, garlic powder, onion powder, and Cajun seasoning. Add in the shrimp and toss to coat. Place the shrimp in the air fryer basket and AirFry for 6 minutes, shaking the basket once until pink and crispy. Serve with lime wedges.

Turnip & Seafood Pie

Total Time: 60 min | **Serves:** 3 | **Per serving:** Cal 318; Net Carbs 2.7g; Fat 22.5g; Protein 24.6g

Ingredients

1 cup seafood marinara mix

1 lb turnips, peeled and quartered

1 cup water

1 carrot, grated

½ head baby fennel, grated

1 bunch dill sprigs, chopped

1 sprig parsley, chopped

A handful of baby spinach

1 small tomato, diced

½ celery sticks, grated

2 tbsp butter

1 tbsp coconut milk

½ cup grated cheddar cheese

1 small red chili, minced

½ lemon, juiced

Salt and black pepper to taste

Directions

Pour the turnips into a pan, add the water, and bring it to a boil over medium heat. Use a fork to check that it is soft and mash-able after about 12 minutes. Drain the water and use a potato masher to mash it. Add butter, coconut milk, salt, and pepper. Mash until smooth and well mixed. Set aside. In a bowl, add the celery, carrots, cheese, chili, fennel, parsley, lemon juice, seafood mix, dill, tomato, spinach, salt, and pepper. Mix well.

Preheat the Air Fryer to 330°F. In a casserole dish, add half of the carrots mixture. Top with half of the turnip mixture. Bake for 20 minutes, ensuring that the mash is golden brown and the seafood is cooked properly. Remove the dish and add the remaining seafood mixture and level it out. Top with the remaining turnip mash and level it too. Place the dish back into the Air Fryer and cook at 330°F for 20 more minutes. Slice and serve.

Easy Coconut Shrimp

Total Time: 15 min | **Serves:** 4 | **Per serving:** Cal 156; Net Carbs 3.2g; Fat 2g; Protein 17g

Ingredients

½ cup water

½ tbsp baking powder

1 tbsp salt

½ cup almond flour

½ tbsp red pepper flakes

4 tbsp rice wine vinegar

½ cup sugar-free strawberry marmalade

2 cups shredded sweetened coconut

½ cup pork rinds, crushed

1 lb large shrimp, peeled and deveined

Directions

For the dipping sauce: add red pepper flakes, vinegar, and marmalade to a saucepan. Heat around 10 minutes on low heat. Keep stirring until the mixture is combined. In a deep bowl, whisk the salt, the flour, and the baking powder. Add water. Whisk everything until the mixture becomes smooth. Set the batter aside for 15 minutes.

In another bowl, toss the coconut and pork rinds. Dip each shrimp into batter and then coat it with coconut mixture. Set the heat to 390°F and fry them for 3 minutes. Serve with the dipping sauce.

Jumbo Prawns in Bacon Rolls

Total Time: 35 min | **Serves**: 3 | **Per serving**: Cal 133; Net Carbs 0.1g; Fat 12.1g; Protein 13.6g

Ingredients

8 bacon slices   8 Jumbo prawns, peeled and deveined Lemon wedges for garnishing

Directions

Wrap each prawn from head to tail with each bacon slice overlapping to keep the bacon in place. Secure the end of the bacon with a toothpick. It's ok not to cover the ends of the cheese with bacon. Refrigerate for 15 minutes.

Preheat the Air Fryer to 400°F. Arrange the bacon-wrapped prawns in the fryer basket. Close the Air Fryer and cook for 7 minutes or until the bacon has browned and crispy. Transfer prawns to a paper towel to cool for 2 minutes. Remove the toothpicks and serve the bacon-wrapped prawns with lemon wedges.

Delicious Octopus with Green Chilies

Total Time: 20 min | **Serves**: 3 | **Per serving**: Cal 195; Net Carbs 4.2g; Fat 7g; Protein 25g

Ingredients

¼ root coriander, peeled	A pinch of salt	1 tbsp olive oil
7 medium green chilies	2 drops liquid stevia	1 lb cooked octopus
2 cloves garlic	2 small limes, juiced	1 tsp fish sauce

Directions

Mash the washed roots of coriander in the mortar. Add the green chilies, garlic, salt, stevia, fish sauce, lime juice and olive oil. Stir until a smooth dip is formed. Set aside in a bowl.

Preheat your Air Fryer to 370°F. Cut the octopus into tentacles. Arrange them in the air fryer basket and set the heat to 370°F. Cook them for 4 minutes, flipping once. Serve with the prepared dip.

Cayenne-Spiced Jumbo Shrimp

Total Time: 15 min | **Serves**: 3 | **Per serving**: Cal 112; Net Carbs 1g; Fat 5g; Protein 15g

Ingredients

1 tbsp coconut oil	¼ tsp fish seasoning
1 lb jumbo shrimp	¼ tsp cayenne pepper

Directions

Preheat your Air Fryer to 390°F. Combine the shrimp, coconut oil, fish seasoning and cayenne pepper in a bowl. Place in the fryer basket and cook for 5 minutes. Transfer to a plate and serve.

Scallops Fritters

Total Time: 20 min | **Serves**: 4 | **Per serving**: Cal 121; Net Carbs 1.5g; Fat 5.5g; Protein 14g

Ingredients

1 lb scallops, cubed	⅓ cup chives, chopped	½ tsp paprika
2 eggs, beaten	1 tbsp mayonnaise	Salt and black pepper to taste
½ cup pork rinds, crushed	1 tsp chili sauce	

Directions

Preheat your Air Fryer to 400°F. Grind the scallops in the food processor. In a bowl, combine the meat, eggs, pork rinds, chives, mayo, chili sauce, paprika, salt, and black pepper. Mould 8 cakes out of the mixture. Sprinkle with cooking spray. Place in the fryer basket and cook for 8 minutes, flipping once. Serve and enjoy!

Hot Mussels with Sweet Potato Fries

Total Time: 40 min | **Serves:** 4 | **Per serving:** Cal 649; Net Carbs 19.4g; Fat 29.2g; Protein 43.1g

Ingredients

1 lb sweet potatoes, cut into fries
3 tbsp olive oil
¼ fennel bulb, chopped
1 shallot, finely chopped

1 red chili, minced
1 garlic clove, minced
½ cup white wine
1 (14-oz) can diced tomatoes

1 tsp tabasco sauce
3 lb cleaned mussels, beard removed
2 tbsp parsley, chopped

Directions

Preheat your Air Fryer to 380°F. Arrange the sweet potato fries on the greased air fryer basket. Drizzle with some olive oil. AirFry for 6-8 minutes, flip, and continue cooking for 5-6 more minutes until golden.

Warm the remaining olive oil in a saucepan over medium heat. Stir-fry the fennel, shallot, chili, and garlic for 1-2 minutes. Pour in the white wine and simmer until reduced by half, about 2 minutes. Add the tomatoes, 1 cup of water, and tabasco sauce. Cook for a further 10 minutes. Add the mussels, cover with lid, and shake the saucepan. Steam for 5 minutes; discard any unopened mussels. Top with parsley. Serve with the potato fruies.

Shrimp & Ham Rolls

Total Time: 20 min | **Serves:** 4 | **Per serving:** Cal 95; Net Carbs 3.2g; Fat 7g; Protein 6g

Ingredients

16 deli ham slices

2 pounds king shrimp

Barbecue sauce, to serve

Directions

Preheat the Air Fryer to 390°F. Tightly wrap a ham slice around the shrimp. Repeat with the rest of the shrimp. Secure with toothpicks. AirFry in the fryer for 5 minutes, tossing once. Serve with BBQ Sauce. Enjoy!

Cayenne & Garlic Prawns

Total Time: 20 min | **Serves:** 2 | **Per serving:** Cal 151; Net Carbs 3.2g; Fat 2g; Protein 23g

Ingredients

8 prawns, cleaned
½ tsp ground cumin

Salt and black pepper to taste
½ tsp ground cayenne pepper

1 garlic clove, minced
1 tbsp parsley, chopped

Directions

Preheat the Air Fryer to 340°F. Mix the cayenne pepper, cumin, parsley, salt, and pepper in a bowl. Rub the prawns with the mixture. Arrange them on a greased air fryer basket AirFry for 8-10 minutes, flipping once.

Hot Crab Cakes with Green Onions

Total Time: 20 min | **Serves:** 8 | **Per serving:** Cal 121; Net Carbs 1.5g; Fat 5.5g; Protein 14g

Ingredients

1 lb crab meat, shredded
2 eggs, beaten
½ cup pork rinds, crushed

⅓ cup green onions, chopped
¼ cup parsley, chopped
1 tbsp mayonnaise

1 tsp chili sauce
½ tsp paprika
Salt and black pepper to taste

Directions

In a bowl, add meat, eggs, pork rinds, green onion, parsley, mayo, chili sauce, paprika, salt and pepper and mix well with hands. Shape into 8 cakes and grease them lightly with cooking spray. Arrange the cakes into the greased air fryer basket without overcrowding. Cook for 8 minutes at 400°F, turning once halfway through cooking.

Sambal Chili Shrimp

Total Time: 20 min | **Serves:** 2 | **Per serving:** Cal 405; Net Carbs 5.2g; Fat 27g; Protein 31g

Ingredients

½ tsp sambal oelek chili paste

½ lb shrimp, peeled and deveined

½ cup soy sauce

2 eggs

2 tbsp peanut oil

1 cup onions, chopped

A pinch of ground ginger

¼ cup almond flour

Directions

Preheat your Air Fryer to 390°F. Pour water in a pot over high heat and bring to a boil. Put in the shrimps for 5 minutes. Combine the ginger, peanut oil, and onion to create a paste. Whisk the eggs and add ginger-onion paste, soy sauce, chili paste, and almond flour. Dip the shrimps in the mixture to coat. Cook for 10 minutes. Serve.

Delicious Crab Cakes

Total Time: 25 min | **Serves:** 6 | **Per serving:** Cal 306; Net Carbs 0.4g; Fat 15.3g; Protein 14g

Ingredients

3 egg whites, beaten

⅓ cup buttermilk

1 ½ lb lump crab meat

⅓ cup mayonnaise

1 red bell pepper, chopped finely

⅓ cup onion, chopped

2 ½ tbsp celery, chopped

½ tsp chives, chopped

1 tsp parsley, chopped

1 tsp hot paprika

1 ½ cup pork rinds, crushed

2 tsp olive oil

1 cup almond flour

4 eggs, beaten

Salt to taste

Directions

Warm 1 ½ tbsp of olive oil in a skillet over medium heat and sauté onion, bell pepper, and celery for 3 minutes. Turn the heat off. In a food processor, blitz the pork rinds, remaining olive oil, and salt. Put the almond flour in a bowl and in another bowl the beaten eggs. In a third bowl, combine the crab meat, mayonnaise, egg whites, buttermilk, chives, parsley, hot paprika, and the celery sauté. Shape bite-sized balls out of the mixture. Preheat your Air Fryer to 390°F. Dip the balls in the eggs, then in the rinds. AirFry the balls for 10 minutes until golden.

Easy Bacon Wrapped Shrimp

Total Time: 15 min | **Serves:** 4 | **Per serving:** Cal 95; Net Carbs 3.2g; Fat 7g; Protein 6g

Ingredients

2 pounds king shrimp

16 bacon strips, cooked

Barbecue sauce, to serve

Directions

Wrap the shrimp with bacon strips, then secure with toothpicks. Cook at 390°F for 5 minutes. Shake the basket from time to time. Serve the shrimp with the BBQ sauce.

Shellfish Platter with Garlic Aioli Sauce

Total Time: 15 min | **Serves:** 4 | **Per serving:** Cal 211; Net Carbs 5.2g; Fat 8.1g; Protein 24g

Ingredients

2 eggs, lightly beaten

1 lb mixed seafood

Salt and black pepper to taste

1 cup pork rinds, crushed

Zest of 1 lemon

1 cup garlic aioli sauce

Directions

Preheat your Air Fryer to 400°F. Mix the pork rinds with lemon zest. Dip each seafood piece in the eggs. Sprinkle with salt and pepper. Then dip in the pork rinds. Spray with some oil. AirFry for 6 minutes. Serve and enjoy!

Veggie & Seafood Tart

Total Time: 45 min | **Serves:** 4 | **Per serving:** Cal 318; Net Carbs 2.7g; Fat 22.5g; Protein 24.6g

Ingredients

1 lb parsnips, peeled and quartered
1 carrot, grated
1 cup bok choy, chopped
1 cup seafood mix
2 tbsp dill, chopped

1 sprig parsley, chopped
1 cup spinach, chopped
1 tomato, diced
½ celery sticks, chopped
2 tbsp butter

1 tbsp coconut milk
½ cup grated cheddar cheese
1 red chili, minced
½ lemon, juiced
Salt and black pepper to taste

Directions

Bring to boil water over medium heat. Add in the parsnips and cook for 12 minutes until soft and mashable. Drain and mash them. Add in butter, coconut milk, salt, and pepper. Mash until smooth. Combine celery, carrots, cheese, chili, bok choy, parsley, lemon juice, seafood mix, dill, tomato, spinach, salt, and pepper in a bowl.

Preheat your Air Fryer to 330°F. Pour the seafood mixture into a casserole. Top with the turnip mixture. Place the dish in the fryer and bake for 20 minutes until it is golden brown. Cut into slices and serve.

Coconut Prawns with Blueberry Dip

Total Time: 15 min | **Serves:** 4 | **Per serving:** Cal 156; Net Carbs 3.2g; Fat 2g; Protein 17g

Ingredients

1 lb large prawns, peeled and deveined
½ cup water
½ tbsp baking powder
1 tbsp salt

½ cup almond flour
½ tbsp red pepper flakes
4 tbsp rice wine vinegar

½ cup blueberry sugar-free preserves
2 cups shredded sweetened coconut
½ cup pork rinds, crushed

Directions

In a saucepan over low heat, place the red pepper flakes, vinegar, and blueberry preserves. Cook for 10 minutes until the mixture is combined. In a bowl, combine the salt, almond flour, and baking powder. Pour in water and stir until the mixture is smooth. Let sit for 15 minutes. In another bowl, mix the coconut and pork rinds.

Preheat your Air Fryer to 390°F. Dip each prawn in the flour mix, then in the coconut mix. Place in the fryer basket and fry for 3 minutes. Serve with the dipping sauce.

Balsamic Baby Octopus Salad

Total Time: 35 min + marinating time | **Serves:** 3 | **Per serving:** Cal 299; Net Carbs 3.4g; Fat 20.8g; Protein 17.7g

Ingredients

1 lb baby octopus, cut into bite-sized pieces
1 ½ tbsp olive oil
2 cloves garlic, minced
1 ½ tbsp capers
1 ¼ tbsp balsamic vinegar

1 tbsp parsley, chopped
1 small fennel bulb, chopped
1 cup dried tomatoes, chopped
1 medium red onion, sliced

2 handfuls arugula
Salt and black pepper to taste
¼ cup grilled halloumi, chopped
1 long red chili, minced

Directions

Bring to a boil 2 cups of water in a pot over medium heat. Add the octopus and cook for 2-3 minutes; drain. Add the octopus, garlic, and olive oil to a bowl and stir to combine. Leave to marinate for 20 minutes.

Preheat the Air Fryer to 390°F. Place the octopus in the air fryer basket and Bake for 5 minutes until slightly charred on both sides. Let it cool. Add the capers, halloumi cheese, red chili, dried tomatoes, parsley, red onion, fennel, cooled octopus, arugula, and balsamic vinegar in a salad bowl. Season with salt and pepper and mix.

Crispy Coconut Scallops

Total Time: 15 min | **Serves:** 6 | **Per serving:** Cal 105; Net Carbs 2.7g; Fat 3.4g; Protein 14g

Ingredients

12 fresh sea scallops
3 tbsp coconut flour

1 egg, lightly beaten
1 cup pork rinds, crushed

Directions

Preheat your Air Fryer to 360°F. Dip the scallops in the coconut flour, toss to coat. Dip in the eggs and in the pork rinds. Sprinkle with cooking spray. Place the scallops in the fryer basket and cook for 6 minutes. Turn once.

Mixed Seafood with Yogurt

Total Time: 15 min | **Serves:** 4 | **Per serving:** Cal 211; Net Carbs 5.2g; Fat 8.1g; Protein 24g

Ingredients

1 lb of mixed seafood
2 eggs, lightly beaten

Salt and black pepper to taste
1 cup pork rinds, crushed mixed with

the zest of 1 lemon
Yogurt, for dipping

Directions

Clean the seafood as needed. Dip each piece into the egg. Season with salt and pepper. Coat in the pork rinds and spray with oil. Arrange into your air fryer and cook for 6 minutes at 400°F, turning once. Serve with yogurt.

Pork Rind & Almond-Coated Scallops

Total Time: 20 min | **Serves:** 6 | **Per serving:** Cal 105; Net Carbs 2.7g; Fat 3.4g; Protein 14g

Ingredients

12 fresh scallops
3 tbsp almond flour

1 egg, lightly beaten
1 cup pork rinds, crushed

Directions

Coat the scallops with almond flour. Dip into the egg, then into the pork rinds. Spray them with cooking spray and arrange them in the air. Cook for 6 minutes at 360°F, turning once halfway through cooking.

Paprika-Rubbed Jumbo Shrimp

Total Time: 15 min | **Serves:** 3 | **Per serving:** Cal 112; Net Carbs 1g; Fat 5g; Protein 15g

Ingredients

1 lb jumbo shrimp
Salt to taste

¼ tsp old bay seasoning
⅓ tsp smoked paprika

¼ tsp cayenne pepper
1 tbsp olive oil

Directions

Preheat the Air Fryer to 390°F. In a bowl, add the shrimp, paprika, oil, salt, old bay seasoning, and cayenne pepper. Combine well. Place the shrimp in the fryer basket, close the Air Fryer, and cook for 5 minutes. Serve.

Garlic & Chili Prawns

Total Time: 20 min | **Serves:** 1 | **Per serving:** Cal 151; Net Carbs 3.2g; Fat 2g; Protein 23g

Ingredients

8 prawns, cleaned
Salt and black pepper to taste

½ tsp ground cayenne pepper
½ tsp chili flakes

½ tsp ground cumin
½ tsp garlic powder

In a bowl, season the prawns with salt and pepper. Sprinkle cayenne, flakes, cumin and garlic and stir to coat. Grease the air fryer basket and arrange the prawns in an even layer. Cook for 8 minutes at 340°F, turning once.

Savory Bacon Wrapped Crab Sticks

Total Time: 25 min | **Serves:** 3 | **Per serving:** Cal 133; Net Carbs 0.1g; Fat 12.1g; Protein 13.6g

Ingredients

8 crab sticks	8 bacon slices	Lemon wedges for garnishing

Directions

Lay the bacon slices on a flat surface and wrap each stick on it. Secure the end of the bacon with toothpicks. Preheat your Air Fryer to 400°F. Place the wrapped sticks in the fryer basket and cook for 7 minutes until the bacon has browned. Remove the toothpicks and serve with lemon wedges.

Restaurant-Style Dragon Shrimp

Total Time: 20 min | **Serves:** 2 | **Per serving:** Cal 405; Net Carbs 5.2g; Fat 27g; Protein 31g

Ingredients

½ lb shrimp	2 eggs	A pinch of ginger, grated
½ cup soy sauce	1 cup onions, chopped	¼ cup almond flour

Directions

Beat the eggs and add ginger, onion, soy sauce, almond flour and mix them very well. Add shrimp to the mixture and place in the fryer basket; AirFry them for 10 minutes at 390°F, turning once. Serve and enjoy!

Fritto Misto with Picante Aïoli

Total Time: 20 min | **Serves:** 4 | **Per serving:** Cal 597; Net Carbs 18.2g; Fat 39g; Protein 31g

Ingredients

½ lb shrimp, pelled and deveined	1 egg	1 cup mayonnaise
½ lb mussels, shelles removed	1 ¼ cups almond milk	1 tbsp chili oil
½ lb calamari, cut into rings	1 lemon, juiced	2 garlic cloves, minced
Salt and black pepper to taste	1 cup almond flour	2 tbsp parsley, chopped

Directions

Preheat your Air Fryer to 390°F. Whisk the egg with almond milk in a bowl. Season with salt and pepper. Add the seafood and toss to coat. Place the almond flour on a large shallow plate.

Dip the seafood in the flour mix, coat well, and shake off any excess flour. Place them into the greased air fryer basket. AirFry for 14-16 minutes, shaking them halfway through the cooking time.

Mix the mayo, garlic, chili oil, and lemon juice from in a serving bowl. Sprinkle fried seafood with parsley. Serve with the prepared aïoli and enjoy!

POULTRY RECIPES

Italian-Style Lemon Chicken Thighs

Total Time: 25 min | **Serves:** 4 | **Per serving:** Cal 598; Net Carbs 0.2g; Fat 31g; Protein 68g

Ingredients

4 chicken thighs
4 tbsp butter, melted
½ tsp Italian seasoning
¼ tsp dried oregano

1 tsp dried basil
½ tsp garlic powder
¼ tsp onion powder
Salt and black pepper to taste

1 lemon, zested and juiced
2 tbsp capers

Directions

Preheat the Air Fryer to 380°F. Toss the chicken thighs with half of the melted butter, Italian seasoning, oregano, basil, garlic powder, onion powder, salt, and pepper. Add the chicken to the air fryer basket and AirFry for 18-20 minutes, flipping once or twice until the skin is browned and crispy.

Meanwhile, place the remaining butter in a small saucepan over medium heat. Cook for 3 minutes until the butter is golden brown. Stir in capers for 1 minute and add in the lemon zest and lemon juice. Simmer until the sauce thickens slightly, about 3 minutes. Pour the sauce over the chicken and serve.

Dinner Chicken Patties

Total Time: 30 min + chilling time | **Serves:** 4 | **Per serving:** Cal 305; Net Carbs 0.2g; Fat 17.2g; Protein 32.9g

Ingredients

1 ¼ lb ground chicken
½ cup mozzarella cheese, shredded
1 tsp dried parsley

1 shallot, finely chopped
½ tsp celery seeds, ground
½ tsp cumin

Salt and black pepper to taste
1 large egg, whisked
2 oz pork rinds, finely ground

Directions

Add the ground chicken, mozzarella cheese, parsley, shallot, ground celery seeds, cumin, salt, and pepper in a bowl; mix until everything is well incorporated. Form the mixture into 4 patties. Place them in the freezer for 30 minutes or until they are firm.

Preheat the Air Fryer to 350°F. Dip the patties into the egg, then roll them in the pork rinds until fully covered. Arrange the cakes on the greased frying basket and AirFry for 15 minutes, turning once halfway through cooking, until nicely browned. Serve and enjoy!

Mustard-Crusted Chicken

Total Time: 40 min | **Serves:** 4 | **Per serving:** Cal 196; Net Carbs 0.2g; Fat 10.1g; Protein 21g

Ingredients

¼ cup ground almonds
2 chicken breasts, halved lengthwise
2 tbsp mayonnaise

1 tsp Dijon mustard
1 lemon, zested
Salt and black pepper to taste

1 tbsp parsley leaves

Directions

Preheat the Air Fryer to 350°F. In a bowl, whisk the mayonnaise, mustard, lemon zest, salt, and pepper. Add in the chicken breasts and toss to coat. Carefully place the coated chicken in the frying basket. Cover with ground almonds, pressing them slightly down to form a crust. AirFry for 20-25 minutes, flipping once until the crust is golden and the chicken is cooked through. Serve topped with parsley.

Cheese & Spinach Stuffed Chicken Breasts

Total Time: 40 min | **Serves:** 4 | **Per serving:** Cal 392; Net Carbs 2.3g; Fat 18.3g; Protein 44g

Ingredients

2 tbsp butter
½ yellow onion, chopped
2 garlic cloves, minced

10 oz fresh spinach, torn
Salt and cayenne pepper to taste
½ cup ricotta cheese, crumbled

2 tbsp fresh cilantro, chopped
4 chicken breasts
2 tbsp coconut oil

Directions

Melt the butter in a pan over medium heat and sauté the onion and garlic for 3 minutes until translucent. Add in the spinach and cook for 3-4 minutes, stirring often until wilted. Season with salt and cayenne pepper; remove from the heat. Let cool slightly, then mix in the ricotta cheese and cilantro.

Preheat the Air Fryer to 350°F. Salt the chicken breasts. Cut a pocket into each chicken breast and stuff it with the spinach mixture. Secure each opening with toothpicks. Arrange the stuffed breasts on the air fryer basket and brush them with coconut oil. AirFry for 23-25 minutes, turning once, until cooked through. Rest for 5 minutes and cut into slices. Serve and enjoy!

Chipotle Chicken Enchiladas

Total Time: 30 min | **Serves:** 4 | **Per serving:** Cal 415; Net Carbs 0.9g; Fat 25.1g; Protein 34.1g

Ingredients

2 tbsp olive oil
1 onion, chopped
1 ¼ lb chicken breasts, cut into strips
1 tsp chipotle seasoning
½ cup chicken stock

Salt and black pepper to taste
⅓ cup low-carb enchilada sauce
½ lb deli ham, thinly sliced
1 cup medium cheddar cheese, shredded

½ cup Monterey Jack cheese, shredded
½ cup sour cream
1 avocado, peeled, pitted, and sliced

Directions

Warm the olive oil in a frying pan over medium heat and sauté the onion for 3 minutes until softened. Add in the chicken and chipotle seasoning. Cook for a further 5-6 minutes, stirring often until the chicken turns golden. Pour in the stock and simmer for 14-16 minutes until thickened. Remove from the heat and stir in half of the enchilada sauce. Adjust the seasoning with salt and pepper.

Preheat the Air Fryer to 350°F. Divide the chicken mixture between the ham slices and top with cheddar cheese. Roll them up and put them in a baking dish. Cover with the remaining enchilada sauce and sprinkle with Monterey Jack cheese. Place the dish in the air fryer basket. Bake for 10 minutes until the cheese is golden and bubbling. Serve with avocado and sour cream. Enjoy!

Almost Famous Southern-Fried Chicken

Total Time: 40 min | **Serves:** 4 | **Per serving:** Cal 190; Net Carbs 0.3g; Fat 7.1g; Protein 27.9g

Ingredients

1 lb chicken drumsticks
2 tbsp hot chili sauce
2 oz pork rinds, finely ground

1 tbsp cayenne pepper
½ tsp cumin
¼ tsp onion powder

Salt and black pepper to taste
1 lemon, cut into wedges

Directions

Preheat the Air Fryer to 350°F. Coat the chicken with hot chili sauce in a bowl. Combine the pork rinds, cayenne pepper, cumin, onion powder, salt, and black pepper in a separate bowl. Roll the chicken into the pork rind mixture and press gently to adhere. Transfer the drumsticks to the greased frying basket. AirFry for 20-25 minutes, flipping once, until golden brown. Serve with lemon wedges.

Jerk Chicken Fajitas

Total Time: 25 min | **Serves**: 4 | **Per serving**: Cal 327; Net Carbs 3.2g; Fat 10.1g; Protein 16g

Ingredients

1 lb chicken breasts, cut into strips
3 tbsp coconut oil, melted
1 tsp Jerk seasoning
½ tsp Anco chili powder

½ tsp cumin
½ tsp paprika
½ tsp garlic powder
¼ white onion, sliced

1 green bell pepper, seeded and sliced
1 red bell pepper, seeded and sliced
1 tbsp cilantro, chopped

Directions

Preheat the Air Fryer to 350°F. In a mixing bowl, thoroughly combine the coconut oil, Jerk seasoning, chili powder, cumin, paprika, and garlic powder. Add in the chicken strips and toss to coat. Arrange them on the greased frying basket in a single layer. Work in batches if necessary. AirFry for 15 minutes. At the 7-minute mark, flip them and add the onion and bell peppers; cook for the remaining 8 minutes until the chicken is cooked through and the vegetables are tender. Scatter over the cilantro and serve.

Louisiana-Style Blackened Chicken Tenders

Total Time: 30 min | **Serves**: 4 | **Per serving**: Cal 165; Net Carbs 0.3g; Fat 7.1g; Protein 21.3g

Ingredients

2 tsp Cajun seasoning
½ tsp garlic powder
½ tsp dried thyme

¼ tsp onion powder
2 tbsp coconut oil
1 ¼ lb chicken tenders

¼ cup ranch dressing

Directions

Preheat the Air Fryer to 370°F. Brush the chicken tenderloins with coconut oil. Rub them with Cajun seasoning, garlic powder, thyme, and onion powder. Arrange the coated tenders on the air fryer basket. AirFry for 16-18 minutes, turning once until the top is blackened. Serve with ranch dressing on the side.

Fajita Chicken Breast Rolls

Total Time: 30 min | **Serves**: 4 | **Per serving**: Cal 145; Net Carbs 1.1g; Fat 5g; Protein 20g

Ingredients

2 chicken breasts, halved lengthwise
1 onion, sliced
1 green bell pepper, seeded and sliced

1 tbsp coconut oil
2 tsp chili powder
1 tsp ground cumin

½ tsp garlic powder
1 tsp fajita seasoning
2 tbsp fresh chives, chopped

Directions

Preheat the Air Fryer to 360°F. Place the chicken breast halves between two plastic wraps and pound them with a rolling pin to an even ¼-inch thickness. Rub the mix of chili powder, cumin, garlic powder, and fajita seasoning onto the chicken. Place them on a clean flat surface and top with bell pepper, onion, and chives. Roll them up, sealing the edges with toothpicks. Arrange the rolls on the air fryer basket and brush them with coconut oil. AirFry for 23-25 minutes, turning once until golden. Serve and enjoy!

Teriyaki Chicken Tenders

Total Time: 30 min + marinating time | **Serves**: 4 | **Per serving**: Cal 445; Net Carbs 0.1g; Fat 30g; Protein 41.9g

Ingredients

1 ¼ lb chicken tenders
½ cup sugar-free teriyaki sauce

½ tbsp soy sauce
2 garlic cloves, minced

¼ tsp ground ginger
2 tsp cayenne pepper

Directions

In a large bowl, combine the teriyaki sauce, soy sauce, garlic, ginger, and cayenne pepper. Add the chicken tenders and toss to coat. Cover with plastic foil and place in the refrigerator for 2 hours.

Preheat the Air Fryer to 395°F. Arrange the chicken tenders on the air fryer basket. AirFry for 23-25 minutes, flipping once until golden and cooked through. Serve and enjoy!

Hot Hasselback Chicken

Total Time: 40 min | **Serves:** 4 | **Per serving:** Cal 499; Net Carbs 1g; Fat 25g; Protein 54.1g

Ingredients

4 oz cream cheese, softened	½ cup pickled jalapeños, sliced	2 tsp chicken seasoning
1 cup sharp cheddar cheese, shredded	4 chicken breasts	Salt and black pepper to taste
8 bacon slices, cooked and crumbled	2 tbsp basil, chopped	

Directions

Preheat the Air Fryer to 350°F. Mix together the cream cheese and half of the cheddar. Add the cooked bacon and sliced jalapeñosand mix well. Season with salt and pepper. Season the breasts with chicken seasoning. Make a few slits in the breasts about ¾ of the way across the chicken; make sure not to slice all the way through.

Fill the slits with the cheese mixture and top with the remaining cheddar cheese. Place the chicken in the air fryer basket. Bake for 18-20 minutes until golden and crispy. Sprinkle with basil and serve.

Crispy Chicken Parmigiana

Total Time: 25 min | **Serves:** 4 | **Per serving:** Cal 392; Net Carbs 2.1g; Fat 23g; Protein 34.3g

Ingredients

2 chicken breasts, sliced lengthwise	1 tsp chicken seasoning	1 oz pork rinds, crushed
½ tsp garlic powder	4 tbsp mayonnaise	½ cup Parmesan cheese, grated
2 tbsp fresh basil, chopped	1 cup mozzarella cheese, shredded	1 cup sugar-free tomato sauce

Directions

Preheat the Air Fryer to 330°F. Flatten the chicken breasts out using a meat tenderizer to an even ¾-inch thickness. Shake the garlic powder and chicken seasoning over the breasts. Mix the pork rinds and Parmesan cheese in a small bowl. Spread each breast with mayonnaise and cover with mozzarella cheese.

Top with the Parmesan mixture. Pour tomato sauce into a baking dish and scatter over the basil. Add the chicken on top and place the dish in the air fryer basket. Bake for 25 minutes until bubbling and golden.

Seven-Spice Chicken Drumsticks

Total Time: 30 min | **Serves:** 4 | **Per serving:** Cal 531; Net Carbs 0.1g; Fat 32.1g; Protein 48g

Ingredients

½ tsp onion powder	4 tbsp butter, melted	Salt and black pepper to taste
½ tsp garlic powder	1 tbsp Japanese seven-spice seasoning	
8 chicken drumsticks	(Togarashi)	

Directions

Preheat the Air Fryer to 375°F. Brush the chicken drumsticks with some melted butter all over. Mix together the spices and rub them onto the chicken. Arrange them on the frying basket and AirFry for 25 minutes, flipping once until golden. Pour the remaining butter over the drumsticks and serve.

Moroccan-Style Chicken Thighs

Total Time: 40 min | **Serves**: 4 | **Per serving**: Cal 435; Net Carbs 0.4g; Fat 29g; Protein 31.9g

Ingredients

4 chicken thighs	2 tsp chili powder	½ lemon, zested
1 tsp baking powder	1 tbsp ras el hanout	¼ cup chopped fresh cilantro
½ tsp garlic powder	1 tsp cumin	½ cup green olives, sliced

Directions

Preheat the Air Fryer to 375°F. Add the baking powder, garlic powder, chili powder, ras el hanout, cumin, and lemon zest to a large bowl. Add the chicken and toss to coat. Place the thighs in the fryer basket and Bake for 20-23 minutes, turning once, until golden. Top with green olives and cilantro. Serve.

Famous Buffalo Chicken Wings

Total Time: 35 min | **Serves**: 4 | **Per serving**: Cal 165; Net Carbs 0.3g; Fat 4g; Protein 27.4g

Ingredients

1 ½ lb chicken wings	½ cup pork rinds, finely ground	1 tsp garlic powder
¼ cup hot sauce	1 tsp chili powder	½ tsp smoked paprika

Directions

Preheat the Air Fryer to 375°F. Mix the pork rinds, chili powder, garlic powder, and smoked paprika in a mixing bowl. Place the wings in another bowl and cover them with hot sauce; toss to coat. Roll the wings in the pork rind mixture, pressing gently to adhere. Add the chicken wings to the air fryer basket. AirFry for 18-20 minutes, turning once, until golden and cooked through. Serve and enjoy!

Sweet Chili Chicken Breasts

Total Time: 55 min | **Serves**: 3 | **Per serving**: Cal 226; Net Carbs 2g; Fat 8g; Protein 18.2g

Ingredients

2 chicken breasts, cubed	½ tsp ginger paste	1 red pepper
Salt and black pepper to taste	½ tsp garlic paste	1 green pepper
1 cup almond flour	1 tbsp swerve sweetener	1 tsp paprika
3 eggs	2 red chilies, minced	4 tbsp water
½ cup Apple Cider vinegar	2 tbsp tomato puree	

Directions

Preheat the Air Fryer to 350°F. Pour the almond flour into a bowl, add the eggs, salt, and pepper. Whisk the mixture with a fork. Put the chicken in the flour mixture. Mix to coat the chicken with it using a wooden spatula. Place the chicken in the fryer basket, spray them with cooking spray, and fry them for 8 minutes.

Pull out the fryer basket, shake it to toss the chicken, and spray again with cooking spray. Keep cooking for 7 minutes or until golden and crispy. Remove the chicken to a plate and set aside. Put the red, and green peppers on a chopping board. Using a knife, cut them open and deseed them. Cut the flesh in long strips.

In a bowl, add the water, apple cider vinegar, swerve sweetener, ginger and garlic puree, red chili, tomato puree, and paprika. Mix with a fork. Place a skillet over medium heat and spray it with cooking spray.

Add the chicken to it and the pepper strips. Stir and cook until the peppers are sweaty but still crunchy. Pour the chili mixture on the chicken, stir, and bring it to simmer for 10 minutes. Turn off the heat. Dish the chicken chili sauce into a serving bowl and serve with a side of steamed cauli rice.

Homemade Jerk Chicken Wings

Total Time: 45 min + marinating time | **Serves:** 4 | **Per serving:** Cal 351; Net Carbs 4.2g; Fat 13.8g; Protein 50.7g

Ingredients

2 lb chicken wings
1 tbsp olive oil
3 cloves garlic, minced
1 tsp chili powder
½ tsp cinnamon powder
½ tsp allspice

1 habanero pepper, seeded
1 tbsp soy sauce, sugar-free
½ tsp white pepper
¼ cup red wine vinegar
3 tbsp lime juice
2 scallions, chopped

½ tbsp grated ginger
½ tbsp chopped fresh thyme
⅓ tbsp erythritol
½ tsp salt

Directions

In a large bowl, add the olive oil, soy sauce, garlic, habanero pepper, allspice, chili powder, cinnamon powder, white pepper, salt, erythritol, thyme, ginger, scallions, lime juice, and red wine vinegar. Use a spoon to mix them well. Add the chicken wings to the marinade mixture and coat it well with the mixture. Cover the bowl with cling film and refrigerate the chicken to marinate it for 16 hours.

Preheat the Air Fryer to 400°F. Remove the chicken from the fridge, drain all the liquid, and pat each wing dry using a paper towel. Place half of the wings in the fryer basket and cook it for 16 minutes. Shake the fryer basket to toss the chicken halfway through. Remove onto a serving platter and repeat the cooking process for the remaining chicken. Serve the jerk wings with a blue cheese dip or ranch dressing.

Herby Chicken Thighs with Tomatoes

Total Time: 20 min | **Serves:** 2 | **Per serving:** Cal 285; Net Carbs 2.1g; Fat 15g; Protein 21g

Ingredients

2 chicken thighs
1 cup tomatoes, quartered

4 cloves garlic, minced
½ tsp dried tarragon

½ tsp olive oil
¼ tsp red pepper flakes

Directions

Preheat the Air Fryer to 390°F. Add the tomatoes, red pepper flakes, tarragon, garlic, and olive oil to a medium bowl. Mix it well. In a large ramekin, add the chicken and top it with the tomato mixture.

Place the ramekin in the fryer basket and roast for 10 minutes. After baking, carefully remove the ramekin. Plate the chicken thighs, spoon the cooking juice over and serve.

Saturday Garlic Stuffed Chicken

Total Time: 55 min | **Serves:** 3 | **Per serving:** Cal 343; Net Carbs 2.5g; Fat 15.8g; Protein 35g

Ingredients

1 (3 lb) small chicken
1 ½ tbsp olive oil
Salt and black pepper to taste

⅓ cup chopped sage
⅓ cup chopped thyme
2 cloves garlic, crushed

1 brown onion, chopped
3 tbsp butter
2 eggs, beaten

Directions

melt the butter in a pan over medium heat. Add the garlic and onion and sauté until softened, about 3 minutes. Add the eggs, sage, thyme, pepper, and salt. Mix well. Cook for 20 seconds and turn the heat off. Stuff the chicken with the mixture into the cavity. Then, tie the legs of the spatchcock with a butcher's twine and brush with olive oil. Rub the top and sides of the chicken generously with salt and pepper.

Preheat the Air Fryer to 390°F. Place the spatchcock into the fryer basket and roast it for 25 minutes. Turn the chicken over and continue cooking for a further 10-15 minutes but you can check it throughout the cooking time to ensure it doesn't dry or overcooks. Remove and wrap it with aluminum foil. Let it rest for 10 minutes.

Chicken Drumsticks with Blue Cheese Sauce

Total Time: 2 hrs 30 min | **Serves:** 4 | **Per serving:** Cal 281; Net Carbs 2g; Fat 14.2g; Protein 14.8g

Ingredients

Drumsticks:

1 lb mini chicken drumsticks
3 tbsp butter
3 tbsp paprika

2 tsp powdered cumin
¼ cup hot sauce
1 tbsp erythritol

2 tbsp onion powder
2 tbsp garlic powder

Blue cheese sauce:

½ cup mayonnaise
1 cup blue cheese, crumbled
1 cup sour cream
1 ½ tsp garlic powder

1 ½ tsp onion powder
Salt and black pepper to taste
1 ½ tsp cayenne pepper
1 ½ tsp white wine vinegar

2 tbsp buttermilk
1 ½ Worcestershire sauce, sugar-free

Directions

Start with the drumstick sauce; place a pan over medium heat. Melt the butter and add the hot sauce, paprika, garlic powder, onion powder, erythritol, and cumin; mix well. Cook the mixture for 5 minutes or until the sauce reduces. Turn off the heat and let it cool. Put the drumsticks in a bowl, pour half of the sauce on it, and mix. Save the remaining sauce for serving. Refrigerate the drumsticks to marinate them for 2 hours.

Make the blue cheese sauce: in a jug, add the sour cream, blue cheese, mayonnaise, garlic powder, onion powder, buttermilk, cayenne pepper, vinegar, Worcestershire sauce, pepper, and salt. Using a stick blender, blend the ingredients until they are well mixed with no large lumps. Adjust the salt and pepper taste as desired.

Preheat the Air Fryer to 350°F. Remove the drumsticks from the fridge and place them in the fryer basket. Cook for 15 minutes. Turn the drumsticks with tongs every 5 minutes to ensure that they are evenly cooked. Remove the drumsticks into a serving bowl and pour the remaining sauce over it. Serve the drumsticks with the blue cheese sauce and a side of celery sticks.

Tasty Barbecued Satay

Total Time: 15 min | **Serves:** 3 | **Per serving:** Cal 434; Net Carbs 6.8g; Fat 31g; Protein 29g

Ingredients

1 lb chicken tenders
½ cup soy sauce
¼ cup sesame oil

4 cloves garlic, chopped
4 scallions, chopped
1 tbsp fresh ginger, grated

2 tbsp sesame seeds, toasted
A pinch of black pepper

Directions

Start by skewering each tender and trim any excess fat. Mix the rest of the ingredients in one large bowl. Add the skewered chicken and place them in the fridge for a period of 4 to 24 hours. Preheat the Air Fryer to 390°F. Pat the chicken until it is completely dry using a paper towel. Cook for 7-10 minutes.

Amazing Chicken Lollipop

Total Time: 20 min | **Serves:** 3 | **Per serving:** Cal 276; Net Carbs 2g; Fat 10.4g; Protein 14.9g

Ingredients

1 lb chicken drumsticks
½ tsp soy sauce, sugar-free
1 tsp lime juice
Salt and black pepper to taste
1 tsp arrowroot starch

½ tsp minced garlic
½ tsp chili powder
½ tsp chopped cilantro
½ tsp garlic-ginger paste
1 tsp vinegar

1 tsp chili paste
½ tsp egg, beaten
1 tsp paprika
1 tsp almond flour
2 tsp erythritol

Directions

Mix the garlic-ginger paste, chili powder, erythritol, chili paste, soy sauce, paprika, cilantro, vinegar, egg, garlic, black pepper, and salt in a bowl. Add the chicken drumsticks and toss to coat thoroughly. Stir in the arrowroot starch, almond flour, and lime juice.

Preheat the Air Fryer to 350°F. Remove each drumstick, shake off the excess marinade, and place in a single layer in the fryer basket. Cook them for 5 minutes. Slide out the fryer basket, spray the chicken with cooking spray and continue cooking for 5 minutes. Remove to a serving platter and serve with a tomato dip.

Chicken Tenders with Tarragon

Total Time: 20 min | **Serves**: 2 | **Per serving**: Cal 230; Net Carbs 2g; Fat 12.5g; Protein 18g

Ingredients

2 chicken tenders
Salt and black pepper to taste

½ cup dried tarragon
1 tsp unsalted butter

Directions

Preheat the Air Fryer to 390°F. Lay out a 12 X 12 inch cut of foil on a flat surface. Place the chicken tenders on the foil, sprinkle with tarragon, and share the butter onto both tenders. Sprinkle salt and pepper on them.

Loosely wrap the foil around the tenders to enable air flow. Place the wrapped chicken in the fryer basket and cook for 12 minutes. Serve the chicken with the sauce extract and steamed mixed veggies.

Turmeric Chicken Breasts

Total Time: 25 min | **Serves**: 3 | **Per serving**: Cal 164; Net Carbs 2g; Fat 6.8g; Protein 24.8g

Ingredients

3 chicken breasts
Salt to taste

¼ cup chili sauce, reduced sugar
3 tbsp turmeric

Directions

Preheat the Air Fryer to 390°F. In a bowl, add the salt, chili sauce, and turmeric. Mix evenly with a spoon. Place the chicken breasts on a clean flat surface and with a brush, apply the turmeric sauce lightly on the chicken. Place them in the fryer basket and grill for 18 minutes. Turn them halfway through. Serve with steamed greens.

Rosemary Chicken with Egg Noodles

Total Time: 30 min + resting time | **Serves**: 4 | **Per serving**: Cal 523; Net Carbs 1.8g; Fat 34g; Protein 41g

Ingredients

4 chicken breasts
Salt and black pepper to taste

1 tbsp rosemary
1 tbsp tomato paste

1 tbsp red pepper
1 tbsp butter, melted

Noodles:

2 cups almond flour

½ tbsp salt

2 eggs, beaten

Directions

Preheat the Air Fryer to 350°F. Coat the chicken breasts with butter, salt, and pepper. Arrange them on the air fryer basket and cook for 18-20 minutes. When ready, remove the chicken and set aside.

For the noodles, combine flour, salt, and egg, and make a dough. Place the dough on a floured surface. Knead and cover it. Set aside for 30 minutes. Roll the dough on a floured surface. When the batter thins, cut into thin strips and let dry for 1 hour. Boil 4 cups of water and add the noodles, tomato paste, and red pepper. Cook for 5 minutes. Season with rosemary, red pepper, salt, and pepper and stir. Serve the noodles topped with the chicken.

Asian-Style Marinated Chicken

Total Time: 20 min | **Serves:** 6 | **Per serving:** Cal 523; Net Carbs 2.5g; Fat 46g; Protein 31g

Ingredients

2 lbs chicken breasts, cut into cubes
¼ cup pork rinds, crushed
2 large eggs
6 tbsp almond flour
1 tbsp baking powder

4 tbsp sesame oil
2 tbsp fresh ginger root, grated
½ cup green onion, chopped
½ cup water
¼ cup white vinegar

1 ½ tbsp liquid stevia
2 tbsp soy sauce
¼ cup oyster sauce

Directions

Preheat the Air Fryer to 390°F. Coat the chicken cubes with the pork rinds, then set aside. In a large bowl, beat eggs. Add flour and baking powder, and beat until there are no lumps. Coat the chicken and place it the Air Fryer. Cook for 15 minutes, shaking the basket halfway through.

Heat the sesame oil in a skillet over medium heat. Add onion and ginger and cook, stirring for 2-3 minutes. Add the water, vinegar, stevia and bring the mixture to a boil. Dissolve the pork rinds in soy sauce and add-oyster sauce. Keep stirring until the sauce thickens. Add the chicken and let simmer for 10-15 minutes.

Prosciutto & Brie Chicken Breasts

Total Time: 25 min | **Serves:** 2 | **Per serving:** Cal 262; Net Carbs 3g; Fat 16g; Protein 24g

Ingredients

2 chicken breasts
1 tbsp olive oil

Salt and black pepper to taste
1 cup semi-dried tomatoes, sliced

½ cup brie cheese, halved
4 slices thin prosciutto

Directions

Preheat the Air Fryer to 370°F. Put the chicken on a chopping board. With a knife, cut a small incision deep enough to make stuffing on both. Insert one slice of cheese and 4 to 5 tomato slices into each chicken.

Lay the prosciutto on the chopping board. Put the chicken on one side of it and roll the prosciutto over the chicken, making sure that both ends of the prosciutto meet under the chicken. Drizzle the olive oil and sprinkle it with salt and pepper. Put the chicken in the fryer basket. Cook it for 10 minutes. Turn the breasts over and cook for another 5 minutes. Slice each chicken breast in half and serve with green tomato salad.

Oregano Chicken Marsala

Total Time: 30 min | **Serves:** 4 | **Per serving:** Cal 488; Net Carbs 3.2g; Fat 43g; Protein 37g

Ingredients

¼ cup almond flour
½ tbsp dried oregano
4 chicken breasts

1 tbsp olive oil
1 cup mushrooms, sliced
½ cup Marsala wine

Salt and black pepper to taste
¼ cup cooking sherry

Directions

Preheat the Air Fryer to 350°F. In a bowl, combine the flour, salt, pepper, and oregano. Coat the chicken with flour and arrange it on the rack of the Air Fryer. Pour over one tablespoon of oil and cook for 12 minutes. When done, add the mushrooms and cook for 5 minutes. Transfer to a pan over medium heat and pour wine and sherry. Let simmer for 10 minutes.

Sweet & Spicy Chicken Wings

Total Time: 25 min | **Serves:** 2 | **Per serving:** Cal 235; Net Carbs 1g; Fat 7g; Protein 37g

Ingredients

1 ½ tbsp hot chili sauce
½ tbsp liquid stevia

¼ tbsp lime juice
12 oz chicken wings

Salt and black pepper to taste

Directions

Preheat the Air Fryer to 390°F. Mix the lime juice, stevia, salt, pepper, and sauce. Toss the chicken wings with the lime and the chili sauce mixture. Put the chicken wings in the Air Fryer basket and cook for around 20 minutes. Shake the basket every 4 to 5 minutes. Serve hot.

Power Green Hot Drumsticks

Total Time: 25 min | **Serves:** 4 | **Per serving:** Cal 275; Net Carbs 1.9g; Fat 17.5g; Protein 26g

Ingredients

4 chicken drumsticks
2 tbsp green curry paste
3 tbsp coconut cream

Salt and black pepper to taste
½ fresh jalapeno chili, finely chopped
A handful of fresh parsley, roughly

chopped

Directions

In a bowl, add the drumsticks, paste, cream, salt, pepper, and jalapeño and toss to coat. Arrange the drumsticks into the air fryer and cook for 6 minutes at 400°F, flipping once halfway through cooking. Serve with parsley.

Divina's Chicken Tenders

Total Time: 15 min | **Serves:** 20 | **Per serving:** Cal 54; Net Carbs 0.2g; Fat 3g; Protein 6g

Ingredients

1 ½ lb chicken tenders
20 skewers bamboo party

2 zested lemons
3 tbsp extra virgin olive oil

Salt and black pepper to taste

Directions

Preheat the Air Fryer to 350°F. Season the chicken pieces with salt and black pepper. Thread the pieces onto skewers. In a dish, mix the lemon zest and olive oil. Coat the chicken tenders and cook the chicken tenders in the preheated Air Fryer for about 12 minutes. Serve with tomato sauce.

Broccoli Chicken Cheesy Casserole

Total Time: 35 min | **Serves:** 3 | **Per serving:** Cal 321; Net Carbs 2g; Fat 13.4g; Protein 35g

Ingredients

3 chicken breasts
Salt and black pepper to taste

1 cup shredded cheddar cheese
1 broccoli head, cut into florets

1 cup cream mushroom soup

Directions

Preheat the Air Fryer to 390°F. Place the chicken breasts on a clean flat surface and season them with salt and pepper. Grease with cooking spray and place them in the air fryer basket. AirFry for 13 minutes, flipping once.

Add the fried chicken, broccoli, cheddar cheese, and mushroom soup cream in a casserole dish and mix well. Put the dish in the air fryer basket and Bake for 10-12 minutes. Serve and enjoy!

Chicken with Cilantro Adobo

Total Time: 15 min | **Serves:** 2 | **Per serving:** Cal 419; Net Carbs 5.1g; Fat 19g; Protein 34g

Ingredients

2 chicken breasts
2 tbsp lime juice
1 tbsp fresh cilantro, minced
1 tbsp olive oil

3 garlic cloves, minced
1 green onion, minced
¼ tbsp ground cumin
¼ tbsp fresh thyme, minced

¼ tbsp fresh oregano, minced
Salt and black pepper to taste

Directions

Mix the ingredients in a resealable plastic bag and seal the bag. Refrigerate for at least 3 hours. Then drain the marinade. Using long tongs, moist paper toweling with the oil and coat the Air Fryer's rack. Set the heat to 340°F and time to 20 minutes. Don't forget to flip the chicken at least once in the cooking process.

Chicken Breast with Tarragon

Total Time: 20 min | **Serves:** 2 | **Per serving:** Cal 187; Net Carbs 0.3g; Fat 5g; Protein 31g

Ingredients

2 chicken breasts
¼ cup dried tarragon

½ tbsp unsalted butter
Kosher salt and black pepper to taste

Directions

Preheat the Air Fryer to 390°F. Place each of the chicken breasts on a foil wrap, 12x12 inches. Top the chicken with the tarragon sprig and the butter. Season with salt and pepper.

Wrap the foil around the chicken breast in a loose way so there is a flow of air. Cook the foil-wrapped chicken in the Air Fryer for 14-16 minutes. Slowly and carefully unwrap the chicken and serve hot.

Garlic Chicken Tenders with Hot Mayo Sauce

Total Time: 15 min | **Serves:** 4 | **Per serving:** Cal 498; Net Carbs 2.1g; Fat 38g; Protein 41g

Ingredients

3 chicken breasts, cut into strips
4 tbsp olive oil

1 cup pork rinds, crushed
Salt and black pepper to taste

½ tsp garlic powder
½ tsp ground chili

Mayo Sauce:

½ cup mayonnaise

2 tbsp lemon juice

½ tsp ground chili

Directions

Preheat the Air Fryer to 380°F. Mix pork rinds, salt, pepper, garlic powder and chili, and spread onto a plate. Brush the chicken with some olive oil. Roll the strips in the pork rind mixture until well coated.

Drizzle them with a little bit of oil. Arrange an even layer of strips into your air fryer basket. AirFry for 6 minutes, turning once. For the mayo sauce: combine mayo with lemon juice and ground chili. Serve with the chicken.

Dijon Thighs

Total Time: 30 min | **Serves:** 4 | **Per serving:** Cal 452; Net Carbs 1.2g; Fat 27g; Protein 49g

Ingredients

4 chicken thighs, skin-on
3 tbsp stevia
2 tbsp Dijon mustard

½ tsp garlic powder
Salt and black pepper to taste

Directions

In a bowl, mix stevia, mustard, garlic, salt and black pepper. Coat the thighs in the mixture and arrange in your air fryer. Cook for 16 minutes at 400°F, turning once halfway through cooking.

Paprika Roasted Whole Chicken

Total Time: 70 min | **Serves:** 4 | **Per serving:** Cal 317; Net Carbs 3g; Fat 21.4g; Protein 18.9g

Ingredients

1 (3 lb) whole chicken, on the bone
Salt and black pepper to taste
1 tsp chili powder
1 tsp garlic powder

4 tsp oregano
2 tsp coriander powder
2 tsp cumin powder
2 tbsp olive oil

4 tsp paprika
1 lime, juiced

Directions

Preheat the Air Fryer to 350°F. In a bowl, pour the oregano, garlic powder, chili powder, ground coriander, paprika, cumin powder, pepper, salt, and olive oil. Mix well to create a rub for the chicken. Add the chicken and rub the spice mixture well on it. Place it in the greased air fryer basket and Bake for 50 minutes.

Use a skewer to poke the chicken to ensure that it is clear of juices. If not, cook the chicken further for 5-10 minutes. Allow the chicken to sit for 10 minutes. After, drizzle the lime juice over it. Serve with salad if desired.

Best Homemade Chicken Fingers

Total Time: 20 min | **Serves:** 2 | **Per serving:** Cal 132; Net Carbs 0.7g; Fat 4g; Protein 18g

Ingredients

¼ tsp fresh chives, chopped
1 tbsp Parmesan cheese, shredded
¼ tsp fresh thyme, chopped

¼ tsp black pepper
½ cup pork rinds, crushed
1 egg white

1 tsp water
½ lb chicken breasts

Directions

Preheat the Air Fryer to 390°F. Mix the chives, the Parmesan, the thyme, the pepper, and the rinds. Whisk and mix the egg white and the water. Cut the chicken breasts in large strips. Carefully dip chicken strips into egg mixture and pork rinds mixture. Place the strips one by one in the Air Fryer basket. Cook for 8 minutes.

Curried Chicken Breasts

Total Time: 25 min + marinating time | **Serves:** 2 | **Per serving:** Cal 428; Net Carbs 6.8g; Fat 23.5g; Protein 42g

Ingredients

2 chicken breasts
1 tbsp mayonnaise
2 eggs

1 tsp chili pepper
1 tsp curry powder
1 tbsp swerve sweetener

1 tsp soy sauce, sugar-free

Directions

Put the chicken cutlets on a clean flat surface and use a knife to slice in diagonal pieces. Gently pound them to become thinner using a rolling pin. Place them in a bowl and add soy sauce, swerve sweetener, curry powder, and chili pepper. Mix well and leave to marinate in the fridge for around 1 hour.

Preheat the Air Fryer to 350°F. Remove the chicken and crack the eggs into it. Add the mayonnaise and mix. Remove each chicken piece and shake it well to remove as much liquid from it. Place in the fryer basket and cook for 8 minutes. Turn and cook further for 6 minutes. Serve the curried chicken with a side of steamed greens.

Chicken Breasts Wrapped in Turkey Bacon

Total Time: 20 min | **Serves**: 4 | **Per serving**: Cal 408; Net Carbs 1.5g; Fat 28g; Protein 27g

Ingredients

2 chicken breasts
8 oz onion and chive cream cheese
1 tbsp butter

6 turkey bacon
Salt to taste
1 tbsp fresh parsley, finely chopped

Juice from ½ lemon

Directions

Preheat the Air Fryer to 390°F. Stretch out the bacon slightly and lay them on in 2 sets, that is 3 bacon strips together on each side. Place the chicken on each bacon set and use a knife to smear the cream cheese on both.

Share the butter on top of each chicken and sprinkle with salt. Wrap the bacon around the chicken and secure the ends. Place in the fryer basket and cook for 14 minutes. Turn the chicken halfway through. Remove the chicken to a platter and top with parsley and lemon juice. Serve with steamed greens.

Lemon Chicken with Fresh Herbs

Total Time: 70 min | **Serves**: 5 | **Per serving**: Cal 398; Net Carbs 2.1g; Fat 28g; Protein 33g

Ingredients

1 (3-lb) whole chicken, cut into pieces
½ cup olive oil
3 cloves garlic, minced

1 tbsp fresh rosemary, chopped
1 tbsp fresh thyme, chopped
1 tbsp fresh oregano, chopped

2 large lemons
½ cup white wine
Salt and black pepper to taste

Directions

In a large bowl, combine garlic, olive oil, oregano, rosemary, thyme, lemon juice, salt, and pepper. Mix the ingredients very well. Spread the mixture into a baking dish. Add the chicken. Keep stirring.

Preheat the Air Fryer to 350°F and place in the chicken. Sprinkle with white wine and cook it for 50-60 minutes.

Korean-Style Chicken

Total Time: 25 min | **Serves**: 3 | **Per serving**: Cal 243; Net Carbs 6.1g; Fat 13g; Protein 18g

Ingredients

3 cloves garlic, minced
½ lb chicken breasts, sliced
1 tbsp cumin powder
1 large onion, chopped

2 tbsp oil
1 tbsp mustard
3 green chili peppers
A pinch of ground ginger

A pinch of fresh coriander, chopped
2 tomatoes, chopped
Salt and black pepper to taste

Directions

Start by heating the oil in a deep pan. Add mustard, cumin, garlic, onion, ginger, and green chili peppers. Sauté the mixture for a few minutes. Add tomatoes, coriander, pepper, and salt, and keep stirring.

Preheat the Air Fryer to 360°F. Coat the chicken with oil, salt, and pepper and cook it for 14-16 minutes. Remove from the Air Fryer and pour the sauce over and around it.

Yummy Chicken Snacks

Total Time: 25 min | **Serves**: 4 | **Per serving**: Cal 346; Net Carbs 1.6g; Fat 21g; Protein 40g

Ingredients

2 chicken breasts, cut into 2 pieces each
1 egg, beaten

¼ cup buttermilk
1 cup pork rinds, crushed

Salt and black pepper to taste

Directions

In a bowl, whisk egg and buttermilk. Add in chicken pieces and stir to coat. On a plate, spread the pork rinds out and mix with salt and pepper. Coat the chicken pieces in the pork rinds. Spray the air fryer with oil spray. Arrange the chicken pieces in an even layer inside your air fryer and cook for 12 minutes at 360°F, turning once. Serve.

Crispy Chicken Schnitzel with Herbs

Total Time: 25 min | **Serves**: 2 | **Per serving**: Cal 415; Net Carbs 2.1g; Fat 34g; Protein 17g

Ingredients

2 chicken breasts
2 eggs, cracked into a bowl
2 cups coconut milk

4 tbsp tomato sauce
2 tbsp mixed herbs
2 cups mozzarella cheese

1 cup almond flour
¾ cup shaved ham
1 cup pork rinds, crushed

Directions

Place the chicken breast between 2 plastic wraps and use a rolling pin to pound them to flatten them out. Whisk the coconut milk and eggs together in a bowl. Pour the flour into a plate, the pork rinds in another dish, and let's start coating the chicken. Toss the chicken in flour, then in the egg mixture, and then in the pork rinds.

Preheat the Air Fryer to 350°F. Put the chicken in the fryer basket and cook for 10 minutes. Remove them onto a plate and top the chicken with the ham, tomato sauce, mozzarella cheese, and mixed herbs. Return the chicken to the fryer basket and bake further for 5 minutes or until the mozzarella cheese has melted. Serve and enjoy!

Mom's Chicken Cordon Bleu

Total Time: 35 min | **Serves**: 4 | **Per serving**: Cal 564; Net Carbs 2.2g; Fat 52g; Protein 48g

Ingredients

4 chicken breasts, skinless and
boneless
4 slices Swiss cheese
4 slices ham

3 tbsp almond flour
1 tbsp paprika
4 tbsp butter
½ cup dry white wine

1 tbsp chicken bouillon granules
1 cup heavy whipping cream

Directions

Preheat the Air Fryer to 390°F. Pound the chicken breasts and put a slice of ham and a slice of Swiss cheese on each of the chicken breasts. Fold the edges of the chicken over the filling and secure the sides with toothpicks. In a bowl, combine flour and paprika and coat the chicken pieces. Set the timer to 15 minutes and cook the chicken.

In a skillet over low heat, melt the butter and add the bouillon, heavy cream, and wine. Remove the chicken from the Air Fryer and add it to the skillet. Let the ingredients simmer for around 30 minutes and serve.

Cilantro Seed Chicken Burgers

Total Time: 25 min | **Serves**: 4 | **Per serving**: Cal 305; Net Carbs 2.3g; Fat 21g; Protein 24g

Ingredients

1 lb ground chicken
½ onion, chopped
2 garlic cloves, chopped

1 egg, beaten
½ cup pork rinds, crushed
½ tsp ground cumin

½ tsp paprika
½ tsp cilantro seeds, crushed
Salt and black pepper to taste

Directions

In a bowl, mix chicken, onion, garlic, egg, pork rinds, cumin, paprika, cilantro, salt and black pepper. Shape into 4 patties. Grease your air fryer oil and arrange the patties inside. Do not layer them. Cook in batches if needed. Cook for 10 minutes at 380°F, turning once halfway through cooking.

Party Roasted Cornish Hen

Total Time: 30 min + marinating time | **Serves:** 4 | **Per serving:** Cal 477; Net Carbs 1.2g; Fat 34.8g; Protein 37g

Ingredients

2 lb cornish hen
1 lemon, zested
¼ tsp swerve sweetener

¼ tsp salt
1 tsp fresh rosemary, chopped
1 tsp fresh thyme, chopped

¼ tsp red pepper flakes
½ cup olive oil

Directions

Place the hen on a chopping board with its back facing you and use a knife to cut through from the top of the backbone to the bottom of the spine, making 2 cuts. Remove the backbone. Divide the hen into two lengthwise while cutting through the breastplate. In a bowl, add the lemon zest, swerve sweetener, salt, rosemary, thyme, red pepper flakes, and olive oil; mix it well. Add the hen pieces, coat them, and place in the refrigerator for 14 hours.

Preheat the Air Fryer to 390°F. After the marinating time, remove the hen pieces from the marinade and pat them dry using a paper towel. Place them in the fryer basket and roast them for 16 minutes. Remove the hen onto a serving platter and serve with veggies.

Garlic Chicken Fingers with Parmesan

Total Time: 25 min + marinating time | **Serves:** 2 | **Per serving:** Cal 370; Net Carbs 2g; Fat 25g; Protein 33g

Ingredients

2 chicken breasts, cut into strips
Salt and black pepper to taste
2 cloves garlic, crushed

3 tbsp xanthan gum
4 tbsp pork rinds, crushed
4 tbsp Parmesan cheese, grated

2 eggs, beaten

Directions

Mix salt, garlic, and pepper in a bowl. Add the chicken and stir to coat thoroughly. Let it stay for 1 hour to marinate in the fridge. Mix the pork rinds with cheese evenly. Set aside. After the marinating time has passed, remove the chicken from the fridge, lightly toss in xanthan gum, dip in egg and coat them in the cheese mixture.

Preheat the Air Fryer to 350°F. Lightly spray the fryer basket with cooking spray and place the chicken in it. Cook for 15 minutes. Serve the chicken with a side of vegetable fries and cheese dip. Yum!

Chicken Skewers with Power Green Sauce

Total Time: 35 min | **Serves:** 4 | **Per serving:** Cal 468; Net Carbs 6.1g; Fat 29g; Protein 43g

Ingredients

1 lb chicken breasts, cut in 2-inch cubes
4 tbsp olive oil
Salt to taste

1 tbsp chili powder
¼ cup xylitol
½ cup Worcestershire sauce
2 green peppers, chopped

8 mushrooms, halved
1 garlic clove
Zest and juice from 1 lime
¼ cup fresh parsley, chopped

Directions

In a bowl, add chicken cubes, chili powder, salt, xylitol, half of the olive oil, and Worcestershire sauce and toss to coat; leave to marinate for 10 minutes. Stick 1 pepper piece, 1 chicken cube, and 1 mushroom half. Repeat until the skewer is full. Repeat the process with the remaining ingredients.

Preheat the Air Fryer to 330°F. Brush the skewers with the marinade and place into the basket. Grease with cooking spray and cook for 20 minutes. Flip halfway through. Blend garlic, remaining olive oil, lemon zest and juice, parsley, and salt in a food processor until a chunky paste. Top the skewers with the green sauce.

Hot Chicken with Cheese Sauce

Total Time: 30 min + marinating time | **Serves**: 4 | **Per serving**: Cal 281; Net Carbs 2g; Fat 14.2g; Protein 14.8g

Ingredients

Drumsticks:

3 tbsp chili powder

2 tsp powdered cumin

3 tbsp butter

1 lb chicken drumsticks

¼ cup Tabasco sauce

1 tbsp erythritol

2 tbsp onion powder

2 tbsp garlic powder

Cheese sauce:

½ cup Greek yogurt

1 cup Roqueford cheese, crumbled

1 cup sour cream

1 ½ tsp garlic powder

1 ½ tsp onion powder

Salt and black pepper to taste

1 ½ tsp cayenne pepper

1 ½ tsp lemon juice

2 tbsp buttermilk

1 ½ Worcestershire sauce, sugar-free

Directions

In a saucepan over medium heat, melt the butter. Add in the Tabasco sauce, chili powder, garlic powder, onion powder, erythritol, and cumin and cook for 5 minutes until the sauce reduces. Turn off the heat and let cool. In a bowl, combine the drumsticks with half of the sauce. Leave in the fridge for 2 hours. Reserve the remaining sauce.

In a blender, blitz the sour cream, Roquefort cheese, Greek Yogurt, garlic powder, onion powder, buttermilk, cayenne pepper, lemon juice, Worcestershire sauce, pepper, and salt until there are no lumps. Adjust the taste.

Preheat your Air Fryer to 350°F. Remove the drumsticks from the fridge and place them in the fryer. Cook for 15 minutes. Turn the chicken every 5 minutes. Transfer to a serving bowl and pour the remaining sauce. Serve the chicken with blue cheese and celery sticks.

Sweet Chicken Wings with Poppy Seeds

Total Time: 25 min | **Serves**: 4 | **Per serving**: Cal 215; Net Carbs 1g; Fat 11g; Protein 27g

Ingredients

1 lb chicken wings

2 tsp olive oil

2 tsp stevia

Salt and black pepper to taste

3 tbsp poppy seeds

Directions

In a bowl, add wings, oil, stevia, salt and pepper, and stir to coat well. In another bowl, add the poppy seeds and roll the wings in the seeds to coat thoroughly. Arrange the wings in an even layer inside your air fryer and cook for 12 minutes on 360°F, turning once halfway through cooking.

Basil & Oregano Chicken Legs

Total Time: 50 min | **Serves**: 4 | **Per serving**: Cal 483; Net Carbs 2.6g; Fat 27g; Protein 49g

Ingredients

4 chicken legs

¼ cup olive oil

3 large halved lemons

4 tbsp dried oregano

4 tbsp dried basil

4 tbsp garlic powder

Salt and black pepper to taste

Directions

Preheat the Air Fryer to 350°F. Place the chicken legs in a deep bowl. Brush the chicken legs with a tbsp of extra virgin olive oil. Squeeze lemon juice over the chicken and arrange in the Fryer's rack. Place the lemons around the chicken. In a medium bowl, combine oregano, basil, garlic, salt, and pepper. Sprinkle the mixture on the chicken legs. Cook the chicken in the preheated Air Fryer for 18-22 minutes. Serve and enjoy!

Crispy Parmesan Chicken

Total Time: 35 min | **Serves:** 2 | **Per serving:** Cal 286; Net Carbs 2.3g; Fat 15g; Protein 25g

Ingredients

2 chicken breasts
¼ cup butter
¼ cup Parmesan cheese, grated

2 cloves garlic, minced
½ tsp dried oregano
½ tsp dried rosemary

Salt and black pepper to taste
¼ tsp paprika

Directions

Preheat the Air Fryer to 370°F. Place the chicken on a plate and season with salt and pepper. Put the chicken in the air fryer basket and AirFry for 14-16 minutes, flipping them halfway through the cooking time.

Warm the butter in a skillet over medium heat and add the garlic. Stir and cook for 1 minute. Add paprika, oregano, and rosemary to the garlic and cook for 1 minute. Turn off the heat. Pour the sauce over the chicken in the air fryer, sprinkle with Parmesan cheese, and Bake for 5 minutes. Serve and enjoy!

Coconut Chicken Drumsticks

Total Time: 25 min | **Serves:** 4 | **Per serving:** Cal 275; Net Carbs 1.9g; Fat 17.5g; Protein 26g

Ingredients

2 tbsp Thai curry paste
4 chicken drumsticks, boneless,

skinless
3 tbsp coconut cream

Salt and black pepper to taste
A handful of fresh cilantro, chopped

Directions

Preheat your Air Fryer to 4000°F. In a bowl, combine the drumsticks with the curry paste, coconut cream, salt, and pepper to coat. Align the drumsticks in the fryer basket and cook for 6 minutes. Turn once during cooking time. Garnish with fresh cilantro and serve.

Tarragon Chicken Legs

Total Time: 20 min | **Serves:** 2 | **Per serving:** Cal 285; Net Carbs 2.1g; Fat 15g; Protein 21g

Ingredients

2 chicken legs
1 cup tomatoes, quartered

½ tsp dried marjoram
½ tsp olive oil

¼ tsp red pepper flakes

Directions

Preheat your Air Fryer to 390°F. In a bowl, combine the tomatoes, red pepper flakes, marjoram, and olive oil. Put the chicken in a large ramekin and pour the tomato mixture over. Place the ramekin in the fryer and cook for 10 minutes. Remove to a plate and top with cooking juices. Serve with cauli rice.

Air Fryer Chicken Nuggets

Total Time: 15 min | **Serves:** 4 | **Per serving:** Cal 311; Net Carbs 3.4g; Fat 20g; Protein 31g

Ingredients

2 chicken breasts, cut into nuggets
4 tbsp sour cream

½ cup pork rinds, crushed
½ tsp garlic powder

½ tsp cayenne pepper
Salt and black pepper to taste

Directions

In a bowl, add sour cream and place the chicken. Stir well. Mix the pork rinds, garlic, cayenne, salt and black pepper and scatter onto a plate. Roll up the chicken in the pork rinds to coat well. Grease the air with cooking spray. Arrange the nuggets in an even layer and cook for 10 minutes on 360°F, turning once.

Tasty Chicken Thighs

Total Time: 20 min | **Serves:** 3 | **Per serving:** Cal 276; Net Carbs 2g; Fat 10.4g; Protein 14.9g

Ingredients

1 lb mini chicken thighs	½ tsp chopped cilantro	½ tsp egg, beaten
Salt and black pepper to taste	½ tsp garlic-ginger paste	1 tsp paprika
1 tsp arrowroot starch	1 tsp vinegar	1 tsp almond flour
½ tsp minced garlic	1 tsp hot sauce	2 tbsp erythritol

Directions

In a bowl, combine the garlic-ginger paste, erythritol, paprika powder, chopped cilantro, plain vinegar, hot sauce, egg, garlic, pepper, and salt. Add the thighs and toss to coat. Put in the arrowroot starch and almond flour, stir.

Preheat your Air Fryer to 350°F. Remove the excess of the marinade and place in the fryer basket. Cook for 4 minutes. Turn the chicken and cook for another 5 minutes. Remove to a serving platter. Serve with a tomato dip.

Bell Pepper & Egg Turkey with Walnuts

Total Time: 45 min | **Serves:** 4 | **Per serving:** Cal 290; Net Carbs 3g; Fat 23g; Protein 16g

Ingredients

¼ cup walnuts, chopped	Salt and black pepper to taste	1 roasted bell peppers
¼ cup pork rinds, crushed	¼ cup chicken soup cream	2 boiled eggs, chopped
2 chopped spring onions	¼ cup mayonnaise	½ cup diced celery
1 lb turkey breast	2 tbsp lemon juice	

Directions

Preheat your Air Fryer to 390°F. Sprinkle the turkey with salt and pepper. Brush with cooking spray. Place the turkey in the fryer basket and cook for 12-14 minutes. Allow to cool before slicing into cubes.

In a bowl, combine the celery, chopped eggs, bell peppers, spring onions, walnuts, lemon juice, mayonnaise, turkey cubes, and chicken soup cream. Grease a casserole dish with cooking spray and pour the mixture into the dish. Sprinkle with pork rinds and cooking spray. Place the dish in the fryer and bake for 20 minutes.

Stuffed Whole Chicken with Herbs

Total Time: 60 min | **Serves:** 3 | **Per serving:** Cal 343; Net Carbs 2.5g; Fat 15.8g; Protein 35g

Ingredients

3 tbsp butter	1 ½ tbsp olive oil	⅓ cup chopped rosemary
2 eggs, beaten	Salt and black pepper to taste	2 cloves garlic, crushed
1 (3 lb) small chicken	⅓ cup chopped sage	1 onion, chopped

Directions

Clean the chicken with a paper towel and discard the excess fat. Set aside. In a saucepan over medium heat, melt butter and sauté garlic and onion until brown. Add in the eggs, sage, rosemary, pepper, and salt, cook for 20 seconds. Turn the heat off. Stuff the chicken with the egg mixture and brush with oil. Season with salt and pepper.

Preheat your Air Fryer to 390°F. Place the chicken in the fryer basket and roast for 25 minutes. Turn the chicken and cook for another 10-15 minutes. Do not overcook. Remove onto a chopping board and wrap in foil. Let rest for 10 minutes before slicing. Serve and enjoy!

Sicilian Chicken Breasts

Total Time: 30 min | **Serves:** 4 | **Per serving:** Cal 488; Net Carbs 3.2g; Fat 43g; Protein 37g

Ingredients

1 cup Sicilian olives, sliced
½ cup white wine
¼ cup almond flour

½ tbsp dried oregano
4 chicken breasts, skinless and boneless

1 tbsp olive oil
Salt and black pepper to taste
1 tbsp balsamic vinegar

Directions

Preheat your Air Fryer to 350°F. In a bowl, combine flour, salt, pepper, and oregano. Add in the chicken and roll up to coat. Put on the Air Fryer basket. Drizzle with 1 tablespoon of oil and cook for 12 minutes, turning once. When done, add in the olives and cook for another 5 minutes. Transfer to a hot skillet and add in the wine and balsamic vinegar. Cook for 10 minutes until the sauce bubbles.

Saucy Chicken & Zucchini Skewers

Total Time: 35 min | **Serves:** 4 | **Per serving:** Cal 468; Net Carbs 6.1g; Fat 29g; Protein 43g

Ingredients

1 jalapeño pepper
1 onion, quartered
1 zucchini, cut into bite-sized pieces

2 chicken breasts, halved
Salt to taste
1 tbsp chili powder

¼ cup erythritol
½ cup soy sauce, sugar-free
2 tbsp sesame seeds

Sauce

1 garlic clove
2 tbsp olive oil

Zest and juice from 1 lime
A pinch of salt

¼ cup fresh parsley, chopped

Directions

Slice chicken into cubes. In a bowl, combine the cubes with chili powder, salt, erythritol, soy sauce, and sesame seeds. Rub with cooking spray. Set aside. Put the jalapeño on the flat surface and deseed. Chop into cubes. Cut the zucchini in bite-sized pieces. Chop the onion in quarters. Stick 1 jalapeño, 1 onion, 1 chicken cube and 1 zucchini cube. Repeat the process until all the ingredients are finished.

Preheat Air Fryer to 330°F. Rub the skewers with soy sauce mixture and place in the fryer basket. Grease with cooking spray and cook for 20 minutes. Turn the skewers once during the cooking time. In a food processor, blend all the salsa ingredients until obtaining a chunky paste. Remove the skewers and serve with the salsa verde.

Cheesy Chicken Sticks

Total Time: 30 min + marinating time | **Serves:** 2 | **Per serving:** Cal 370; Net Carbs 2g; Fat 25g; Protein 33g

Ingredients

2 eggs, beaten
2 chicken breasts, cut into strips
2 tbsp rosemary, chopped

Salt and black pepper to taste
2 cloves garlic, crushed
3 tbsp xanthan gum

4 tbsp pork rinds, crushed
4 tbsp Romano cheese, grated

Directions

In a bowl, combine salt, garlic, rosemary, and pepper. Add in the chicken and toss to coat. Transfer to the fridge for 1 hour. In the meantime, combine the pork rinds with the cheese. Once the chicken is ready, remove from the fridge and combine with the xanthan gum. Dip the chicken in the egg, then in the cheese mixture.

Preheat your Air Fryer to 350°F. Grease the basket with cooking spray. Place the chicken in the basket and cook for 15 minutes. Serve with fried vegetables and cheese dip. Yummy!

Banana Pepper Chicken Wings

Total Time: 40 min + marinating time | **Serves**: 4 | **Per serving**: Cal 351; Net Carbs 4.2g; Fat 13.8g; Protein 50.7g

Ingredients

1 banana pepper, seeded	2 lb chicken wings	½ tbsp grated ginger
1 tbsp soy sauce, sugar-free	1 tbsp olive oil	½ tbsp chopped fresh thyme
¼ cup red wine vinegar	2 cloves garlic, minced	⅓ tbsp erythritol
2 spring onions, chopped	½ tsp allspice	Salt and white pepper to taste

Directions

In a bowl, combine the olive oil, soy sauce, garlic, banana pepper, allspice, white pepper, salt, erythritol, thyme, ginger, spring onions, and red wine vinegar. Add the chicken wings and toss to coat. Put in the fridge for 2 hours.

Preheat your Air Fryer to 400°F. Remove the wings from the fridge and drain the liquid. Reserve the marinade. Pat dry the chicken wings and place them in the air fryer basket. Cook for 16-18 minutes, shaking once. Serve.

Sweet Ginger Chicken Bites

Total Time: 30 min | **Serves**: 4 | **Per serving**: Cal 226; Net Carbs 2g; Fat 8g; Protein 18.2g

Ingredients

1 cup colored bell peppers	3 eggs	1 tbsp xylitol
2 chicken breasts, cubed	½ cup white wine vinegar	2 tbsp tomato puree
Salt and black pepper to taste	½ tsp ginger paste	1 tsp hot paprika
1 cup almond flour	½ tsp garlic paste	4 tbsp water

Directions

Preheat your Air Fryer to 350°F. Beat the eggs with almond flour, salt, and pepper. Dip the chicken in the mixture and place in the basket with cooking spray. Cook for 8 minutes. Turn them and brush more cooking spray. Cook for another 7 minutes until golden and crispy. Transfer to a plate and set aside.

Slice and deseed the bell peppers into long strips. In a bowl, combine the water, white wine vinegar, xylitol, ginger and garlic puree, tomato puree, and hot paprika.

Place a skillet over medium heat greased with cooking spray. Add the chicken and pepper strips and cook until the peppers are soft. Add in the chili mixture and cook for 10 minutes. Transfer to a serving bowl. Serve.

Garam Masala Chicken Breasts

Total Time: 25 min + marinating time | **Serves**: 2 | **Per serving**: Cal 428; Net Carbs 6.8g; Fat 23.5g; Protein 42g

Ingredients

1 tbsp peanut butter	1 tsp chili pepper	1 tsp soy sauce, sugar-free
2 chicken breasts	1 tsp garam masala	
2 eggs	1 tbsp swerve sweetener	

Directions

Lay the chicken on a flat surface and cut into diagonal pieces. Roll the pieces to make thinner. In a bowl, combine the pieces with soy sauce, swerve sweetener, garam masala, and chili pepper. Marinate in the fridge for 1 hour.

Preheat your Air Fryer to 350°F. Remove the chicken and break in the eggs. Add in the peanut butter and combine. Remove each piece and without any liquid place in the fryer basket. Cook for 8 minutes. Turn the breasts and cook for another 6 minutes. Serve the chicken with steamed greens if desired.

Chicken Breasts Wrapped in Jamón Serrano

Total Time: 25 min | **Serves:** 2 | **Per serving:** Cal 262; Net Carbs 3g; Fat 16g; Protein 24g

Ingredients

4 Jamon serrano slices
2 chicken breasts

1 tbsp olive oil
Salt and black pepper to taste

1 cup dried tomatoes, sliced
½ cup brie cheese, halved

Directions

Preheat your Air Fryer to 365°F. Lay the chicken on a chopping board and make a small incision, deep enough to make the stuffing. Put into each chicken one slice of cheese and 4-5 tomato slices. Place the serrano on the surface and put the chicken on one slice and roll the serrano over the chicken.

Brush with olive oil and season with salt and pepper. Place the chicken in the fryer basket and cook for 10 minutes. Turn over and cook for another 5 minutes. Slice the chicken by half. Serve with tomato salad.

Fried Chicken with Zoodles

Total Time: 30 min | **Serves:** 4 | **Per serving:** Cal 523; Net Carbs 1.8g; Fat 34g; Protein 41g

Ingredients

1 tbsp ground nutmeg
2 cups zoodles
4 chicken breasts, skinless and

boneless
Salt and black pepper to taste
1 tbsp tomato paste

2 tbsp olive oil

Directions

Preheat your Air Fryer to 350°F. Season the chicken with salt and pepper. Place it in the air fryer basket, spray with cooking spray, and AirFry for 14-16 minutes. Once ready, remove the chicken from the fryer and set aside.

Heat the olive oil in a skillet over medium heat and stir-fry in the zoodles and tomato paste for 5 minutes. Add in the ground nutmeg and season with salt and pepper. Serve the zoodles topped with the fried chicken.

Roasted Chicken with Pancetta & Lemon

Total Time: 60 min | **Serves:** 4 | **Per serving:** Cal 315; Net Carbs 3.6g; Fat 9.5g; Protein 52g

Ingredients

1 (3 lb) small whole chicken
1 lemon

4 slices of pancetta, chopped
1 onion, chopped

1 fresh rosemary sprig
Salt and black pepper to taste

Directions

In a bowl, mix pancetta, onion, rosemary, salt and pepper. Insert the pancetta mixture into chicken cavity and press tight. Place in the whole lemon, and rub the top and sides of the chicken with salt. Grease the air fryer's basket with cooking spray and put the chicken inside. Cook for 30 minutes on 400°F, turning once. Serve.

Chicken in Sweet Oriental-Sauce

Total Time: 20 min | **Serves:** 6 | **Per serving:** Cal 523; Net Carbs 2.5g; Fat 46g; Protein 31g

Ingredients

½ cup chives, chopped
2 lb chicken breasts, cubed
¼ cup pork rinds, crushed
2 eggs, beaten
6 tbsp almond flour

1 tbsp baking powder
½ cup vegetable oil
2 tbsp sesame oil
2 tbsp fresh ginger root, grated
½ cup water

¼ cup white vinegar
1 ½ tbsp liquid stevia
2 tbsp Worcestershire sauce
¼ cup oyster sauce

Directions

Preheat your Air Fryer to 390°F. Dip the cubes in the pork rinds. In a bowl, place the eggs, almond flour, and baking powder. Whisk until there are no lumps. Dip the cubes in the egg mixture and place in the fryer basket. Drizzle with sesame oil and AirFry for 15 minutes, shaking the basket halfway through. Set aside.

Warm the vegetable oil in a saucepan over medium heat and cook the ginger and chives for 2-3 minutes. Add the water, vinegar, and stevia and bring to a boil. Dissolve the pork rinds with Worcestershire sauce and put in oyster sauce. Cook until the sauce thickens. Add in the chicken and let simmer for 10-15 minutes. Serve and enjoy!

Herbs-Lemon Chicken Breasts

Total Time: 15 min | **Serves:** 2 | **Per serving:** Cal 419; Net Carbs 5.1g; Fat 19g; Protein 34g

Ingredients

1 spring onion, chopped
¼ tbsp ground coriander
¼ tbsp fresh thyme, minced
¼ tbsp fresh oregano, minced

2 chicken breasts, boneless and skinless
2 tbsp lemon juice
1 tbsp olive oil

1 garlic clove, minced
Salt and black pepper to taste

Directions

Place all the ingredients in a Ziploc bag and seal it. Transfer to the fridge for at least 3 hours. Preheat the Air Fryer to 340°F. Grease a rack with moist paper toweling with olive oil and place the chicken in it. Put in the fryer and cook for 20 minutes. Turn the chicken at least once during the cooking time.

Bacon-Wrapped Chicken Breasts

Total Time: 21 min | **Serves:** 4 | **Per serving:** Cal 408; Net Carbs 1.5g; Fat 28g; Protein 27g

Ingredients

2 chicken breasts, halved
8 oz ricotta cheese
1 tbsp butter

6 smoky bacon
Salt to taste
1 tbsp parsley, finely chopped

Juice from ½ lemon

Directions

Preheat your Air Fryer to 390°F. Lay the bacon on a flat surface in 2 sets of 3 bacon strips. Place the chicken over the bacon and spread the ricotta cheese on both. Top with butter and season with salt. Wrap the bacon around the chicken and secure the ends. Transfer into the fryer and cook for 14 minutes. Flip the chicken once during the cooking time. Remove to a plate and sprinkle with parsley and lemon juice. Serve with steamed greens if desired.

Sesame Chicken Tenders

Total Time: 15 min + marinating time | **Serves:** 4 | **Per serving:** Cal 434; Net Carbs 6.8g; Fat 31g; Protein 29g

Ingredients

¼ cup sesame oil
1 lb chicken tenders
½ cup soy sauce

4 cloves garlic, minced
1 onion, chopped
1 tbsp ground allspice

2 tbsp sesame seeds, toasted
Salt and black pepper to taste

Directions

In an bowl, combine soy sauce, sesame oil, garlic, onion, ground allspice, salt, and pepper and mix well. Add in the chicken; toss to coat. Transfer to the fridge and let sit for 2 hours.

Preheat Air Fryer to 390°F. Remove the chicken from the fridge. Place in the fryer and cook for 7-10 minutes, shaking once during the cooking time. Serve sprinkled with sesame seeds.

Lemon Chicken Breast with Herbs

Total Time: 25 min + marinating time | **Serves:** 4 | **Per serving:** Cal 477; Net Carbs 1.2g; Fat 34.8g; Protein 37g

Ingredients

2 lb chicken breasts
1 lemon, zested
¼ tsp swerve sweetener

¼ tsp salt
1 tsp fresh rosemary, chopped
1 tsp fresh thyme, chopped

¼ tsp red pepper flakes
½ cup olive oil

Directions

Combine the lemon zest, swerve sweetener, salt, rosemary, thyme, red pepper flakes, and olive oil in a bowl. Add in the chicken and toss to coat. Marinate in the fridge for 1 hour. Preheat your Air Fryer to 390°F. Remove the chicken and place in the air fryer basket. AirFry for 14-16 minutes. Serve and enjoy!

Mozzarella & Grana Padano Chicken

Total Time: 25 min | **Serves:** 2 | **Per serving:** Cal 443; Net Carbs 3.2g; Fat 25g; Protein 49g

Ingredients

2 chicken breasts, ½ inch thick
1 egg, beaten

½ cup pork rinds, crushed
2 tbsp marinara sauce

2 tbsp Grana Padano cheese, grated
2 slices mozzarella cheese

Directions

Dip breasts into the egg, then into the pork rinds and put in the air fryer. Cook for 5 minutes at 400°F. Turn over and drizzle with marinara sauce, Grana Padano and mozzarella cheeses. Cook for 5 minutes.

Celery & Cauliflower Chicken Bake

Total Time: 30 min | **Serves:** 3 | **Per serving:** Cal 321; Net Carbs 2g; Fat 13.4g; Protein 35g

Ingredients

1 cauliflower head, cut into florets
3 chicken breasts

Salt and black pepper to taste
1 cup shredded cheddar cheese

½ cup celery soup cream

Directions

Preheat your Air Fryer to 390°F. Brush the chicken with cooking spray and season with salt and pepper. Place in the fryer basket and AirFry for 13 minutes. Combine the chicken with cauliflower, cheddar cheese, and celery soup cream. Place the mixture in a baking dish. Place the dish in the fryer basket and Bake for 10 minutes. Serve.

Thyme Chicken Fingers

Total Time: 20 min | **Serves:** 2 | **Per serving:** Cal 132; Net Carbs 0.7g; Fat 4g; Protein 18g

Ingredients

¼ tsp fresh scallions, chopped
1 tbsp mozzarella cheese, shredded
¼ tsp fresh thyme, chopped

Salt and black pepper to taste
½ cup pork rinds, crushed
1 egg white

1 tsp water
5 oz chicken breasts

Directions

Preheat your Air Fryer to 390°F. Combine the scallions, mozzarella cheese, thyme, salt, pepper, and pork rinds. Beat the egg white with water. Slice the chicken into large strips. Dip the strips in the egg, then in the rinds. Place in the fryer basket and cook for 8-10 minutes, shaking the basket halfway through. Serve and enjoy!

Oregano Chicken Roast

Total Time: 70 min + marinating time | **Serves:** 4 | **Per serving:** Cal 317; Net Carbs 3g; Fat 21.4g; Protein 18.9g

Ingredients

1 tsp cayenne pepper powder
1 tsp garlic powder
4 tsp oregano

2 tsp fennel powder
2 tbsp canola oil
1 (3 lb) whole chicken

Salt and black pepper to taste
2 tsp paprika
3 tbsp butter, melted

Directions

Combine the oregano, garlic powder, cayenne powder, fennel powder, paprika, pepper, salt, and canola oil in a bowl. Rub the chicken with the mixture. Marinate in the fridge for 1-2 hours.

Preheat your Air Fryer to 350°F. Remove the chicken from the fridge and place it in the fryer. Cook for 50 minutes. Turn and cook for another 5-10 minutes. Let sit for 10 minutes. Drizzle the melted butter and serve.

Jalapeño Peppered Chicken

Total Time: 25 min | **Serves:** 4 | **Per serving:** Cal 363; Net Carbs 3.4g; Fat 27g; Protein 26g

Ingredients

4 chicken thighs, boneless
2 garlic cloves, crushed

1 jalapeno pepper, finely chopped
4 tbsp chili sauce

Salt and black pepper to taste

Directions

In a bowl, add thighs, garlic, jalapeno, chili sauce, salt and black pepper, and stir to coat. Arrange the thighs in an even layer on the air fryer and cook for 12 minutes at 360°F, turning once halfway cooking. Serve and enjoy!

Basil Chicken Tenders

Total Time: 20 min | **Serves:** 2 | **Per serving:** Cal 230; Net Carbs 2g; Fat 12.5g; Protein 18g

Ingredients

1 tsp ghee
2 chicken tenders

Salt and black pepper to taste
½ cup dried basil

Directions

Preheat your Air Fryer to 390°F. Place a 12x12 foil on a flat surface. Lay the chicken on the foil and season with the basil. Brush with the ghee and sprinkle salt and pepper. Wrap the foil and place in the fryer basket. Cook for 12 minutes. Remove the chicken and unwrap the foil. Serve with the cooking juices and steamed mixed veggies.

Crispy Chicken Strips with Chili Mayo Dip

Total Time: 15 min | **Serves:** 4 | **Per serving:** Cal 498; Net Carbs 2.1g; Fat 38g; Protein 41g

Ingredients

4 tbsp canola oil
3 chicken breasts, cut into strips
1 cup pork rinds, crushed

Salt and black pepper to taste
½ tsp garlic powder
½ tsp paprika

½ cup mayonnaise
2 tbsp lemon juice
½ tsp ground chili

Directions

Preheat your Air Fryer to 360°F. On a plate, combine the pork rinds, salt, pepper, garlic powder, and paprika. Brush the chicken with oil and dip in the rinds mixture. Grease the fryer basket with oil and place in the chicken. Cook for 6 minutes. Flip the chicken once during the cooking time. Combine the mayo with 2 tbsp of lemon juice and ground chili. Serve the chicken with the dip.

Herby & Paprika Chicken

Total Time: 33 min | **Serves:** 2 | **Per serving:** Cal 286; Net Carbs 2.3g; Fat 15g; Protein 25g

Ingredients

1 lb chicken breasts
¼ cup butter
2 cloves garlic, minced

½ tsp dried thyme
½ tsp dried rosemary
Salt and black pepper to taste

¼ tsp paprika

Directions

Preheat your Air Fryer to 370°F. Sprinkle the chicken with salt and pepper. Place the chicken in the fryer basket and sear for 5 minutes. In the meantime, melt the butter in a skillet over medium heat and sauté the garlic for 1 minute. In a bowl, mix the paprika, thyme, and rosemary. Pour the mixture over the garlic and stir. Turn the heat off. When the chicken is ready, pour the sauce over it, and cook for 5 minutes. Serve and enjoy!

Chipotle Chicken Breasts

Total Time: 22 min | **Serves:** 4 | **Per serving:** Cal 164; Net Carbs 2g; Fat 6.8g; Protein 24.8g

Ingredients

¼ cup chipotle sauce
3 tbsp curry powder

4 chicken breasts
Salt to taste

Directions

Preheat Air Fryer to 390°F. In a bowl, combine salt, chipotle sauce, and curry powder. Rub chicken with the curry mix. Place in the fryer basket and cook for 18 minutes. Turn once during cooking time.

Chicken Escalopes with Herby Tomato Sauce

Total Time: 25 min | **Serves:** 2 | **Per serving:** Cal 415; Net Carbs 2.1g; Fat 34g; Protein 17g

Ingredients

1 cup almond flour
¾ cup shaved ham
2 chicken breasts

2 eggs, cracked into a bowl
4 tbsp tomato sauce
2 tbsp basil

2 cups mozzarella cheese
1 cup pork rinds, crushed

Directions

Preheat your Air Fryer to 350°F. Place the flour in a bowl and the pork rinds in another bowl. Dip the chicken in the flour, then in the egg mixture, and finally in the pork rinds. Place the chicken in the fryer basket and AirFry for 10 minutes. Top with ham, tomato sauce, mozzarella, and basil. Bake for another 5 minutes. Serve and enjoy!

Mouth-Watering Chicken Bites

Total Time: 25 min | **Serves:** 4 | **Per serving:** Cal 346; Net Carbs 1.6g; Fat 21g; Protein 40g

Ingredients

1 egg, beaten
2 chicken breasts, cut into 2 pieces each

¼ cup creme fraiche
1 cup pork rinds, crushed

Salt and black pepper to taste
1 tbsp dried sage

Directions

Preheat your Air Fryer to 360°F. Beat the egg with the creme fraiche in a bowl. Place in the chicken and toss to coat. In a bowl, mix the pork rinds with salt, sage and pepper. Dip the chicken in the rinds. Grease the fryer basket with oil spray. Place the pieces in the fryer and cook for 12 minutes. Flip the pieces once during the cooking time.

Chicken Wings with Chili-Garlic Sauce

Total Time: 25 min | **Serves:** 2 | **Per serving:** Cal 235; Net Carbs 1g; Fat 7g; Protein 37g

Ingredients

4 chicken wings
1 ½ tbsp chili-garlic sauce

½ tbsp xylitol
Juice of 1 lime

Salt and black pepper to taste

Directions

Preheat Air Fryer to 390°F. Combine lime juice, salt, pepper, xylitol and chili-garlic sauce. Dip in the wings and toss to coat. Place in the fryer basket and cook for 16 minutes. Turn every 4-5 minutes. Serve.

Rosemary Chicken Rolls

Total Time: 15 min | **Serves:** 2 | **Per serving:** Cal 187; Net Carbs 0.3g; Fat 5g; Protein 31g

Ingredients

½ tbsp unsalted ghee
2 chicken breasts

¼ cup rosemary
Salt and black pepper to taste

Directions

Preheat your Air Fryer to 390°F. Wrap each breast in foil and rub with rosemary and ghee. Sprinkle with salt and pepper. Place in the fryer basket and cook for 13 minutes. Unwrap the foil and serve hot.

Blue Ribbon Chicken

Total Time: 50 min | **Serves:** 4 | **Per serving:** Cal 564; Net Carbs 2.2g; Fat 52g; Protein 48g

Ingredients

4 chicken breasts
4 slices Gruyere cheese
4 slices ham

3 tbsp almond flour
1 tbsp paprika
4 tbsp butter

½ cup Marsala wine
1 tbsp chicken bouillon granules
1 cup heavy whipping cream

Directions

Preheat your Air Fryer to 390°F. Roll each chicken breast. Place a slice of ham and cheese in each breast and wrap it. Secure all sides with toothpicks. In a bowl, combine the flour and paprika. Put in the chicken and toss to coat.

Place the chicken in the fryer basket and cook for 15 minutes. Melt the butter in a skillet over medium heat and pour the bouillon, heavy cream, and wine. Transfer the chicken to the skillet and simmer for 30 minutes. Serve.

Lime Zested Chicken

Total Time: 20 min | **Serves:** 6 | **Per serving:** Cal 54; Net Carbs 0.2g; Fat 3g; Protein 6g

Ingredients

1 cup buttermilk
1 garlic powder
1 tsp Hungarian paprika

1.5 lb chicken tenders, cubed
1 cup almond flour
2 zested lime

3 tbsp extra virgin olive oil
Salt and black pepper to taste

Directions

Preheat your Air Fryer to 350°F. In a bowl, mix well the chicken with buttermilk, garlic, paprika, lime, salt and pepper and place in the fridge to marinate for 30 minutes. Pat dry the chicken with paper towels and dip in the almond flour. Shake to remove any excess flour. Grease the fryer basket with oil and put the chicken inside. Cook for 12 minutes, shaking halfway through. Serve with dip.

Fried Chicken with Lemon

Total Time: 60 min | **Serves:** 5 | **Per serving:** Cal 398; Net Carbs 2.1g; Fat 28g; Protein 33g

Ingredients

½ cup olive oil
2 lb chicken, cut in pieces
3 cloves garlic, minced

1 tbsp fresh oregano, chopped
2 large lemons
½ cup apple cider vinegar

Salt and black pepper to taste

Directions

Preheat your Air Fryer to 350°F. Mix the garlic, olive oil, oregano, salt, and pepper in a bowl. Pour the mixture into a baking dish, put the chicken and stir. Place the dish in the fryer and add in the apple cider vinegar and lemons. Cook for 50 minutes. Serve and enjoy!

Chicken Patties with Cilantro Seeds

Total Time: 20 min | **Serves:** 4 | **Per serving:** Cal 305; Net Carbs 2.3g; Fat 21g; Protein 24g

Ingredients

1 lb ground chicken
½ onion, chopped
2 garlic cloves, chopped

1 egg, beaten
½ cup pork rinds, crushed
½ tsp ground cumin

½ tsp cilantro seeds, crushed
Salt and black pepper to taste

Directions

Preheat your Air Fryer to 380°F. Combine the ground chicken, onion, garlic, egg, pork rinds, cumin, cilantro seeds, salt, and pepper in a bowl. Form 4 patties with the mixture. Grease the fryer basket. Place the patties in the fryer and AirFry for 10 minutes. Flip the patties once during cooking time. Serve and enjoy!

Chicken with Lemon & Basil

Total Time: 30 min | **Serves:** 4 | **Per serving:** Cal 483; Net Carbs 2.6g; Fat 27g; Protein 49g

Ingredients

¼ cup butter
4 chicken legs

3 large halved lemons
4 tbsp dried basil

4 tbsp garlic powder
Salt and black pepper to taste

Directions

Preheat your Air Fryer to 350°F. In a bowl, brush the legs with butter and squeeze the lemon juice over. Lay in the rack and put the lemon wedges around it. Mix the basil, garlic, salt, and pepper in a bowl. Pour the mixture over the chicken and cook for 18-20 minutes. Serve and enjoy!

Cheesy Chicken with Tomato Sauce

Total Time: 25 min | **Serves:** 2 | **Per serving:** Cal 443; Net Carbs 3.2g; Fat 25g; Protein 49g

Ingredients

2 tbsp tomato sauce
2 tbsp Grana Padano cheese, grated
2 slices cheddar cheese

2 chicken breasts, skinless, ½ inch
thick
1 egg, beaten

½ cup pork rinds, crushed

Directions

Preheat your Air Fryer to 400°F. Dip the breasts in the egg, then in the pork rinds. Place the breasts in the fryer basket and cook for 5 minutes. Once ready, remove the basket and pour in the tomato sauce, Grana Padano cheese, and cheddar cheese. Cook for another 5 minutes.

Asian-Style Chicken

Total Time: 30 min | **Serves:** 4 | **Per serving:** Cal 243; Net Carbs 6.1g; Fat 13g; Protein 18g

Ingredients

2 tbsp olive oil
2 cloves garlic, minced
1 lb chicken breasts, sliced
1 tbsp cumin powder

4 pearl onions, sliced
1 tbsp mustard
2 green chili peppers
A pinch of garam masala

A pinch of fresh cilantro, chopped
2 tomatoes, chopped
Salt and black pepper to taste

Directions

Warm the oil in a saucepan over medium heat and sauté the mustard, cumin, garlic, onion, garam masala, and green chili peppers for a few minutes. Place in the tomatoes, cilantro, black pepper, and salt and stir.

Preheat your Air Fryer to 360°F. Grease the chicken with oil and sprinkle with salt and pepper. Place the chicken in the fryer basket and cook for 14-16 minutes. Transfer to a plate and top with the sauce.

Sunday Chicken Nuggets

Total Time: 15 min | **Serves:** 4 | **Per serving:** Cal 311; Net Carbs 3.4g; Fat 20g; Protein 31g

Ingredients

4 tbsp creme fraiche
2 chicken breasts, boneless, cut into nuggets

½ cup pork rinds, crushed
½ tsp onion powder
½ tsp cayenne pepper

Salt and black pepper to taste

Directions

Preheat your Air Fryer to 360°F. In a bowl, place the creme fraiche and the chicken, stir well. In another bowl, combine the pork rinds, onion, cayenne, salt, and black pepper. Transfer to a plate. Dip the chicken into the rinds. Grease the fryer basket with cooking spray. Place the chicken in the basket and cook for 10 minutes, flipping once.

Sesame Seed Chicken Wings

Total Time: 25 min | **Serves:** 4 | **Per serving:** Cal 215; Net Carbs 1g; Fat 11g; Protein 27g

Ingredients

2 tsp olive oil
2 tsp xylitol

1 lb chicken wings
Salt and black pepper to taste

3 tbsp sesame seeds

Directions

Preheat your Air Fryer to 360°F. In a bowl, combine the chicken wings, oil, xylitol, salt, and pepper. Stir to coat. In a second bowl, place the sesame seeds. Dip the wings in the seeds. Place in the air fryer basket and cook for 12 minutes, tossing once. Serve and enjoy!

Best Serrano Chicken

Total Time: 25 min | **Serves:** 4 | **Per serving:** Cal 363; Net Carbs 3.4g; Fat 27g; Protein 26g

Ingredients

1 serrano pepper, finely chopped
4 chicken thighs, boneless

2 garlic cloves, crushed
4 tbsp tomato puree

Salt and black pepper to taste

Directions

Preheat your Air Fryer to 360°F. Combine the chicken thighs, garlic, serrano pepper, tomato sauce, salt, and black pepper in a bowl and toss to coat. Place the thighs in the fryer basket and cook for 12 minutes. Turn once.

Horseradish Chicken Thighs

Total Time: 30 min | **Serves:** 4 | **Per serving:** Cal 452; Net Carbs 1.2g; Fat 27g; Protein 49g

Ingredients

2 tbsp horseradish
½ tsp garlic powder

4 chicken thighs, skin-on
3 tbsp stevia

Salt and black pepper to taste

Directions

Preheat Air Fryer to 400°F. Combine stevia, horseradish, garlic, salt, and pepper in a bowl. Dip the thighs in the mixture. Place in the fryer basket and cook for 16 minutes, flipping once during the cooking time.

Bacon & Oregano Chicken Roast

Total Time: 60 min | **Serves:** 4 | **Per serving:** Cal 315; Net Carbs 3.6g; Fat 9.5g; Protein 52g

Ingredients

4 slices bacon, chopped
1 onion, chopped

1 fresh oregano sprig
1 (3 lb) small whole chicken

1 lemon
Salt and black pepper to taste

Directions

Preheat your Air Fryer to 400°F. Combine the bacon, onion, oregano, salt, and black pepper in a bowl. Pat dry the chicken. Stuff the chicken cavity with the mixture. Put in the whole lemon and sprinkle with salt and pepper. Grease the fryer basket with cooking spray. Place the chicken in the basket and cook for 30 minutes. Turn once during the cooking time. Serve and enjoy!

Broccoli with Turkey Ham

Total Time: 20 min | **Serves:** 4 | **Per serving:** Cal 123; Net Carbs 6.2g; Fat 7.5g; Protein 3.4g

Ingredients

1 broccoli head, cut into florets
½ cup Maggi seasoning sauce
3 tbsp stevia

1 tsp sesame oil
⅓ cup water
½ chili powder

2 cloves garlic, chopped
1 tsp psyllium husk
4 slices turkey ham, cubed

Directions

Preheat your Air Fryer to 340°F. In a bowl, beat the Magi sauce, stevia, sesame oil, water, chili powder, garlic, and psyllium husk until smooth. In a second bowl, mix the broccoli with the teriyaki sauce and toss to coat.

Place the broccoli in the fryer and cook for 14 minutes. Flip them once during the cooking time. Transfer to a plate and scatter with the turkey ham.

Green Onion & Pimento Turkey with Almonds

Total Time: 55 min | **Serves:** 3 | **Per serving:** Cal 290; Net Carbs 3g; Fat 23g; Protein 16g

Ingredients

1 lb turkey breasts
Salt and black pepper to taste
¼ cup chicken soup cream
¼ cup mayonnaise

2 tbsp lemon juice
¼ cup slivered almonds, chopped
¼ cup pork rinds, crushed
2 tbsp chopped green onion

2 tbsp chopped pimentos
2 boiled eggs, chopped
½ cup diced celery

Directions

Preheat the Air Fryer to 390°F. Place the turkey breasts on a clean flat surface and season with salt and pepper. Grease with cooking spray and place them in the fryer basket. Close the Air Fryer and cook for 13 minutes.

Remove turkey back onto the chopping board, let cool, and use a knife to cut into cubes. In a bowl, add the celery, chopped eggs, pimentos, green onions, almonds, lemon juice, mayonnaise, turkey, and chicken soup cream; mix.

Grease a casserole dish with cooking spray, scoop the turkey mixture into the bowl, sprinkle the pork rinds on it, and spray it with cooking spray. Put the dish in the fryer basket and Bake the ingredients for 20 minutes.

Sweet-Soy Cauliflower with Turkey Ham

Total Time: 20 min | **Serves:** 4 | **Per serving:** Cal 123; Net Carbs 6.2g; Fat 7.5g; Protein 3.4g

Ingredients

1 big cauliflower head, cut into florets	1 tsp sesame oil	2 cloves garlic, chopped
½ cup soy sauce, sugar-free	⅓ cup water	1 tsp psyllium husk
3 tbsp stevia	½ chili powder	4 slices turkey ham, cubed

Directions

In a bowl, whisk soy sauce, stevia, sesame oil, water, chili powder, garlic and psyllium husk until smooth. In a separate bowl, add cauliflower and pour teriyaki sauce. Toss until well-coated. Take the cauliflower to the air fryer basket and cook for 14 minutes at 340°F, turning once halfway through cooking. When ready, check if the cauliflower is cooked but not too soft. Remove to a serving plate and sprinkle with turkey ham cubes to serve.

Party Turkey Meatballs with Parmesan

Total Time: 40 min | **Serves:** 4 | **Per serving:** Cal 245; Net Carbs 1.8g; Fat 15.7g; Protein 15.4g

Ingredients

1 lb ground turkey	1 tsp garlic powder	¼ cup Parmesan cheese, shredded
1 egg	1 tsp Italian seasoning	Salt and black pepper to taste
½ cup pork rinds, crushed	1 tsp onion powder	

Directions

Preheat the Air Fryer to 400°F. In a bowl, add the ground turkey, crack the egg onto it, add the pork rinds, garlic powder, onion powder, Italian seasoning, parmesan cheese, salt, and pepper. Mix well. Spoon out portions and make bite-size balls out of the mixture.

Grease the fryer basket with cooking spray and add the turkey balls to the air fryer basket. Cook for 12 minutes. Slide out the fryer basket halfway through and shake it to toss the turkey. Remove them onto a serving platter and continue the cooking process for the remaining balls. Serve the turkey balls with marinara sauce.

Italian Turkey Meatballs

Total Time: 40 min | **Serves:** 3 | **Per serving:** Cal 245; Net Carbs 1.8g; Fat 15.7g; Protein 15.4g

Ingredients

1 egg	1 tsp garlic powder	¼ cup Parmesan cheese, shredded
1 lb ground turkey	1 tsp Italian seasoning	Salt and black pepper to taste
½ cup pork rinds, crushed	1 red onion, chopped	

Directions

Preheat your Air Fryer to 400°F. In a bowl, put the ground turkey and crack the egg onto it. Stir in the pork rinds, garlic powder, onion, Italian seasoning, Parmesan, salt, and pepper. Shape bite-sized balls out of the mixture.

Grease the fryer basket with cooking spray. Place 10 turkey balls in the fryer and cook for 12 minutes. Toss evenly. Repeat the process for the remaining balls. Serve with marinara sauce and zoodles.

MEAT RECIPES

Pork Chop & Cheese Salad

Total Time: 25 min | **Serves**: 4 | **Per serving**: Cal 253; Net Carbs 2.9g; Fat 36.9g; Protein 34.5g

Ingredients

2 tbsp coconut oil
2 pork chops, cubed
2 tsp chili powder
1 tsp paprika
½ tsp garlic powder

¼ tsp onion powder
¼ tsp ground allspice
4 cups romaine lettuce, shredded
1 ripe tomato, chopped
1 tbsp chopped cilantro

¼ cup ranch dressing
½ cup cheddar cheese, shredded
1 avocado, peeled, pitted, and sliced
½ red chili, finely chopped

Directions

Preheat the air fryer to 390°F. In a mixing bowl, thoroughly combine the coconut oil, chili powder, paprika, garlic powder, onion powder, and allspice. Add in the pork cubes and toss to coat. Transfer the meat to the air fryer basket and AirFry for 8-10 minutes, shaking the basket once until crispy.

Put the lettuce, tomato, and cilantro in a salad bowl. Drizzle with ranch dressing. Top with pork cubes, cheddar cheese, and avocado slices. Scatter the red chili over. Serve and enjoy!

Herby Breaded Pork Chops

Total Time: 25 min | **Serves**: 4 | **Per serving**: Cal 296; Net Carbs 0.2g; Fat 18.9g; Protein 29.8g

Ingredients

Salt and black pepper to taste
1 tsp cayenne pepper
1 tsp dried basil

1 tsp dried rosemary
1 tsp dried thyme
½ tsp garlic powder

1 tbsp coconut oil, melted
4 pork chops
1 ½ oz pork rinds, finely ground

Directions

Preheat the air fryer to 390°F. Season the pork chops with salt, black pepper, cayenne pepper, basil, rosemary, thyme, and garlic powder. Brush with coconut oil, then coat them with the pork rinds. Set the chops in the frying basket. AirFry for 14-16 minutes, flipping once until the top is golden. Serve hot.

Pigs in a Blanket

Total Time: 15 min | **Serves**: 4 | **Per serving**: Cal 620; Net Carbs 0.7g; Fat 56g; Protein 28g

Ingredients

8 Vienna sausages

8 thin bacon slices

Directions

Preheat the Air Fryer to 380°F. Wrap each sausage tightly with a slice of bacon. Lay the bacon-wrapped sausages on the fryer basket and AirFry for 10 minutes, turning once until the bacon is crisp and golden.

Buffalo Hot Dogs

Total Time: 20 min | **Serves**: 4 | **Per serving**: Cal 403; Net Carbs 1.2g; Fat 32g; Protein 17.6g

Ingredients

1 cup mozzarella cheese, shredded
4 tbsp almond flour

2 oz cream cheese
4 beef smoked sausages

¼ cup buffalo hot sauce

Directions

Preheat the Air Fryer to 395°F. Microwave mozzarella, almond flour, and cream cheese for 30-40 seconds. Remove and form the dough into a ball. Lay wax paper on a flat surface, place the dough on top, and cover with another piece of wax paper. Roll the dough into a rectangle shape, about ¼-inch thick.

Take the parchment paper off. Cut the dough into 4 pieces. Divide the sausages between them and drizzle with buffalo hot sauce. Wrap hot dogs into the dough pieces. Transfer them to the air fryer basket. Bake for 6-8 minutes, turning over halfway through cooking. Serve and enjoy!

Spicy & Tender Pork Chops

Total Time: 20 min | **Serves**: 4 | **Per serving**: Cal 312; Net Carbs 0.2g; Fat 22.8g; Protein 24.6g

Ingredients

½ tsp cayenne pepper	½ tsp cumin	¼ tsp dried thyme
1 tsp ancho chili powder	Salt and black pepper to taste	4 boneless pork chops
½ tsp garlic powder	¼ tsp dried oregano	2 tbsp butter

Directions

Preheat the Air Fryer to 380°F. Combine cayenne pepper, chili powder, garlic powder, cumin, salt, pepper, thyme, and oregano in a bowl; stir well. Massage the mixture into the pork chops to coat them on both sides. Transfer them to the air fryer basket. Bake for 14-16 minutes, turning once. Spread the butter all over the chops. Serve.

St. Louis-Style Baby Back Ribs

Total Time: 30 min | **Serves**: 4 | **Per serving**: Cal 649; Net Carbs 0.3g; Fat 51.6g; Protein 39.9g

Ingredients

2 lb baby back ribs, individually cut	½ tsp garlic powder	½ tbsp mustard powder
2 teaspoons chili powder	¼ tsp ground cayenne pepper	Salt and black pepper to taste
1 tsp paprika	½ cup sugar-free barbecue sauce	
½ tsp onion powder	½ tbsp oregano	

Directions

Preheat the Air Fryer to 390°F. Mix all the ingredients, except for the barbecue sauce, in a bowl and toss to coat. Transfer the ribs to the air fryer basket. Bake for 23-25 minutes, flipping once until they are tender inside and crisp on the outside. Pour the barbecue sauce over the ribs. Serve and enjoy!

Sausage-Stuffed Bell Peppers

Total Time: 30 min | **Serves**: 4 | **Per serving**: Cal 359; Net Carbs 4.7g; Fat 24g; Protein 21g

Ingredients

2 tbsp butter	1 tsp Italian seasoning	deseeded
2 garlic cloves, minced	½ tsp dried basil	1 cup mozzarella cheese, shredded
1 onion, chopped	1 medium Roma tomato, diced	Salt and black pepper to taste
1 lb pork sausage, casings removed	4 green bell peppers, halved and	

Directions

Preheat the Air Fryer to 350°F. Melt the butter in a skillet over medium heat and sauté the onion and garlic for 2 minutes. Add in the sausage and cook for 7-9 minutes until no longer pink. Stir in Italian seasoning, basil, salt, and black pepper. Pour in the tomato and cook for 3-4 more minutes. Stuff the pepper halves with the sausage filling. Top with grated mozzarella. Place the peppers in the air fryer basket. Bake for 15 minutes or until the peppers are tender and the cheese has melted. Serve.

Basic Pulled Pork

Total Time: 2 hours 40 min | **Serves:** 4 | **Per serving:** Cal 538; Net Carbs 0.3g; Fat 35.6g; Protein 42.8g

Ingredients

¼ tsp dried cilantro
1 tbsp chili powder
½ tsp garlic powder

¼ tsp shallot powder
Salt and black pepper to taste
¼ tsp cumin

2 lb pork shoulder

Directions

Preheat the Air Fryer to 340°F. Combine all the ingredients, except for the pork, in a bowl and stir well. Massage the mixture onto the pork to coat it on all sides. Transfer the shoulder to the air fryer basket. Bake for 2 ½ hours. When cooking is complete, the meat should be easily flaked apart with 2 forks.

Stuffed Pork Loins in Bacon Wraps

Total Time: 45 min | **Serves:** 4 | **Per serving:** Cal 604; Net Carbs 2.8g; Fat 51.8g; Protein 30g

Ingredients

16 bacon slices
16 oz pork tenderloin
Salt and black pepper to season
1 cup spinach

3 oz cream cheese
1 small onion, sliced
1 tbsp olive oil
1 clove garlic, minced

½ tsp dried thyme
½ tsp dried rosemary

Directions

Place the tenderloin on a chopping board, cover it with plastic wrap and pound it using a kitchen hammer to be 2-inches flat and square. Trim the uneven sides with a knife to have a perfect square. On the same chopping board, place and weave the bacon slices into a square of the size of the pork. Place the pork on the bacon weave and leave them aside for now.

Heat olive oil in a skillet over medium heat, add onions and garlic, and sauté until transparent. Add spinach, rosemary, thyme, salt, and pepper. Stir in cream cheese until the mixture is even.

Preheat the Air Fryer to 360°F. Spoon and spread the spinach mixture onto the pork loin. Roll up the bacon and pork over the spinach stuffing. Secure the ends with toothpicks. Season with more salt and pepper. Place in the fryer basket and cook it for 15 minutes. Flip to other side and cook for another 5 minutes. Let it sit before slicing.

Paprika Pork Chops

Total Time: 25 min | **Serves:** 3 | **Per serving:** Cal 376; Net Carbs 2.6g; Fat 16.9g; Protein 33.9g

Ingredients

3 lean pork chops
Salt and black pepper to taste
2 eggs, cracked into a bowl
1 tbsp water

1 cup pork rinds, crushed
½ tsp garlic powder
3 tsp paprika
1 ½ tsp oregano

½ tsp cayenne pepper
¼ tsp dry mustard
1 lemon, zested

Directions

Put the pork chops on a chopping board and use a knife to trim off any excess fat. Add the water to the eggs and whisk them. Set aside. In another bowl, add the pork rinds, salt, pepper, garlic powder, paprika, oregano, cayenne pepper, lemon zest, and dry mustard. Use a fork to mix evenly.

Preheat the Air Fryer to 380°F and after grease the fryer basket with cooking spray. In the egg mixture, dip each pork chop and then in the pork rind mixture. Place the breaded chops in the fryer basket. Don't spray with cooking spray. The fat in the chops will be enough oil to cook them. Close the Air Fryer and cook for 10 minutes. Flip and cook for 5 minutes. Place the chops on a chopping board to rest for 3 minutes before slicing.

Cheddar Shredded Pork with Bacon

Total Time: 50 min | **Serves**: 2 | **Per serving**: Cal 765; Net Carbs 6.3g; Fat 68g; Protein 34g

Ingredients

½ pound pork steak
1 tsp steak seasoning
Salt and black pepper to taste

5 thick bacon slices, chopped
1 cup grated cheddar cheese
½ tbsp Worcestershire sauce

2 hamburger buns, zero carbs, halved

Directions

Preheat the Air Fryer to 400°F.

Place the pork steak on a plate and season with pepper, salt, and the steak seasoning. Pat it with your hands. Slide out the fryer basket and place the pork in it. Grill it for 15 minutes, turn it using tongs, slide the fryer in and continue cooking for 6 minutes.

Once ready, remove the steak onto a chopping board and use two forks to shred the pork into small pieces. Place the chopped bacon in a small heatproof bowl and place the bowl in the fryer basket. Close the Air Fryer and cook the bacon at 370°F for 10 minutes.

Remove the bacon into a heatproof bowl, add the pulled pork, Worcestershire sauce, and the cheddar cheese. Season with salt and pepper as desired. Place the bowl in the fryer basket and cook at 350°For 4 minutes. Slide out the fryer basket, stir the mixture with a spoon, slide the fryer basket back in and cook further for 1 minute. Spoon to scoop the meat into the halved buns and serve with a cheese or tomato dip if desired.

BBQ Pork Ribs

Total Time: 35 min + chilling time | **Serves**: 3 | **Per serving**: Cal 376; Net Carbs 3.3g; Fat 29.3g; Protein 21.7g

Ingredients

1 lb pork ribs
1 tsp soy sauce, sugar-free
Salt and black pepper to taste

1 tsp oregano
1 tbsp + 1 tbsp erythritol
3 tbsp reduced sugar barbecue sauce

2 cloves garlic, minced
1 tbsp cayenne pepper
1 tsp sesame oil

Directions

Put the chops on a chopping board and use a knife to cut them into smaller pieces of desired sizes. Put them in a mixing bowl, add the soy sauce, salt, pepper, oregano, one tablespoon of erythritol, barbecue sauce, garlic, cayenne pepper, and sesame oil. Mix well and place the pork in the fridge to marinate in the spices for 5 hours.

Preheat the Air Fryer to 350°F. Open the Air Fryer and place the ribs in the fryer basket. Slide the fryer basket in and cook for 15 minutes. Turn the ribs, apply the remaining erythritol on them, and cook for 10 minutes.

Herby Mushroom Filled Pork Chops

Total Time: 40 min | **Serves**: 3 | **Per serving**: Cal 412; Net Carbs 1.2g; Fat 28g; Protein 28g

Ingredients

3 thick pork chops
A pinch of herbs

7 mushrooms, chopped
1 tbsp almond flour

1 tbsp lemon juice
Salt and black pepper to taste

Directions

Preheat the Air Fryer to 350°F. Season each side of the meat with salt and pepper. Arrange the chops in the Air Fryer and cook for 15 minutes at 350°F. Cook the mushroom for 3 minutes in a skillet and stir in the lemon juice. Add the flour and then mix the herbs. Cook the mixture for 4 minutes. Then set aside.

Cut five pieces of foil. On every piece of foil, put a chop in the middle and cover with the mushroom mixture. Fold the foil and seal around the chop. Cook the chops in the Air Fryer for 30 minutes.

Bacon Rolls with Sausage Sticks

Total Time: 30 min + chilling time | **Serves**: 8 | **Per serving**: Cal 455; Net Carbs 8.3g; Fat 39.6g; Protein 18.7g

Ingredients

Sausage:

8 bacon strips

8 pork sausages

8 medium-length bamboo skewers

Relish:

8 large tomatoes

1 clove garlic, peeled

1 small onion, peeled

3 tbsp chopped parsley

Salt and black pepper to taste

2 tbsp swerve sugar

1 tsp smoked paprika

1 tbsp vinegar

Directions

Start with the relish; add the tomatoes, garlic, and onion in a food processor. Blitz them for 10 seconds until the mixture is pulpy. Pour the pulp into a saucepan, add the vinegar, salt, pepper, and place it over medium heat. Bring it to simmer for 10 minutes. Add the paprika and sugar. Stir with a spoon and simmer for 10 minutes until pulpy and thick. Turn off the heat, transfer the relish to a bowl and chill it for an hour.

In 30 minutes after putting the relish in the refrigerator, move on to the sausages. Wrap each sausage with a bacon strip neatly and stick in a bamboo skewer at the end of the sausage to secure the bacon ends. Open the Air Fryer, place 4 wrapped sausages in the fryer basket and cook for 12 minutes at 350°F. Repeat the cooking process for the remaining sausages. Remove the relish from the refrigerator. Serve the sausages and relish with turnip mash.

Basil Pork Burgers

Total Time: 35 min | **Serves**: 2 | **Per serving**: Cal 470; Net Carbs 6g; Fat 42g; Protein 22g

Ingredients

½ lb minced pork

1 medium onion, chopped

1 tbsp mixed herbs

2 tsp garlic powder

1 tsp dried basil

1 tbsp tomato puree

1 tsp mustard

Salt and black pepper to taste

2 zero carbs bread Buns, halved

Assembling:

1 large onion, sliced in 2-inch rings

1 large tomato, sliced in 2-inch rings

2 small lettuce leaves, cleaned

4 slices cheddar cheese

Directions

In a bowl, add the minced pork, chopped onion, mixed herbs, garlic powder, dried basil, tomato puree, mustard, salt, and pepper. Use your hands to mix them evenly. Form two patties out of the mixture.

Preheat the Air Fryer to 370°F. Place the pork patties in the fryer basket, close the Air Fryer, and cook them for 15 minutes. Slide out the fryer basket and turn the patties. Reduce the temperature to 350°F and continue cooking for 5 minutes. Once ready, remove them onto a plate and start assembling the burger.

Place two halves of the bun on a clean flat surface. Add the lettuce in both, then a patty each, followed by an onion ring each, a tomato ring each, and then 2 slices of cheddar cheese each. Cover the buns with their other halves. Serve with a side of sugar-free ketchup and some turnip fries.

Bacon & Cheese Pork

Total Time: 25 min | **Serves**: 4 | **Per serving**: Cal 262; Net Carbs 3g; Fat 16g; Protein 24g

Ingredients

1 lb pork tenderloin

1 tbsp olive oil

Salt and black pepper to taste

1 cup semi-dried tomatoes, sliced

½ lb Camembert cheese, sliced

4 slices bacon

Directions

Preheat the Air Fryer to 365°F. Put the pork on a chopping board. With a knife, cut a small incision deep enough to make stuffing on both. Insert the cheese and tomato slices into the pork tenderloin. Lay the bacon slices on the chopping board. Put the pork over and roll the bacon over the pork. Drizzle with olive oil and sprinkle with salt and pepper. Put the pork in the fryer basket. Cook for 15 minutes, turning once. Slice and serve.

Aromatic Pork Chops

Total Time: 20 min + marinating time | **Serves**: 3 | **Per serving**: Cal 373; Net Carbs 3.1g; Fat 21.3g; Protein 24.2g

Ingredients

3 slices pork chops
2 garlic cloves, minced
4 stalks lemongrass, chopped

2 shallots, chopped
2 tbsp olive oil
1 ¼ tsp soy sauce, sugar-free

1 ¼ tsp fish sauce
1 ½ tsp black pepper

Directions

In a bowl, add the garlic, lemongrass, shallots, olive oil, soy sauce, fish sauce, and black pepper; mix well. Add the pork chops, coat them with the mixture and allow to marinate for around 2 hours to get nice and savory.

Preheat the Air Fryer to 400°F. Cooking in 2 to 3 batches, remove and shake each pork chop from the marinade and place it in the fryer basket. Cook it for 7 minutes. Turn the pork chops and cook further for 5 minutes. Remove the chops and serve with sautéed asparagus.

Herby Pork Roast

Total Time: 40 min | **Serves**: 4 | **Per serving**: Cal 587; Net Carbs 1g; Fat 54.2g; Protein 22g

Ingredients

1 ½ lb pork belly
1 ½ tsp garlic powder
1 ½ tsp coriander powder

Salt and black pepper to taste
1 ½ dried thyme
1 ½ tsp dried oregano

1 ½ tsp cumin powder
1 lemon, halved

Directions

In a small bowl, add garlic powder, coriander powder, salt, black pepper, thyme, oregano, and cumin powder. After the pork is well dried, poke holes all around it using a fork. Smear the oregano rub thoroughly on all sides with your hands and squeeze the lemon juice all over it. Leave to sit for 5 minutes.

Preheat the Air Fryer to 340 F. Put the pork in the center of the fryer basket, close the Air Fryer and cook for 30 minutes. Turn the pork and continue cooking for 25 minutes. Once ready, remove it and place it on a chopping board to sit for 4 minutes before slicing. Serve the pork with a side of sautéed asparagus and hot sauce.

Mustard-Sweet Pork Balls

Total Time: 25 min | **Serves**: 6 | **Per serving**: Cal 225; Net Carbs 1g; Fat 17g; Protein 13g

Ingredients

1 lb ground pork
1 large onion, chopped
½ tsp erythritol

2 tsp mustard
½ cup chopped basil leaves
Salt and black pepper to taste

2 tbsp cheddar cheese, grated

Directions

In a mixing bowl, add the ground pork, onion, erythritol, mustard, basil leaves, salt, pepper, and cheddar cheese. Mix everything well. Use your hands to form bite-size balls. Place them in the fryer basket and cook them at 400°F for 10 minutes. Slide out the fryer basket and shake it to toss the meatballs. Cook for 5 minutes. Remove to a wire rack and serve with marinara sauce.

Chili Tri-Color Pork Kebabs

Total Time: 25 min + marinating time | **Serves:** 4 | **Per serving:** Cal 247; Net Carbs 2.5g; Fat 14.9g; Protein 28g

Ingredients

1 lb pork chops, cut into cubes
¼ cup soy sauce, sugar-free
2 tsp smoked paprika

1 tsp powdered chili
1 tsp garlic salt
1 tsp red chili flakes

1 tbsp vinegar
3 tbsp hot sauce

Skewing:

1 green pepper, cut into cubes
1 red pepper, cut into cubes

1 yellow squash, seeded and cubed
1 green squash, seeded and cubed

Directions

In a mixing bowl, add the pork cubes, soy sauce, smoked paprika, powdered chili, garlic salt, red chili flakes, white wine vinegar, and hot sauce. Mix them using a spoon. Place in the fridge to marinate for at least 1 hour.

Preheat the Air Fryer to 370°F. On each skewer, stick the pork cubes and vegetables in the order that you prefer. Once the pork cubes and vegetables are finished, arrange the skewers in the fryer basket and Grill them for 12-14 minutes. You can do them in batches. Serve with a green salad if desired.

Rosemary Pork Rack with Nuts

Total Time: 55 min | **Serves:** 3 | **Per serving:** Cal 319; Net Carbs 1g; Fat 18g; Protein 27g

Ingredients

1 lb rack of pork
2 tbsp olive oil
1 clove garlic, minced

Salt and black pepper to taste
1 cup macadamia nuts, chopped
1 tbsp pork rinds, crushed

1 egg, beaten in a bowl
1 tbsp fresh rosemary, chopped

Directions

Add the olive oil and garlic to a bowl. Mix vigorously with a spoon to make garlic oil. Place the rack of pork on a chopping board and brush it with the garlic oil using a brush. Sprinkle with salt and pepper.

Preheat the Air Fryer to 320°F. In a bowl, add the pork rinds, nuts, and rosemary. Mix with a spoon and set aside. Brush the meat with the egg on all sides and sprinkle the nut mixture generously over the pork. Press with your hands to avoid the nut mixture from falling off. Put the coated pork in the fryer basket and Roast for 30 minutes.

Increase the temperature to 390°F and cook for 5 minutes. Once ready, remove the meat onto a chopping board. Allow sitting for 10 minutes before slicing it. Serve with a side of parsnip fries and tomato dip.

Oregano Pork Chops

Total Time: 25 min | **Serves:** 4 | **Per serving:** Cal 376; Net Carbs 2.6g; Fat 16.9g; Protein 33.9g

Ingredients

¼ tsp ground fennel
4 pork chops
Salt and black pepper to taste
2 eggs, beaten

1 tbsp water
1 cup pork rinds, crushed
½ tsp garlic powder
3 tsp hot paprika

1 ½ tsp oregano
1 lemon, zested

Directions

Remove the excess fat from the chops. Beat the eggs with water and set aside. In another bowl, mix the pork rinds, salt, pepper, garlic powder, paprika, oregano, lemon zest, and ground fennel.

Preheat your Air Fryer to 380°F. Grease the fryer basket with cooking spray. Dip the chops in the egg, then in the pork rinds. Transfer to the fryer and cook for 15 minutes, flipping once. Let rest 3 minutes before slicing.

Tasty Marinated Pork

Total Time: 20 min | **Serves:** 6 | **Per serving:** Cal 523; Net Carbs 2.5g; Fat 46g; Protein 31g

Ingredients

2 large eggs
2 lb pork tenderloin, cut into cubes
¼ cup pork rinds, crushed
1 cup almond flour

1 tbsp baking powder
4 tbsp sesame oil
2 tbsp fresh ginger root, grated
½ cup spring onions, chopped

½ cup water
¼ cup white vinegar
1 ½ tbsp liquid stevia
¼ cup soy sauce

Directions

Preheat the Air Fryer to 390°F. Coat the pork cubes with the pork rinds, then set aside. In a large bowl, beat eggs with a fork. Add the almond flour and baking powder and beat until there are no lumps. Dip the pork in the egg mixture and place in the air fryer basket. Brush with some sesame oil and cook it for 15 minutes. Set aside.

Heat the remaining sesame oil in a skillet over medium heat. Stir in the spring onions and ginger. Cook for 2-3 minutes. Add the water, vinegar, soy sauce, and stevia and boil the mixture. Keep stirring until the sauce thickens. Add the pork and let simmer for 10-15 minutes. Serve and enjoy!

Pancetta Wrapped Cheese Stuffed Tenderloin

Total Time: 30 min | **Serves:** 4 | **Per serving:** Cal 604; Net Carbs 2.8g; Fat 51.8g; Protein 30g

Ingredients

16 pancetta slices
16 oz pork tenderloin
Salt and black pepper to season

1 cup spinach
3 oz cream cheese
2 shallots, sliced

1 tbsp olive oil
1 clove garlic, minced
½ tsp dried thyme

Directions

Cover the tenderloin with plastic foil and pound it to flatten in 2-inches size. Slice into squares and transfer onto a flat plate. Lay the pancetta slices on a flat surface and cut into squares too. Remove to the same flat plate.

Warm olive oil in a skillet over medium heat and sauté shallots and garlic until transparent. Stir in spinach, thyme, salt, and pepper until the spinach wilts. Add in cream cheese and stir.

Preheat your Air Fryer to 360°F. Put the mixture over the tenderloin. Roll the pancetta and pork over the stuffing and secure the ends with toothpicks. Season with salt and pepper. Place it in the fryer basket and cook for 15 minutes. Turn the pork over and cook for 5 more minutes. Transfer onto a chopping board and let sit for 4 minutes before slicing. Serve with steamed green veggies.

Pork Rack with Almonds

Total Time: 35 min | **Serves:** 3 | **Per serving:** Cal 319; Net Carbs 1g; Fat 18g; Protein 27g

Ingredients

1 cup unsalted almonds, chopped
1 lb rack of pork
2 tbsp olive oil

1 clove garlic, minced
Salt and black pepper to taste
1 tbsp pork rinds, crushed

1 egg, beaten
1 tbsp sage, chopped

Directions

Preheat your Air Fryer to 320°F. Combine the olive oil with the garlic in a bowl. Brush the rack with the mixture and season with salt and pepper. In another bowl, combine the pork rinds, almonds, and sage. Set aside.

Brush the rack with egg on all sides and dip in the almond mixture. Place the rack in the fryer basket and Roast for 25-30 minutes. Increase the Fryer to 390°F and cook for 5 more minutes. Let rest for 10 minutes before slicing.

Smoked Sausage & Cheese Pork

Total Time: 50 min | **Serves**: 2 | **Per serving**: Cal 765; Net Carbs 6.3g; Fat 68g; Protein 34g

Ingredients

1 smoked sausage, chopped
½ pound pork steak
1 tsp steak seasoning

Salt and black pepper to taste
1 cup grated mozzarella cheese
½ tbsp Worcestershire sauce

2 zero carbs hamburger buns, halved

Directions

Preheat your Air Fryer to 400°F. Season the pork with salt, pepper, and steak seasoning. Place it in the basket and grill for 15 minutes. Turn and cook for 6 more minutes. When is ready, shred the pork into small pieces.

Set the Air Fryer to 370°F. Put the smoked sausages in an oven-safe bowl and cook for 10 minutes. Transfer to a bowl and combine with the pulled pork, Worcestershire sauce, and mozzarella cheese. Season with salt and pepper. Reduce the heat to 350°F. Place the bowl in the fryer and cook for 4 minutes. Stir and cook for one minute. Scoop the meat into the halved buns and serve with a cheese or tomato dip.

Pork Chops with Hoisin Sauce

Total Time: 35 min + marinating time | **Serves**: 3 | **Per serving**: Cal 376; Net Carbs 3.3g; Fat 29.3g; Protein 21.7g

Ingredients

1 lb pork chops
Salt and black pepper to taste
1 tsp oregano

1 tbsp erythritol
3 tbsp hoisin sauce
2 cloves garlic, minced

1 tbsp cayenne pepper
1 tsp olive oil

Directions

Slice the chops into smaller pieces. Place it in a bowl and combine with the salt, pepper, oregano, 1 tbsp of erythritol, hoisin sauce, garlic, cayenne pepper, and olive oil. Transfer to the fridge and marinate for 2 hours.

Preheat your Air Fryer to 350°F. Place the chops in the basket and cook for 15 minutes. Turn the chops and brush the remaining erythritol. Cook for another 10 minutes.

Sweet Pork Chops

Total Time: 20 min | **Serves**: 3 | **Per serving**: Cal 351; Net Carbs 2g; Fat 19.5g; Protein 41.5g

Ingredients

3 pork chops, ½-inch thick
Salt and black pepper to taste

1 tbsp erythritol
3 tbsp mustard

Directions

In a bowl, add erythritol, mustard, salt, and pepper and mix well. Add the pork and toss to coat. Place in the fryer basket and cook at 350°F for 6 minutes. Flip and cook for 6 minutes.

Cheddar Pork Meatballs

Total Time: 45 min | **Serves**: 6 | **Per serving**: Cal 326; Net Carbs 1g; Fat 26.6g; Protein 19.6g

Ingredients

1 ½ lb ground pork
2 ¼ cups cheddar cheese, shredded
¾ cups almond flour
½ cup coconut flour

4 eggs
¾ cup sour cream
1 tsp dried oregano
1 tsp smoked paprika

2 tsp garlic powder
½ cup melted coconut oil

Directions

In a bowl, combine the almond flour and coconut flour. In a separate bowl, beat the eggs, sour cream, oregano, paprika, coconut oil, and garlic powder. Combine the flour mixture with the egg mixture. Add in the cheese and ground pork. Stir well. Form bite-sized balls out of the mixture. Let them chill in the fridge for 15 minutes.

Preheat Air Fryer to 350°F. Arrange the meatballs on the greased air fryer basket in a single layer. Spritz them with cooking spray. AirFry for 14-16 minutes. Turn over halfway through the cooking time. Serve and enjoy!

Bacon & Sausage Rolls

Total Time: 2 hrs | **Serves:** 8 | **Per serving:** Cal 455; Net Carbs 8.3g; Fat 39.6g; Protein 18.7g

Ingredients

Sausage:

8 Canadian bacon strips	8 pork sausages	8 medium-length bamboo skewers

Seasoning:

8 large tomatoes	Salt and black pepper to taste	1 tbsp vinegar
1 clove garlic, peeled	2 tbsp swerve sugar	
1 small onion, peeled	1 tsp smoked paprika	

Directions

In a food processor, blend the tomatoes, garlic, and onion until the mixture is pulpy. In a saucepan over medium heat, pour the mixture, add in the vinegar, salt, and pepper. Simmer for 10 minutes. Add in the paprika and sugar. Stir and simmer for 10 more minutes. Transfer to a bowl and let chill in the fridge for 1 hour. After 30 minutes, prepare the sausage by wrapping each sausage with a bacon strip. Stick in a bamboo skewer.

Preheat Air Fryer to 350°F. Put skewers in the fryer basket and cook for 12 minutes. Remove the relish from the fridge. Serve the sausage and relish with turnip mash.

Homemade Pork Tenderloins

Total Time: 20 min | **Serves:** 4 | **Per serving:** Cal 312; Net Carbs 0.8g; Fat 17g; Protein 21g

Ingredients

1 pound pork tenderloin, sliced	2 oz pork rinds, crushed
2 tbsp oil	1 large egg, whisked

Directions

Preheat Air Fryer to 365°F. Stir the oil with the pork rinds until the mixture gets crumbly. Dip pork in the egg, then in the rinds mix. Place in the air fryer basket and cook for 12 minutes, flipping once. Serve.

Pork Liver Cheesy Bake

Total Time: 15 min | **Serves:** 4 | **Per serving:** Cal 287; Net Carbs 1.2g; Fat 23g; Protein 12g

Ingredients

1 lb pork liver, sliced	Salt and black pepper to taste	1 tbsp cream cheese
2 eggs	2 tbsp olive oil	

Directions

Preheat your Air Fryer to 340°F. In a bowl, beat the eggs with cream cheese, olive oil, salt, and pepper. Put the liver slices in the air fryer basket. Top with the egg mixture. Cook for 12 minutes. Let cool and serve.

Tangy Pork Cheeseburgers

Total Time: 35 min | **Serves:** 2 | **Per serving:** Cal 470; Net Carbs 6g; Fat 42g; Protein 22g

Ingredients

1 tbsp sugar-free ketchup
½ lb ground pork
1 onion, chopped

1 tbsp old bay seasoning
2 tsp garlic powder
1 tsp mustard

Salt and black pepper to taste
2 zero carbs bread buns, halved

Assembling:

1 onion, sliced
1 tomato, sliced

2 lettuce leaves, cleaned
2 slices mozzarella cheese

Directions

Combine the ground pork, onion, old bay seasoning, garlic powder, ketchup, mustard, salt, and pepper in a bowl. Shape 2 patties out of the mixture. Preheat your Air Fryer to 370°F. Place the patties in the fryer and cook for 15 minutes. Flip the patties and reduce the heat to 350°F and cook for another 5 minutes.

When done, transfer to a plate and assemble the burger. Place two halves of the bun on a flat surface and put the lettuce in both, then a patty each, then an onion ring each, a tomato ring each, and finally 2 slices of mozzarella cheese each. Top with their other halves. Serve with sugar-free ketchup and some turnip fries.

Almond Crusted Pork Chops

Total Time: 25 min | **Serves:** 4 | **Per serving:** Cal 345; Net Carbs 1.2g; Fat 21g; Protein 42g

Ingredients

4 pork chops, center-cut
2 tbsp almond flour

2 tbsp sour cream
½ cup pork rinds, crushed

Directions

Coat the chops with almond flour. Drizzle the cream over the chops. Spread the pork rinds into a bowl, and coat each pork chop with them. Spray with oil and arrange them into the air fryer. Cook for 14 minutes at 380°F, turning once halfway through cooking.

Soy & Cinnamon Marinated Pork Tenderloins

Total Time: 40 min | **Serves:** 4 | **Per serving:** Cal 522; Net Carbs 1.6g; Fat 18g; Protein 74g

Ingredients

4 pork tenderloins
1 cinnamon quill

1 tbsp olive oil
1 tbsp soy sauce, sugar-free

Salt and black pepper to taste

Directions

In a bowl, add pork, cinnamon, olive oil, soy sauce, salt and black pepper. Stir to coat well. Let sit at room temperature for 20 minutes. Put the pork into the air fryer and add a little bit of marinade. Cook at 380°F for 14 minutes, turning once halfway through cooking. Serve hot!

Mouth-Watering Pork Sticks

Total Time: 15 min + marinating time | **Serves:** 2 | **Per serving:** Cal 418; Net Carbs 0.5g; Fat 32.5g; Protein 29.2g

Ingredients

1 lb ground pork
3 tbsp erythritol

½ tsp garlic powder
½ tsp chili powder

Salt to taste
1 tsp liquid smoke

Directions

Place the meat, erythritol, garlic powder, chili powder, salt and liquid smoke in a bowl. Mix well. Mold out four sticks with your hands, place them on a plate, and refrigerate approximately for 2 hours.

Preheat the Air Fryer to 350°F. Slide out the fryer basket and add the salami sticks to it. Cook for 10 minutes.

Pork & Mushroom Skewers

Total Time: 90 min | **Serves**: 4 | **Per serving**: Cal 247; Net Carbs 2.5g; Fat 14.9g; Protein 28g

Ingredients

1 lb pork tenderloin, cubed	1 tsp powdered chili	1 tbsp vinegar
¼ cup soy sauce, sugar-free	1 tsp garlic salt	3 tbsp hot sauce
2 tsp smoked paprika	1 tsp red chili flakes	

Skewing:

1 lb mushrooms, quartered	1 green squash, seeded and cubed

Directions

In a bowl, combine the pork cubes, soy sauce, smoked paprika, powdered chili, garlic salt, red chili flakes, vinegar, and hot sauce. Marinate in the fridge for 1 hour.

Preheat your Air Fryer to 370°F. Remove the marinated pork and assemble the skewers with the vegetables. When the pork and veggies are done, transfer to the fryer and grill for 8 minutes. Serve with salad.

Simple Shirred Eggs

Total Time: 20 min | **Serves**: 2 | **Per serving**: Cal 279; Net Carbs 1.8g; Fat 20g; Protein 21g

Ingredients

2 tsp butter, melted	4 slices pork ham	Salt and black pepper to taste
4 eggs, divided	3 tbsp Parmesan cheese, shredded	2 tsp chives, chopped
2 tbsp heavy cream	¼ tsp paprika	

Directions

Preheat the air fryer to 320°F. Grease a pie pan with butter. Arrange the ham slices on the bottom of the pan to cover it completely. Whisk one egg along with the heavy cream, salt, and pepper in a small bowl. Pour the mixture over the ham slices. Crack the other eggs over the ham. Sprinkle the Parmesan cheese and cook for 14 minutes. Sprinkle with paprika and garnish with chives. Serve and enjoy!

Thyme Pork Belly Bites

Total Time: 30 min | **Serves**: 4 | **Per serving**: Cal 587; Net Carbs 1g; Fat 54.2g; Protein 22g

Ingredients

1 ½ tsp garlic powder	dry	1 tbsp soy sauce
1 ½ tsp coriander powder	Salt and black pepper to taste	1 lemon, halved
1 ½ lb pork belly, rinsed and patted	1 ½ dried thyme	

Directions

In a bowl, combine the garlic powder, soy sauce, coriander powder, salt, black pepper, and thyme. Cut the pork belly into cubes. Rub with the mixture. Squeeze the lemon juice all over. Let sit for 5 minutes.

Preheat your Air Fryer to 350°F. Place the pork in the fryer and cook for 20 minutes, shaking twice through the cooking process. Serve with sautéed asparagus and hot sauce.

Sunday Meatballs in Marinara Sauce

Total Time: 25 min | **Serves:** 4 | **Per serving:** Cal 441; Net Carbs 3.2g; Fat 37g; Protein 22g

Ingredients

1 lb ground pork
1 onion, chopped
1 tbsp fresh parsley, chopped

½ tbsp thyme leaves, chopped
1 egg
3 tbsp pork rinds, crushed

Salt and black pepper to taste
6 oz marinara sauce

Directions

Preheat your Air Fryer to 390°F. Combine all the ingredients, except the marinara sauce, in a bowl. Mould 10-12 balls with the mixture. Place the balls in the fryer and cook for 8-9 minutes. Remove the meatballs and transfer to an oven plate. Lower the Air Fryer to 330°F. Pour the marinara sauce over the meatballs and cook for 4 minutes.

Cinnamon Pork Patties

Total Time: 25 min | **Serves:** 2 | **Per serving:** Cal 505; Net Carbs 2.5g; Fat 21g; Protein 64g

Ingredients

12 oz ground pork
1 cup pork rinds, crushed

2 eggs, beaten
½ tsp ground cumin

½ tsp ground cinnamon
Salt and black pepper to taste

Directions

In a bowl, add all the ingredients. Mix with hands. Shape into patties. Arrange the patties inside the Air Fryer and cook for 14 minutes at 340°F, turning once halfway through cooking.

Kaffir Lime Pork Chops

Total Time: 20 min + marinating time | **Serves:** 4 | **Per serving:** Cal 373; Net Carbs 3.1g; Fat 21.3g; Protein 24.2g

Ingredients

1 tbsp ground kaffir lime leaves
4 slices pork chops
2 garlic cloves, minced

2 shallots, chopped
2 tbsp olive oil
1 ¼ tsp hoisin sauce

1 ½ tsp black pepper

Directions

In a bowl, combine the chops, garlic, kaffir lime, shallots, olive oil, hoisin sauce, and pepper. Marinate for 2 hours.

Preheat your Air Fryer to 400°F. Place the chops in the fryer and cook for 7 minutes. Turn the chops and cook for another 5 minutes. Repeat the process until no chops are left. Serve with sautéed asparagus.

Bell Pepper Stuffed Pork Chops

Total Time: 40 min | **Serves:** 4 | **Per serving:** Cal 412; Net Carbs 1.2g; Fat 28g; Protein 28g

Ingredients

1 cup mixed bell peppers, chopped
1 tbsp almond flour

4 thick pork chops
A pinch of herbs de Provence

1 tbsp lemon juice
Salt and black pepper to taste

Directions

Preheat Air Fryer to 350°F. Sprinkle chops with salt and pepper. Cook for 15 minutes. In a pan over medium heat, cook the mixed bell peppers for 3 minutes. Stir in lemon juice. Add in the flour and the herbs de Provence. Cook for 4 minutes and set aside. Put pork chop in separated pieces of foil. Then cover it with the mushroom mixture and fold. Seal the foil and place in the fryer. Cook for 30 minutes. Serve and enjoy!

Pork Tenderloins in Tamari Marinade

Total Time: 20 min + marinating time | **Serves:** 4 | **Per serving:** Cal 522; Net Carbs 1.6g; Fat 18g; Protein 74g

Ingredients

2 tbsp cumin seeds
4 pork tenderloins

1 tbsp olive oil
1 tbsp Tamari sauce, sugar-free

Salt and black pepper to taste

Directions

Stir the pork, cumin seeds, olive oil, Tamari sauce, salt, and black pepper in a bowl. Let rest for 30 minutes at room temperature. Preheat your Air Fryer to 380°F. Place the pork in the fryer with some marinade and cook for 14 minutes. Turn once during cooking time. Serve warm.

Cheesy Ham Eggs

Total Time: 20 min | **Serves:** 2 | **Per serving:** Cal 279; Net Carbs 1.8g; Fat 20g; Protein 21g

Ingredients

3 tbsp Pecorino Romano cheese, shredded
2 tsp butter
4 eggs, divided
2 tbsp half and half

4 slices pork ham
¼ tsp paprika
Salt and black pepper to taste

2 tsp chives, chopped

Directions

Preheat Air Fryer to 320°F. Grease a pie pan with butter. Align ham slices in the bottom. In a bowl, beat one egg with half and half, salt, and pepper. Pour the mixture over the ham. Break the remaining eggs over the ham. Top with the cheese and cook for 14 minutes. Garnish with chives and paprika and serve.

Wasabi Pork Balls with Monterey Jack Cheese

Total Time: 25 min | **Serves:** 6 | **Per serving:** Cal 225; Net Carbs 1g; Fat 17g; Protein 13g

Ingredients

2 tbsp Monterey Jack cheese, grated
1 lb ground pork
1 large onion, chopped

½ tsp erythritol
2 tsp wasabi sauce
½ cup chopped basil leaves

Salt and black pepper to taste

Directions

Preheat your Air Fryer to 400°F. Combine the ground pork, onion, erythritol, wasabi, basil leaves, salt, pepper, and Monterey jack cheese in a bowl. Form bite-sized balls out of the mixture. Place the balls in the fryer and cook for 10 minutes. Toss the balls and cook for 5 more minutes. Serve with marinara sauce.

Homemade Mustard Pork Chops

Total Time: 20 min | **Serves:** 4 | **Per serving:** Cal 351; Net Carbs 2g; Fat 19.5g; Protein 41.5g

Ingredients

1 tbsp dry mustard
1 tsp white vinegar

4 pork chops
Salt and black pepper to taste

1 tbsp erythritol

Directions

Preheat your Air Fryer to 350°F. In a small bowl, mix dry mustard, white vinegar, and 1 tsp of water to obtain homemade mustard. Add in erythritol, salt, and pepper. Coat in the chops. Place in the fryer basket and cook for 6 minutes. Turn over and cook for 6 more minutes. Serve and enjoy!

Cumin Pork Cakes

Total Time: 25 min | **Serves:** 2 | **Per serving:** Cal 505; Net Carbs 2.5g; Fat 21g; Protein 64g

Ingredients

2 eggs, beaten
½ lb ground pork

1 cup pork rinds, crushed
½ tsp ground cumin

1 tbsp parsley, chopped
Salt and black pepper to taste

Directions

Preheat your Air Fryer to 340°F. Combine all the ingredients in a bowl. Form patties with the mixture. Place in the fryer basket and cook for 14 minutes. Flip the patties once during cooking time. Serve and enjoy!

Pork Chops with Hazelnut Crust

Total Time: 25 min | **Serves:** 4 | **Per serving:** Cal 345; Net Carbs 1.2g; Fat 21g; Protein 42g

Ingredients

2 tbsp hazelnut flour
2 tbsp crème fraîche

4 pork chops, center-cut
½ cup pork rinds, crushed

Directions

Preheat your Air Fryer to 380°F. Dip the chops in hazelnut flour. Pour the crème fraîche over and dip in the pork rinds. Drizzle with oil. Transfer into the fryer and cook for 14 minutes, turning once. Serve and enjoy!

Roasted Ribeye with Hot Aioli

Total Time: 50 min | **Serves:** 2 | **Per serving:** Cal 379; Net Carbs 0g; Fat 30.8g; Protein 22.6g

Ingredients

3 tbsp mayonnaise
1 tsp garlic puree
1 tsp chili oil
1 tbsp lemon juice

1 tsp red pepper flakes
1 (8-oz) ribeye steak
1 tbsp butter, softened
Salt and black pepper to taste

¼ tsp garlic powder
½ tsp dried dill
¼ tsp dried oregano

Directions

In a small bowl, whisk mayonnaise, garlic puree, chili oil, lemon juice, and red pepper flakes; reserve. Preheat the Air Fryer to 245°F. Rub the steak with butter on all sides. Sprinkle with salt, pepper, garlic powder, dill, and oregano and transfer to the fryer basket. Roast for 40-50 minutes, turning once or until the meat reaches an internal temperature of 150 F for medium-rare. Serve the steak sliced with aioli.

Mexican-Style Burgers

Total Time: 25 min | **Serves:** 4 | **Per serving:** Cal 292; Net Carbs 2.6g; Fat 18.6g; Protein 21.7g

Ingredients

1 lb ground beef
¼ lb Mexican ground chorizo
1 onion, chopped
1 jalapeno, seeded and minced

2 tsp ancho chili powder
1 tsp minced garlic
¼ tsp cumin
¼ tsp Mexican oregano

2 tbsp cilantro, chopped
Salt and black pepper to taste

Directions

Preheat the Air Fryer to 370°F. In a mixing bowl, place all ingredients and mix with your hands until everything is thoroughly combined. Shape the mixture into burger patties and transfer them to the air fryer basket. Brush the patties with cooking spray. AirFry for 15 minutes, flipping once. Serve hot.

Beef Empanadas

Total Time: 25 min | **Serves**: 4 | **Per serving**: Cal 461; Net Carbs 1.8g; Fat 31g; Protein 33.1g

Ingredients

2 tbsp olive oil
½ cup green bell peppers, chopped
½ yellow onion, chopped
1 lb ground beef
2 tsp chili powder

½ tsp garlic powder
¼ tsp cumin
Salt and black pepper to taste
¼ cup chunky salsa
1 ½ cups mozzarella cheese, shredded

½ cup almond flour
2 oz cream cheese
1 egg yolk, beaten

Directions

Warm the olive oil in a pan over medium heat and sauté bell peppers and onion for 4 minutes. Add ground beef and stir-fry for 5-6 minutes. Stir in chili powder, garlic powder, cumin, salt, and pepper. Pour in the chunky salsa and cook, stirring occasionally until the sauce thickens, 5 minutes.

Preheat the air fryer to 390°F. Microwave mozzarella, almond flour, and cream cheese 40-50 seconds. Stir the mixture until smooth and form it into a ball. Lay wax paper on a flat surface, place the dough on top, and cover with another piece of wax paper. Roll the dough into a square, about ¼-inch thick.

Take the parchment paper off. Cut the dough into 4 pieces. Divide the meat mixture between them. Fold the dough in half over the filling; press and seal the edges with a fork. Brush with the beaten yolk and transfer to the air fryer. Bake for 10 minutes, turning once, until golden. Let cool slightly before serving.

BBQ Beef & Sausage Meatballs

Total Time: 25 min | **Serves**: 4 | **Per serving**: Cal 335; Net Carbs 0.8g; Fat 19.7g; Protein 28g

Ingredients

1 lb ground beef
¼ lb ground Italian sausage
1 large egg
¼ tsp onion powder
½ tsp garlic powder

1 tsp dried parsley
1 tsp nutmeg
½ tsp fennel seeds
4 bacon slices, cooked and chopped
1 shallot, chopped

Salt and black pepper to taste
¼ cup pickled jalapeños, chopped
½ cup sugar-free barbecue sauce

Directions

Preheat the air fryer to 390°F. In a bowl, combine all ingredients, except for the barbecue sauce. Shape the mixture into balls. Transfer them to the air fryer basket. AirFry for 14 minutes, until they are browned all over. Check the meatballs halfway through the cooking time. Top with barbecue sauce and serve.

Spiced Rib Eye Steak with Avocado Salsa

Total Time: 35 min | **Serves**: 4 | **Per serving**: Cal 523; Net Carbs 2.3g; Fat 45g; Protein 32g

Ingredients

1 ½ lb ribeye steak
2 tsp olive oil

1 tbsp chipotle chili pepper
Salt and black pepper to taste

1 avocado, diced
Juice from ½ lime

Directions

Place the steak on a chopping board. Pour the olive oil over and sprinkle with chipotle pepper, salt, and black pepper. Rub the spices on the meat. Leave to sit and marinate for 10 minutes.

Preheat the Air Fryer to 400°F. Pull out the fryer basket and place the meat in it. Slide it back into the Air Fryer and cook for 14 minutes. Turn the steak and continue cooking for 6 minutes. Remove the steak, cover with foil, and let it sit for 5 minutes before slicing. Mash the avocado with potato mash. Add in the lime juice and mix until smooth. Taste, adjust the seasoning. Slice and serve the steak with salsa.

Almond Flour Beef Burritos

Total Time: 30 min | **Serves**: 4 | **Per serving**: Cal 381; Net Carbs 1.9g; Fat 26.5g; Protein 25g

Ingredients

2 tbsp avocado oil
½ lb ground beef
⅓ cup beef stock
2 tsp cumin
½ tsp garlic powder

¼ tsp dried oregano
½ tsp taco seasoning
1 tbsp red pepper flakes
¼ cup canned diced tomatoes and chiles, drained

1 ½ cups mozzarella cheese, shredded
½ cup almond flour
2 oz cream cheese
1 large egg

Directions

Warm the avocado oil in a pan over medium heat and sauté ground beef for 6-8 minutes until browned. Stir in cumin, garlic powder, oregano, taco seasoning, red pepper flakes, and tomatoes with chiles. Pour in the stock and simmer for 3-4 minutes. Remove from the heat and set aside.

Preheat the air fryer to 350°F. Microwave mozzarella, almond flour, and cream cheese for 30-40 seconds. Remove and stir in the egg; form the dough into a ball. Lay wax paper on a flat surface, place the dough on top, and cover with another piece of wax paper. Roll the dough into a rectangle shape, about ¼-inch thick.

Take the parchment paper off. Cut the dough into 8 rectangles. Divide the beef mixture between them. Roll up and pinch the edge to seal. Place the seam side down on the parchment-lined air fryer basket. Bake for 10-12 minutes, turning once, until golden. Let cool slightly before serving.

Rainbow Peppercorn-Crusted Beef Tenderloin

Total Time: 35 min | **Serves**: 6 | **Per serving**: Cal 290; Net Carbs 0g; Fat 13.9g; Protein 34.8g

Ingredients

¼ tsp chili powder
2 tbsp butter, melted
2 tbsp roasted garlic, minced

3 tbsp rainbow peppercorn blend, crushed
2 lb beef tenderloin

1 tsp sage, chopped
Sea salt to taste

Directions

Preheat the air fryer to 390°F. Whisk the roasted garlic, butter, and chili powder in a small dish. Smear the mixture onto the beef. Roll it in the rainbow peppercorn blend, pressing them slightly down to form a crust. Transfer the tenderloin to the air fryer basket. AirFry for 23-25 minutes, flipping once. Let the tenderloin sit for a few minutes before slicing. Sprinkle with sea salt and sage. Serve and enjoy!

Hot Meatloaf Muffins

Total Time: 35 min | **Serves**: 6 | **Per serving**: Cal 172; Net Carbs 1.6g; Fat 9.6g; Protein 15g

Ingredients

2 tbsp tomato paste
1 tbsp powdered erythritol
1 ½ lb ground beef
1 shallot, chopped
½ green bell pepper, seeded and diced

1 large egg
3 tbsp ground almond flour
1 tbsp Worcestershire sauce
½ tsp garlic powder
1 tsp dried parsley

1 tsp dried oregano
1 tsp chili oil
1 tsp hot paprika
Salt and black pepper to taste

Directions

Preheat the Air Fryer to 350°F. In a bowl, stir the tomato paste, ¼ cup of water, and erythritol; set aside. Mix the ground beef, shallot, bell pepper, egg, almond flour, Worcestershire sauce, garlic powder, parsley, oregano, chili oil, paprika, salt, and pepper in a bowl until everything is well incorporated. Spoon the meat mixture into 6 cupcake liners. Top with tomato glaze. Bake for 23-25 minutes. Serve warm.

Beef Strips with Broccoli

Total Time: 30 min + marinating time | **Serves**: 4 | **Per serving**: Cal 340; Net Carbs 1.7g; Fat 19g; Protein 26.9g

Ingredients

1 lb sirloin steak, cut into strips
2 tbsp soy sauce
1 tsp oyster sauce
¼ tsp grated ginger

1 garlic clove, minced
1 tbsp coconut oil
1 lb broccoli florets
¼ tsp red pepper flakes

⅛ tsp xanthan gum
½ tsp sunflower seeds, lightly toasted
Salt and black pepper to taste
2 tbsp parsley, chopped

Directions

Mix the soy sauce, oyster sauce, ginger, garlic, coconut oil, salt, and pepper in a bowl. Add in the beef and toss to coat. Cover with plastic wrap and place in the refrigerator for at least 2 hours.

Preheat the Air Fryer to 325°F. Put the beef in the air fryer basket. Reserve the marinade. AirFry for 20 minutes. At the 10-minute mark, turn the strips over, add the broccoli, and scatter the red pepper flakes on top; cook for the remaining 10 minutes until the broccoli is tender and beef is crispy.

Place a small saucepan over medium heat and pour in the reserved marinade and bring to a boil. Lower the heat and add in xanthan gum. Stir and simmer for 3-4 minutes until the sauce thickens. Pour the sauce over the beef and sprinkle with sunflower seeds and parsley. Serve warm and enjoy!

Beef-Club Burger

Total Time: 20 min | **Serves**: 4 | **Per serving**: Cal 440; Net Carbs 2.2g; Fat 35g; Protein 22.4g

Ingredients

1 lb ground beef
¼ tsp garlic powder
¼ tsp cumin powder
Salt and black pepper to taste

2 tbsp butter, melted
½ cup mayonnaise
2 tsp sriracha sauce
8 romaine lettuce leaves

4 bacon slices
8 pickle slices
1 red onion, cut into rounds

Directions

Preheat the Air Fryer to 380°F. Place the bacon slices in the air fryer basket and AirFry them for 5 minutes, flipping once. Combine ground beef, garlic powder, cumin, salt, and pepper in a bowl and stir well. Shape the mixture into 4 patties and brush them with butter on both sides. Transfer them to the air fryer basket. Bake for 14-16 minutes, turning over halfway through.

Mix the mayonnaise with sriracha sauce; adjust the seasoning with salt and pepper. Arrange 4 lettuce leaves on a large serving platter and divide the patties between them and top with bacon, onion, and pickles. Spoon the sriracha mayo on top and cover with the remaining lettuce leaves. Serve and enjoy!

Sweet & Spicy Veggie Beef

Total Time: 25 min | **Serves**: 4 | **Per serving**: Cal 235; Net Carbs 6.2g; Fat 11g; Protein 27g

Ingredients

2 beef steaks, sliced into thin strips
2 garlic cloves, chopped
2 tsp stevia
1 tsp oyster sauce

1 tsp cayenne pepper
½ tsp olive oil
Juice of 1 lime
Salt and black pepper to taste

1 cauliflower, cut into florets
2 carrots, cut into chunks
1 cup green beans

Directions

In a bowl, add beef, garlic, stevia, oyster sauce, cayenne, oil, lime juice, salt and black pepper, and stir to combine. Place the beef along with the garlic and some of the juices into your air fryer and top with the veggies. Cook at 400°F for 8 minutes, turning once halfway through cooking.

Beef Lasagna-Style Bake

Total Time: 30 min | **Serves**: 4 | **Per serving**: Cal 370; Net Carbs 1.8g; Fat 21.5g; Protein 31.3g

Ingredients

2 tbsp olive oil
2 garlic cloves, minced
1 onion, diced
1 lb ground beef

1 tsp dried parsley
½ tsp dried oregano
1 tsp grated nutmeg
Salt and black pepper to taste

1 cup sugar-free pasta sauce
½ cup ricotta cheese
¼ cup Parmesan cheese, grated
1 cup mozzarella cheese, shredded

Directions

Warm the olive oil in a pan over medium heat and sauté garlic and onion for 2 minutes. Add ground beef and stir-fry for 5-6 minutes. Stir in parsley, oregano, nutmeg, salt, and pepper. Set aside.

Preheat the air fryer to 390°F. Spread 1/3 of the pasta sauce on the bottom of a baking dish. Top with 1/3 of the ground beef, 1/3 of the ricotta cheese, 1/3 of the Parmesan cheese, and 1/3 of the mozzarella cheese. Repeat the layering process twice. Place the dish in the air fryer and cover it with foil. Bake for 15 minutes. When 3 minutes remain, remove the foil and cook until golden and bubbling. Serve.

American-Style Cheeseburger Casserole with Bacon

Total Time: 25 min | **Serves**: 4 | **Per serving**: Cal 370; Net Carbs 0.6g; Fat 22.7g; Protein 31g

Ingredients

1 tsp olive oil
1 lb ground beef
1 white onion, chopped
2 garlic cloves, minced

1 tsp mustard powder
1 tsp Worcestershire sauce
1 cup American cheese, shredded
1 large egg

4 bacon slices, chopped
2 pickle spears, chopped
Salt and black pepper to taste

Directions

Preheat the Air Fryer to 370°F. Warm the olive oil in a skillet over medium heat and cook the bacon for 4 minutes; remove. Add the onion, garlic, and ground beef to the skillet and stir-fry for 7-9 minutes. Heat off. Stir in mustard powder, Worcestershire sauce, egg, salt, and pepper. Return the cooked bacon.

Pour the mixture into a baking dish and top with the cheese. Place the dish in the air fryer basket. Bake for 18-20 minutes or until the top is golden brown. Scatter pickles over the top and serve immediately.

Family Favorite Taco-Stuffed Peppers

Total Time: 30 min | **Serves**: 4 | **Per serving**: Cal 345; Net Carbs 4.8g; Fat 19g; Protein 27.9g

Ingredients

10 oz canned tomatoes and green chiles, drained
2 tbsp olive oil
1 lb ground beef
1 tbsp chili powder
1 tsp cumin

1 tsp garlic powder
1 tsp taco seasoning
Salt and black pepper to taste
4 green bell peppers, halved

1 cup cheddar cheese, shredded
2 tbsp fresh cilantro, chopped

Directions

Preheat the Air Fryer to 350°F. Warm the olive oil in a skillet over medium heat and stir-fry the ground beef for 7-9 minutes until browned. Stir in chili powder, cumin, garlic powder, taco seasoning, salt, and black pepper. Pour in the tomatoes and chiles and simmer for 3-4 minutes, stirring occasionally.

Arrange the pepper halves on a baking dish and fill them with the beef mixture. Top with cheese and cilantro and place the dish in the fryer basket. Bake for 15 minutes until the top is golden. Serve warm.

Tasty Beef Cauli Rice

Total Time: 40 min | **Serves:** 2 | **Per serving:** Cal 445; Net Carbs 5.2g; Fat 21g; Protein 49g

Ingredients

Beef:

1 lb beef steak   Salt and black pepper to taste

Cauli rice:

2 ½ cups cauli rice   2 tsp ginger, minced   ¼ cup chopped broccoli
1 ½ tbsp soy sauce, sugar-free   2 tsp vinegar   ¼ cup green beans
2 tsp sesame oil   1 clove garlic, minced

Directions

Put the beef on a chopping board and use a knife to cut it into 2-inch strips. Add the beef to a bowl, sprinkle with pepper and salt, and mix it with a spoon. Let sit for 10 minutes.

Preheat the Air Fryer to 400°F. Add the beef to the fryer basket and cook for 5 minutes. Turn the beef strips with kitchen tongs and cook further for 3 minutes. Once ready, remove the beef into a safe oven dish that fits into the fryer basket. Add the cauli rice, broccoli, green beans, garlic, ginger, sesame oil, vinegar and soy sauce.

Mix evenly using a spoon. Place the dish in the fryer basket carefully, close the Air Fryer and cook at 370°F for 10 minutes. Open the Air Fryer, mix the rice well, and cook further for 4 minutes. Season with salt and pepper as desired. Dish the cauli fried rice into a serving bowl. Serve with hot sauce.

Homemade Worcestershire Beef Burgers

Total Time: 25 min | **Serves:** 4 | **Per serving:** Cal 421; Net Carbs 3.2g; Fat 39g; Protein 21g

Ingredients

1 ½ lb ground beef   1 tsp garlic powder   1 large tomato, sliced
Salt and black pepper to taste   1 ½ tbsp Worcestershire sauce 4 slices cheddar cheese
¼ tsp liquid smoke   8 lettuce leaves
2 tsp onion powder   4 tbsp mayonnaise

Directions

Preheat the Air Fryer to 370°F. In a mixing bowl, combine the ground beef, salt, black pepper, liquid smoke, onion powder, garlic powder and Worcestershire sauce using your hands. Form 4 patties out of the mixture.

Place the patties in the fryer basket making sure to leave enough space between them. Cook for 10 minutes. Turn the beef with kitchen tongs and cook further for 5 minutes. Remove the patties onto a plate. Assemble burgers with lettuce, mayonnaise, sliced cheese, and sliced tomato.

Sticky Ginger-Garlic Beef Ribs with Hot Sauce

Total Time: 35 min | **Serves:** 2 | **Per serving:** Cal 616; Net Carbs 2.4g; Fat 53g; Protein 41.7g

Ingredients

1 rack rib steak   1 tsp garlic powder   1 tsp ginger powder
Salt and white pepper to taste   ½ tsp red pepper flakes   ½ cup hot sauce

Directions

Preheat the Air Fryer to 360°F. Place the rib rack on a flat surface and pat dry using a paper towel. Season the ribs with salt, garlic, ginger, white pepper, and red pepper flakes. Place in the fryer basket and cook for 15 minutes. Turn the ribs with kitchen tongs and cook further for 15 minutes. Remove the ribs onto a chopping board and let it sit for 3 minutes before slicing. Plate and drizzle hot sauce over and serve.

Simple Roast Beef with Herbs

Total Time: 60 min | **Serves:** 2 | **Per serving:** Cal 358; Net Carbs 2g; Fat 24.6g; Protein 26.4g

Ingredients

2 tsp olive oil
1 lb beef roast

½ tsp dried rosemary
½ tsp dried thyme

½ tsp dried oregano
Salt and black pepper to taste

Directions

Preheat the Air Fryer to 400°F. Drizzle the oil on the beef and sprinkle the salt, pepper, and herbs. Rub into the meat. Place the meat in the fryer basket and cook it for 20-25 minutes for medium-rare and 25-30 minutes for well done. Check halfway through and flip to ensure they cook evenly. Wrap the beef in foil for 10 minutes after cooking to allow the juices to reabsorb into the meat. Slice the meat using a knife and serve warm.

Beef Baby Back Ribs

Total Time: 65 min | **Serves:** 4 | **Per serving:** Cal 561; Net Carbs 3.15g; Fat 53g; Protein 28g

Ingredients

2 lb baby back ribs
2 tbsp fresh ginger, ground

Salt and black pepper to taste
5 drops liquid stevia

1 tbsp Spanish paprika

Directions

Preheat the Air Fryer to 400°F. Mix the ginger, stevia, paprika, salt, and pepper very well. Coat the beef ribs with the mixture. Place them in the air fryer basket. Bake for 25 minutes until charred. Serve warm.

Holiday Beef Veggie Mix with Hoisin Sauce

Total Time: 55 min | **Serves:** 6 | **Per serving:** Cal 428; Net Carbs 8.7g; Fat 25.5g; Protein 37.8g

Ingredients

Hoisin sauce:

2 tbsp soy sauce, sugar-free
1 tbsp peanut butter

½ tsp sriracha hot sauce
1 tsp stevia sweetener

1 tsp vinegar
3 cloves garlic, minced

Beef veggie mix:

2 lb beef sirloin, cut into strips
2 yellow peppers, cut into strips
2 green peppers, cut into strips
2 green peppers, cut into strips
2 medium white onions, cut into

strips
1 medium red onions, cut into strips
1 lb broccoli, cut in florets
2 tbsp soy sauce, sugar-free
2 tsp sesame oil

3 tsp minced garlic
2 tsp ground ginger
½ cup water
1 tbsp olive oil

Directions

To make the sauce: in a pan, add the soy sauce, peanut butter, stevia sweetener, hot sauce, vinegar, and minced garlic. Bring it to simmer over low heat until reduced, about 15 minutes. Stir occasionally using a vessel and let it cool. Add to the chilled hoisin sauce, garlic, sesame oil, soy sauce, ginger, and water. Mix well. Add the meat, mix with a spoon, and place it in the refrigerator to marinate for 20 minutes.

Add the broccoli florets, the peppers, onions, and olive oil to a bowl, mix to coat well. Pour the veggies in the fryer basket and cook for 5 minutes at 400 degrees F. Open the Air Fryer, stir the veggies, and cook further for 5 minutes if they are not softened. Remove the veggies to a serving plate and set aside.

Remove the meat from the fridge and drain the liquid into a small bowl. Add the beef into the fryer basket, close the Air Fryer, and cook at 380°F for 8 minutes. Slide out the fryer basket and shake it to toss the beef strips. Cook for 7 minutes. Transfer the beef strips to the veggie plate. Pour the cooking sauce over and serve.

Beef Meatloaf with Tomato-Basil Sauce

Total Time: 40 min | **Serves:** 5 | **Per serving:** Cal 260; Net Carbs 1g; Fat 13g; Protein 26g

Ingredients

1 cup sugar-free tomato basil sauce
1 ½ lb ground beef
1 ¼ cup onion, diced
2 tbsp minced garlic

2 tbsp minced ginger
½ cup pork rinds, crushed
½ cup Parmesan cheese, grated
Salt and black pepper to season

2 tsp cayenne pepper
½ tsp dried basil
⅓ cup parsley, chopped
2 egg whites

Directions

Preheat the Air Fryer to 360°F. In a mixing bowl, add the beef, half of the tomato sauce, onion, garlic, ginger, pork rinds, cheese, salt, pepper, cayenne pepper, dried basil, parsley, and egg whites. Mix well. Grease a pan with cooking spray and scoop in the meat mixture. With a spatula, shape the meat into the pan while pressing firmly.

Use a brush to apply the remaining tomato sauce to the meat. Place the pan in the fryer basket and cook for 25 minutes. After 15 minutes, open the Air Fryer and use a meat thermometer to ensure the meat has reached 160 F internally. Otherwise, cook further for 5 minutes. Remove the pan, drain any excess liquid and fat. Let meatloaf cool for 20 minutes before slicing. Serve with a side of sautéed green beans.

Lime Marinated Beef Fajitas

Total Time: 15 min + marinating time | **Serves:** 4 | **Per serving:** Cal 567; Net Carbs 2.1g; Fat 46g; Protein 41g

Ingredients

2 lb beef, cut into thin strips
2 tbsp coconut oil
½ cup lime juice
4 garlic cloves, mashed

½ tbsp chili powder
1 red bell pepper, chopped
1 hot pepper, sliced
2 onions, sliced

12 flaxseed tortillas
2 tbsp butter, melted
1 avocado, sliced

Directions

In a bowl, mix the oil, lime juice, and spices and add the beef; toss to coat well. Marinate for 5 hours in the fridge.

Preheat the Air Fryer to 400°F. Place the beef in the fryer basket and cook for 35 minutes. At the 20-minute mark, add the vegetables and cook for the remaining 15 minutes. Heat the tortillas for a short time in a pan and brush them with melted butter. Serve the beef meat with tortillas and avocado.

Stuffed Savoy Cabbage Rolls

Total Time: 35 min | **Serves:** 4 | **Per serving:** Cal 317; Net Carbs 2.1g; Fat 21.2g; Protein 27.2g

Ingredients

½ lb ground beef
8 savoy cabbage leaves
1 small onion, chopped

¼ packet taco seasoning
1 tbsp cilantro lime rotel
½ cup shredded Mexican cheese

Salt and black pepper to taste
2 cloves garlic, minced
1 tsp chopped cilantro

Directions

Preheat the Air Fryer to 400°F. Grease a skillet with cooking spray and place it over medium heat. Add the onions and garlic. Sauté until fragrant. Add the beef, pepper, salt, and taco seasoning. Cook until the beef browns while breaking the meat with a vessel as it cooks. Add the cilantro Rotel and stir well to combine.

Lay 4 of the savoy cabbage leaves on a flat surface, scoop the beef mixture in their center and sprinkle them with the Mexican cheese. Wrap them diagonally and double wrap them with the remaining 4 cabbage leaves. Arrange the 4 rolls in the fryer basket and spray with cooking spray. Cook for 8 minutes. Flip, spray with cooking spray, and continue cooking for 4 minutes. Garnish with cilantro and allow them to cool. Serve with cheese dip.

Saucy Beef Tenderloin

Total Time: 40 min | **Serves:** 3 | **Per serving:** Cal 235; Net Carbs 4g; Fat 11g; Protein 18g

Ingredients

Beef:

2 lb beef tenderloin, cut into strips   ½ cup almond flour

Sauce:

1 tbsp minced ginger   ½ cup soy sauce, sugar-free   1 tsp arrowroot starch
1 tbsp minced garlic   ½ cup water   ½ tsp red chili flakes
½ cup chopped green onions   ¼ cup vinegar   Salt and black pepper to taste
2 tbsp olive oil   ¼ cup erythritol

Directions

Pour the almond flour into a bowl, add the beef strips and dredge them in the flour. Spray the fryer basket with cooking spray and arrange the beef strips in it. Spray with cooking spray. Cook the beef at 400°F in the Air Fryer for 4 minutes. Slide out and shake the fryer basket to toss the beef strips. Cook further for 3 minutes. Set aside.

To make the sauce, pour the arrowroot starch in a bowl and mix it with 3 tsp of water until well dissolved. Place a saucepan over medium heat and add olive oil, garlic, and ginger. Stir continually for 10 seconds. Add the soy sauce, vinegar, and remaining water. Bring to boil for 2 minutes. Stir in the erythritol, chili flakes, and arrowroot starch mixture. Add the beef strips and cook for 3 minutes. Mix in the green onions and cook for 2 minutes.

Butter Beef Schnitzel with Lemon

Total Time: 25 min | **Serves:** 4 | **Per serving:** Cal 675; Net Carbs 1.9g; Fat 37g; Protein 73g

Ingredients

4 beef schnitzel cutlets   Salt and black pepper to taste   ½ stick butter, sliced
½ cup almond flour   1 cup pork rinds, crushed
2 eggs, beaten   1 lemon, sliced

Directions

Coat the cutlets in almond flour and shake off any excess. Dip the coated cutlets into the beaten egg. Sprinkle with salt and black pepper. Then dip into the pork rinds and coat well. Spray them generously with oil and cook for 10 minutes at 360°F, turning once halfway through cooking. Serve topped with a slice of butter and lemon.

Beef Meatloaf in Passata Sauce

Total Time: 40 min | **Serves:** 5 | **Per serving:** Cal 260; Net Carbs 1g; Fat 13g; Protein 26g

Ingredients

1 cup sugar-free passata   ½ cup pork rinds, crushed   ½ tsp dried basil
1 ½ lb ground beef   ½ cup Grana Padano cheese, grated   ⅓ cup parsley, chopped
1 ¼ cup onion, diced   Salt and black pepper to season   2 egg whites
2 tbsp minced garlic   2 tsp cayenne pepper

Directions

Preheat your Air Fryer to 360°F. In a bowl, combine the beef, half of the passata sauce, onion, garlic, pork rinds, cheese, salt, pepper, cayenne pepper, dried basil, parsley, and egg whites.

Grease a medium-size pan with cooking spray and pour the mixture into it. Pour the remaining passata sauce over the meat and place in the basket. Cook for 25 minutes. Remove the pan and discard any excess liquid and fat. Let cool for 20 minutes before slicing. Serve with sautéed green beans.

Mustard Lamb with Pumpkin

Total Time: 35 min | **Serves:** 2 | **Per serving:** Cal 587; Net Carbs 3.2g; Fat 39g; Protein 46g

Ingredients

1 lb lamb rack
1 tbsp Dijon mustard
2 oz pork rinds, crushed

2 tbsp fresh herbs, chopped
1 oz Parmesan cheese, grated
1 lemon zest

1 tbsp olive oil.
1 medium pumpkin
Salt and black pepper to taste

Directions

Preheat the Air Fryer to 390°F for 3 minutes. Pat the lamb dry using a towel. Remove the fat and rub the meat with mustard. Blitz the rinds with herbs, Parmesan cheese, lemon zest and the seasonings. Season the joint. Place the meat in the Air Fryer and drizzle with oil. Roast the meat for around 15 minutes.

For the wedges, start by peeling and coring the pumpkin, then coat it with oil. Season the pumpkin and set aside. Remove lamb from the Air Fryer and put on a serving dish. Place the pumpkin wedges in the Air Fryer and Roast for 18 minutes. Once ready, serve the meat with the salad and the wedges.

Beef Tenderloin with Zoodles

Total Time: 40 min | **Serves:** 2 | **Per serving:** Cal 445; Net Carbs 5.2g; Fat 21g; Protein 49g

Ingredients

Beef:

1 lb beef tenderloin, cut into strips   Salt and black pepper to taste

Zoodles:

2 ½ cups zoodles
1 ½ tbsp soy sauce, sugar-free
2 tsp sesame oil

2 tsp ginger, minced
2 tsp vinegar
1 clove garlic, minced

¼ cup chopped broccoli
¼ cup green beans

Directions

Preheat your Air Fryer to 400°F. In a bowl, mix the beef with salt and pepper. Let rest for 10 minutes. Place the beef in the basket and cook for 5 minutes. Flip the beef over and cook for another 3 minutes. When done, transfer to a safe-oven dish. Add in the zoodles, broccoli, green beans, garlic, ginger, sesame oil, vinegar, and soy sauce.

Place the dish in the fryer and cook for 10 minutes. Open the Air Fryer and mix. Cook for another 4 minutes. Season with salt and pepper to taste. Remove to a serving bowl. Serve topped with hot sauce.

Sweet Homemade Beef Satay

Total Time: 25 min | **Serves:** 4 | **Per serving:** Cal 441; Net Carbs 6.5g; Fat 25.8g; Protein 53g

Ingredients

2 lb flank steaks, cut in long strips
2 tbsp fish sauce
2 tbsp soy sauce, sugar-free

2 tbsp swerve sweetener
2 tbsp garlic, ground
2 tbsp ginger, ground

2 tsp hot sauce
2 tbsp chopped cilantro
½ cup roasted peanuts, chopped

Directions

Preheat the Air Fryer to 400°F. Add the beef, fish sauce, swerve sweetener, garlic, soy sauce, ginger, half of the cilantro, and hot sauce in a zipper bag. Zip the bag and massage the ingredients with your hands to mix them well.

Open the bag, remove the beef, shake off the excess marinade and place the beef strips in the fryer basket in a single layer. Try to avoid overlapping. Cook for 5 minutes. Turn the beef and cook further for 5 minutes. Dish the cooked meat in a serving platter, garnish with the chopped peanuts and the remaining cilantro. Serve and enjoy!

Turmeric Liver Curry

Total Time: 20 min | **Serves:** 2 | **Per serving:** Cal 212; Net Carbs 7.5g; Fat 7g; Protein 26g

Ingredients

½ lb beef liver
1 onion, sliced
1 large tomato, chopped
1 clove garlic, minced
1 tbsp ginger, grated

1 tbsp paprika
½ tbsp chili powder
1 tbsp cumin powder
½ tbsp ground coriander
½ tbsp turmeric

½ tbsp Garam Masala
4 drops liquid stevia
Cilantro leaves for garnish

Directions

In a skillet, fry the onion on medium heat until it tenders. Add the grated ginger and the garlic. Keep stirring. Add the powdered spices, then fry for 3 more minutes.

Meanwhile, season the liver with salt and pepper. Place the liver in the Air Fryer and cook it for 15 minutes at 350°F. Remove the liver from the Air Fryer and transfer it to the skillet. Add the tomato, stevia and a little bit of water until everything is cooked. Garnish with cilantro.

Beef Sausage & Mozzarella Omelet

Total Time: 20 min | **Serves:** 2 | **Per serving:** Cal 590; Net Carbs 6g; Fat 42.5g; Protein 44g

Ingredients

1 beef sausage, chopped
4 slices prosciutto, chopped
3 oz salami, chopped

1 cup mozzarella cheese, grated
4 eggs
1 tbsp onion, chopped

1 tbsp ketchup, sugar-free

Directions

Preheat the air fryer to 350°F. Whisk the eggs with the ketchup in a bowl. Stir in the onion. Brown the sausage in the air fryer for about 2 minutes. Combine the egg mixture, mozzarella cheese, salami and prosciutto. Pour the egg mixture over the sausage and give it a stir. Cook for about 10 minutes.

Thyme Lamb Chops with Parsnips

Total Time: 25 min | **Serves:** 2 | **Per serving:** Cal 527; Net Carbs 6.5g; Fat 41g; Protein 17g

Ingredients

2 lamb chops
2 tbsp olive oil

2 garlic cloves, crushed
Salt and black pepper to taste

A handful of fresh thyme, chopped
2 parsnips, cubed

Directions

Rub the chops with oil, garlic, salt and black pepper. Put thyme in the fryer, and place the chops on top. Oil the parsnip chunks and sprinkle with salt and pepper. Arrange the parsnips next to the chops, and cook on 360°F for 14 minutes, turning once.

Jalapeño Beef Carnitas

Total Time: 15 min + marinating time | **Serves:** 4 | **Per serving:** Cal 567; Net Carbs 2.1g; Fat 46g; Protein 41g

Ingredients

1 jalapeño pepper, sliced
2 lb beef, cut into thin strips
6 tbsp coconut oil
½ cup lime juice

4 garlic cloves, mashed
½ tbsp chili powder
1 red bell pepper, chopped
2 onions, sliced

12 flaxseed tortillas, warm
1 avocado, sliced

Directions

Combine 3 tbsp of the coconut oil with lime juice. Add in all the spices and the beef. Marinate in the fridge for 2 hours. Preheat your Air Fryer to 390°F. Remove and pat dry the beef. Place it in the air fryer basket and cook for 6-8 minutes. Mix the vegetables with the remaining coconut oil. Add in the fryer. Cook for 8-10 more minutes. Spoon the beef and vegetables on the tortillas and top with avocado slices. Serve and enjoy!

Juicy Tenderloin Strips

Total Time: 40 min | **Serves**: 3 | **Per serving**: Cal 235; Net Carbs 4g; Fat 11g; Protein 18g

Ingredients

Beef:

½ cup almond flour	Salt and black pepper to taste	1 lb beef tenderloin strips

Sauce:

½ cup Worcestershire sauce	2 tbsp olive oil	1 tsp arrowroot starch
1 tbsp minced garlic	¼ cup vinegar	½ tsp red chili flakes
½ cup chopped green onions	¼ cup erythritol	Salt and black pepper to taste

Directions

Preheat your Air Fryer to 400°F. Grease the fryer basket with cooking spray. Put the flour, salt and black pepper in a bowl and coat the beef strips. Place the strips in the basket and spray with cooking spray. Cook for 4 minutes. Flip the strips and cook for another 3 minutes. In a bowl, mix the arrowroot with 3-4 tsp of water until well dissolved. Set aside. Warm the olive oil in a saucepan over medium heat and stir in the garlic for 10 seconds.

Add in the Worcestershire sauce, vinegar, and ½ cup of water and bring to a boil for 2 minutes. Pour in the erythritol, chili flakes, and arrowroot starch mixture and stir. Stir in the beef strip and cook for 3 minutes. Add in the green onions and stir for another 2 minutes. Season with salt and pepper to taste.

Cayenne-Coated Beef Steaks

Total Time: 15 min | **Serves:** 2 | **Per serving:** Cal 568; Net Carbs 1.7g; Fat 42g; Protein 47g

Ingredients

2 beef steaks, 1-inch thick	1 tbsp olive oil
½ tsp cayenne pepper	½ tsp hot paprika
Salt and black pepper to taste	

Directions

Preheat the air fryer to 390°F, if needed. Mix olive oil, cayenne, paprika, salt and pepper and rub onto steaks. Spread evenly. Put the steaks in the fryer, and cook for 6 minutes, turning once.

Thyme Roast Beef

Total Time: 60 min | **Serves:** 2 | **Per serving:** Cal 358; Net Carbs 2g; Fat 24.6g; Protein 26.4g

Ingredients

2 tsp olive oil	½ tsp dried thyme	Salt and black pepper to taste
1 lb beef roast	½ tsp garlic powder	

Directions

Preheat your Air Fryer to 400°F. Brush the beef with oil and season with salt, pepper, garlic powder, and thyme. Place the beef in the basket and cook for 45-50 minutes. Turn the beef once during cooking time. Foil the beef with aluminium and let sit for 10 minutes. With a knife, cut the beef into slices. Serve with steamed asparagus.

Jalapeño Baby Back Ribs

Total Time: 30 min | **Serves**: 4 | **Per serving**: Cal 631; Net Carbs 2.9g; Fat 67g; Protein 57g

Ingredients

1 slab baby back ribs
1 tbsp ginger, grated
1 scallion, minced

½ tbsp fresh cilantro, chopped
1 jalapeño pepper, seeded and
chopped

1 clove garlic, minced
½ cup orange juice
2 tbsp sesame oil

Directions

Put all the ingredients inside a plastic bag overnight. Reserve the marinade. Place the ribs vertically in the Air Fryer. Cook for 30 minutes at 365°F. Put the marinade in a deep cooking pan. Cook the marinade on medium heat for 5 minutes. Brush the ribs with the marinade.

Sirloin & Mixed Bell Peppers with Hot Sauce

Total Time: 55 min | **Serves**: 6 | **Per serving**: Cal 428; Net Carbs 8.7g; Fat 25.5g; Protein 37.8g

Ingredients

Sauce:

2 tbsp soy sauce, sugar-free
1 tbsp peanut butter

½ tsp sriracha sauce
2 tbsp hot sauce

1 tsp rice vinegar
3 cloves garlic, minced

Mix:

2 lb beef sirloin, cut into strips
2 yellow peppers, cut into strips
2 green peppers, cut into strips
2 green peppers, cut into strips
2 medium white onions, cut into

strips
1 red onion, sliced
2 tbsp soy sauce, sugar-free
2 tsp sesame oil
3 tsp minced garlic

2 tsp ground ginger
½ cup water
1 tbsp olive oil

Directions

In a saucepan over low heat, put the soy sauce, peanut butter, sriracha sauce, hot sauce, rice vinegar, and minced garlic Bring to a simmer for 15 minutes until reduced, stirring occasionally. Let cool.

Preheat your Air Fryer to 400°F. Combine the chilled sauce, minced garlic, sesame oil, soy sauce, ground ginger, and water. Add in the beef and stir. Marinate in the fridge for 20 minutes.

In a bowl, combine the bell peppers, onions and olive oil. Place the veggies in the fryer and cook for 10 minutes, until softened. Transfer to a plate and set aside. Remove the meat from the fridge and drain the liquid in a bowl. Place in the fryer and cook for 8 minutes. Turn the strips and cook for 7 minutes. Place the beef with the veggies and top with the cooking juices.

Authentic Wiener Schnitzel

Total Time: 25 min | **Serves**: 4 | **Per serving**: Cal 675; Net Carbs 1.9g; Fat 37g; Protein 73g

Ingredients

4 veal cutlets
½ cup almond flour
2 eggs, beaten

Salt and black pepper to taste
1 cup pork rinds, crushed
1 lemon, sliced

½ stick butter, sliced
2 tbsp parsley, chopped

Directions

Preheat your Air Fryer to 360°F. Dip the cutlets in almond flour, then in the beaten eggs. Season with salt and pepper. Finally, dip in the pork rinds. Rub the cutlets with oil. Place in the fryer and cook for 10 minutes. Turn once during cooking time. Top with a slice of butter, parsley and lemon. Serve warm.

Asian-Style Beef Liver

Total Time: 20 min | **Serves:** 2 | **Per serving:** Cal 212; Net Carbs 7.5g; Fat 7g; Protein 26g

Ingredients

½ tbsp gochugaru powder
½ lb beef liver
1 onion, sliced
1 large tomato, chopped

1 clove garlic, minced
1 tbsp ginger, grated
1 tbsp cumin powder
½ tbsp ground coriander

½ tbsp Garam Masala
4 drops liquid stevia
Cilantro leaves for garnish

Directions

Preheat your Air Fryer to 350°F. In a skillet over medium heat, sauté the onion, until translucent. Add in the grated ginger and the garlic. Put in the powdered spices and cook for another 3 minutes.

Place the liver in the fryer and cook for 15 minutes. Remove to a hot skillet and add in the tomato, stevia, and a bit of water. Garnish with cilantro to serve.

Chili Brussels Sprouts with Beef Sausages

Total Time: 25 min | **Serves:** 4 | **Per serving:** Cal 52; Net Carbs 2.1g; Fat 2.6g; Protein 5.1g

Ingredients

½ lb Brussels sprouts, trimmed
Salt and black pepper to taste
1 ½ tbsp olive oil

2 tsp lemon juice
1 tsp powdered chili
3 cloves garlic

1 lb beef sausages
1 cup mayonnaise

Directions

Heat a greased skillet over medium heat. Add the garlic cloves with the peels on it and roast until lightly brown and fragrant. Remove the skillet with the garlic and place a pot with 2 cups of water over the same heat. Bring it to a boil. Using a knife, cut the brussels sprouts in halves lengthwise. Add to the boiling water to blanch for just 3 minutes. Drain through a sieve and set aside.

Preheat the Air Fryer to 350°F. Remove the garlic from the skillet to a plate; peel and crush and set aside. Add olive oil to the skillet over medium heat. Cook the sausages for 4-5 minutes. Turn off the heat. Pour the brussels sprouts and sausages into the fryer basket and bake for 5 minutes. In a bowl, add the mayonnaise, garlic, lemon juice, powdered chili, pepper and salt. Mix well. Remove the brussels sprouts and sausages to a serving bowl and serve with the garlic sauce. Serve and enjoy!

Beef Dolmas

Total Time: 35 min | **Serves:** 4 | **Per serving:** Cal 317; Net Carbs 2.1g; Fat 21.2g; Protein 27.2g

Ingredients

1 (8-oz) jar grape leaves, drained and rinsed leaves
½ lb ground beef
1 small onion, chopped
1 tbsp cilantro-lime rotel

½ cup shredded mozzarella cheese
2 tsp olive oil
Salt and black pepper to taste

2 cloves garlic, minced
1 tsp chopped cilantro

Directions

Preheat your Air Fryer to 400°F. In a skillet over medium heat with cooking spray, sauté the onion and garlic until fragrant. Add in the beef, pepper and salt cook until the beef browns. Stir in the cilantro rotel.

Place 4 of the grape cabbage leaves on a flat surface and spread the beef mixture in the center. Top with mozzarella cheese. Roll them diagonally and roll them with the remaining leaves to make a double wrap. Place the rolls in the basket and sprinkle some cooking spray. Cook for 8 minutes. Turn the rolls and cook for 4 minutes more. Remove the rolls and top with cilantro. Let cool. Serve with cheese dip.

Ginger Ground Beef Skewers

Total Time: 25 min | **Serves**: 2 | **Per serving**: Cal 331; Net Carbs 2.5g; Fat 22g; Protein 33g

Ingredients

½ lb ground beef
½ large onion
1 medium green chili

½ tbsp chili powder
1 minced clove garlic
A pinch of ginger

1 tbsp Garam Masala
3 tbsp pork rinds, crushed
Salt to taste

Directions

Grate 1 pinch of ginger and garlic. Chop and deseed the chili. Chop the onion. Mix ginger, garlic, chili and onion with ground beef. Add the powdered spices. Add a few pork rinds and salt.

Shape the beef into fat sausages around short wooden skewers. Set the skewers aside for 1 hour, then cook them in a preheated Air Fryer for 25 minutes at 350°F.

Spicy Rib Eye with Avocado

Total Time: 35 min | **Serves**: 4 | **Per serving**: Cal 523; Net Carbs 2.3g; Fat 45g; Protein 32g

Ingredients

1 tomato, chopped
1 ½ lb rib-eye steak
2 tsp olive oil

1 tbsp chili pepper
Salt and black pepper to taste
1 avocado, diced

Juice from ½ lime
1 tbsp cilantro, chopped

Directions

Brush the steak with olive oil. Rub with chili pepper, salt, and pepper. Marinate for 10 minutes.

Preheat your Air Fryer to 400°F. Place the steak in the basket and cook for 14 minutes. Flip the steak and cook for another 6 minutes. Remove the steak and cover with aluminium foil. Let rest for 5 minutes before slicing. Mash the avocado, add in the lime juice, tomato, and cilantro; mix until smooth. Season. Slice the steak and serve.

Easy Beef Meatloaf with Herbs

Total Time: 30 min | **Serves**: 4 | **Per serving**: Cal 312; Net Carbs 5.2g; Fat 15g; Protein 34g

Ingredients

1 lb ground beef
2 eggs, lightly beaten
½ cup pork rinds, crushed

2 garlic cloves, crushed
1 onion, finely chopped
2 tbsp tomato puree, sugar-free

1 tsp mixed dried herbs

Directions

Line a loaf pan with baking paper. In a bowl, mix beef, eggs, pork rinds, garlic, onion, puree, and herbs. Press the mixture into the pan and slide in the air fryer. Cook for 25 minutes at 380°F. Serve and enjoy!

Hungarian Beef Ribs

Total Time: 65 min | **Serves**: 6 | **Per serving**: Cal 561; Net Carbs 3.15g; Fat 53g; Protein 28g

Ingredients

1 tbsp Hungarian paprika
2 racks beef ribs

Salt and black pepper to taste
5 drops liquid stevia

Directions

Preheat your Air Fryer to 390°F. Combine all the seasonings and coat the ribs well. Place the ribs in the fryer and cook for 55 minutes. Top with the seasonings and serve.

Meaty Omelet

Total Time: 20 min | **Serves:** 2 | **Per serving:** Cal 590; Net Carbs 6g; Fat 42.5g; Protein 44g

Ingredients

3 oz kielbasa, chopped
1 beef sausage, chopped

1 cup mozzarella cheese, grated
4 eggs

1 tbsp onion, chopped
1 tbsp ketchup, sugar-free

Directions

Preheat your Air Fryer to 350°F. In a bowl, beat the eggs with the ketchup. Add in the onion and stir. Place the sausage in the fryer and brown for 2 minutes. In the meantime, mix the egg mixture with the mozzarella and kielbasa. Pour the mixture over the sausage and stir. Cook for 10 minutes.

Smoky Cheeseburgers

Total Time: 25 min | **Serves:** 4 | **Per serving:** Cal 421; Net Carbs 3.2g; Fat 39g; Protein 21g

Ingredients

1 ½ lb ground beef
Salt and black pepper to taste

¼ tsp liquid smoke
2 tsp onion powder

1 tsp garlic powder
1 ½ tbsp Worcestershire sauce

Directions

Preheat your Air Fryer to 370°F. In a bowl, mix the ground beef, salt, black pepper, liquid smoke, onion powder, garlic powder, and Worcestershire sauce. Shape 4 patties out of the mixture. Place them in the basket and cook for 10 minutes. Flip them and cook for another 5 minutes. Transfer to a plate. Serve and enjoy!

Baby Back Ribs with Habanero

Total Time: 30 min + chilling time | **Serves:** 4 | **Per serving:** Cal 631; Net Carbs 2.9g; Fat 67g; Protein 57g

Ingredients

1 habanero pepper, chopped
1 slab baby back ribs
1 tbsp ginger, grated

1 scallion, minced
½ tbsp fresh cilantro, chopped
1 clove garlic, minced

½ cup lemon juice
2 tbsp sesame oil

Directions

Place all the ingredients in a plastic bag. Let chill for 2 hours in the refrigerator. Preheat your Air Fryer to 365°F. Place the ribs vertically in the fryer basket and cook for 30 minutes. In a saucepan over medium heat, pour the marinade and cook for 5 minutes. Brush the ribs with the marinade and serve.

Veggie & Beef Slices

Total Time: 25 min | **Serves:** 4 | **Per serving:** Cal 235; Net Carbs 6.2g; Fat 11g; Protein 27g

Ingredients

1 broccoli, cut into florets
2 beef steaks, sliced
2 garlic cloves, chopped
2 tsp stevia

1 tsp oyster sauce
1 tsp cayenne pepper
½ tsp olive oil
Juice of 1 lime

Salt and black pepper to taste
2 carrots, cut into chunks
1 cup haricots vert

Directions

Preheat Air Fryer to 400°F. In a bowl, mix beef, garlic, stevia, oyster sauce, cayenne, oil, lime juice, salt, and pepper. Stir the beef with the garlic and some of the juices. Place in the fryer basket and top with the veggies. Cook for 8 minutes. Turn once during cooking time.

Flank Steaks with Hazelnuts

Total Time: 25 min | **Serves:** 4 | **Per serving:** Cal 441; Net Carbs 6.5g; Fat 25.8g; Protein 53g

Ingredients

½ cup roasted hazelnuts, chopped
2 lb flank steaks, cut in long strips
2 tbsp fish sauce
2 tbsp soy sauce, sugar-free

2 tbsp swerve sweetener
2 tbsp garlic, ground
2 tbsp ginger, ground
2 tsp hot sauce

1 cup chopped cilantro, divided into two

Directions

Preheat your Air Fryer to 400°F. In a sealable bag, place the beef, fish sauce, swerve sweetener, garlic, soy sauce, ginger, half of the cilantro, and hot sauce. Seal and shake to coat. Remove the beef and place in the basket. Do not overlap. Cook for 5 minutes. Flip the beef and cook another 5 minutes. Transfer to a serving plate and garnish with cilantro and hazelnuts. Serve and enjoy!

Paprika Beef Steaks

Total Time: 15 min | **Serves:** 2 | **Per serving:** Cal 568; Net Carbs 1.7g; Fat 42g; Protein 47g

Ingredients

1 tbs rosemary, chopped
2 beef steaks, 1-inch thick

1 tbsp olive oil
½ tsp hot paprika

Salt and black pepper to taste

Directions

Preheat Air Fryer to 390°F. Combine olive oil, black pepper, paprika, rosemary, and salt. Brush the steak with the mixture. Place in the fryer and cook for 6 minutes. Turn once during cooking time. Serve and enjoy!

Greek Sandwiches

Total Time: 15 min | **Serves:** 2 | **Per serving:** Cal 541; Net Carbs 8.3g; Fat 49g; Protein 16.2g

Ingredients

¼ cup halloumi cheese, grated
¼ cup dill, chopped
1 tomato, sliced
1 beef kielbasa, sliced

1 green onion, thinly sliced
1 clove garlic
Salt to taste
2 tsp + ¼ cup olive oil

1 ½ tbsp pine nuts, toasted
¼ cup parsley, chopped

Directions

In a food processor, blend the dill, pine nuts, garlic, and salt. Pour in 1/4 cup of olive oil. Transfer the mixture into a bowl and put in the fridge for 30 minutes.

Preheat your Air Fryer to 390°F. Remove the pesto. Lay the tomato slices on a flat surface and spoon some pesto on each slice. Top with kielbasa slices. In a bowl, mix the green onion and remaining olive oil. Pour over the halloumi cheese. Place the tomato sandwiches in the fryer basket and bake for 8 minutes. Transfer to a plate and sprinkle with salt. Top with the remaining pesto to serve.

Jicama Salad with Mozzarella

Total Time: 35 min | **Serves:** 4 | **Per serving:** Cal 235; Net Carbs 2.6g; Fat 15g; Protein 19g

Ingredients

1 lb jicama
2 tbsp olive oil

Salt and black pepper to taste
½ lb mozzarella cheese

2 tbsp balsamic vinegar
2 smoked beef sausages

Directions

Preheat your Air Fryer to 350°F. Wash and dry the jicama. In a bowl, sprinkle the jicama with oil, salt, and black pepper. Place in the fryer basket and cook for 35 minutes. Dress with balsamic vinegar and top with mozzarella cheese and beef sausages. Serve and enjoy!

Beef & Cauliflower Cheddar Quiche

Total Time: 50 min | **Serves:** 2 | **Per serving:** Cal 316; Net Carbs 1g; Fat 24g; Protein 10g

Ingredients

2 cauliflower, cut into florets
4 eggs
2 oz mortadella, chopped
1 cup almond milk

2 tomatoes, diced
4 carrots, diced
¼ cup ricotta cheese, crumbled
1 cup cheddar cheese, grated

Salt and black pepper to taste
1 tsp parsley, chopped
1 tsp dried thyme

Directions

Place the cauliflower and carrots in a steamer and cook for 10 minutes until soft. Break the eggs in a jug and whisk with parsley, salt, thyme, and pepper. Add in the almond milk and beat until obtain a pale mixture.

Preheat your Air Fryer to 350°F. Once the veggies are ready, drain them and set aside. In a quiche dish, place the carrots and cauliflower. Add in the tomatoes, mortadella, ricotta, and cheddar cheese, and the egg mixture on top.

Scatter with the remaining cheddar. Place in the fryer and cook for 20 minutes. When it is ready, remove the dish and cut into slices.

Mustard Squash Lamb

Total Time: 35 min | **Serves:** 2 | **Per serving:** Cal 587; Net Carbs 3.2g; Fat 39g; Protein 46g

Ingredients

1 tbsp hot English mustard
1 lb lamb rack
2 oz pork rinds, crushed

2 tbsp fresh thyme, chopped
1 oz Parmesan cheese, grated
1 lemon zest

1 tbsp olive oil
1 medium butternut squash, cubed
Salt and black pepper to taste

Directions

Preheat your Air Fryer to 390°F. Dry the lamb with a paper towel. Rub the lamb with mustard. Combine the pork rinds with the thyme, Parmesan cheese, lemon zest, and the seasonings. Dip the lamb in the mixture. Place the lamb in the basket. Spray with oil and cook for 15 minutes.

Grease butternut squash with oil and season with salt and pepper. Set aside. Remove the lamb and transfer to a serving plate. Place the squash in the fryer and roast for 18 minutes. Serve with salad and roasted wedges.

Holiday Lamb Meatloaf

Total Time: 30 min | **Serves:** 4 | **Per serving:** Cal 312; Net Carbs 5.2g; Fat 15g; Protein 34g

Ingredients

1 lb ground lamb
2 eggs, lightly beaten
½ cup pork rinds, crushed

2 garlic cloves, crushed
1 onion, finely chopped
2 tbsp tomato puree, sugar-free

2 tsp mint, chopped

Directions

Preheat your Air Fryer to 380°F. Line a loaf pan with baking paper. Combine the lamb, eggs, pork rinds, garlic, onion, tomato puree, and mint. Place in the pan, transfer to the Fryer and cook for 25 minutes. Serve and enjoy!

Veggie & Lamb Kebabs

Total Time: 25 min | **Serves:** 2 | **Per serving:** Cal 331; Net Carbs 2.5g; Fat 22g; Protein 33g

Ingredients

½ lb ground lamb
½ large onion, chopped
1 medium green chili

½ tbsp chili powder
1 minced clove garlic
A pinch of ginger

½ tbsp allspice
½ ground cumin
3 tbsp pork rinds, crushed

Directions

Preheat your Air Fryer to 350°F. Grate a pinch of ginger and garlic. Cut and deseed the chili. Combine the ginger, onion, garlic, and green chili with the ground lamb. Season with spices. Add in the pork rinds. Shape fat sausages out of the mixture around wooden skewers. Place in the fryer basket and cook for 25 minutes. Serve and enjoy!

Prosciutto Wrapped Lamb Chops

Total Time: 20 min | **Serves:** 4 | **Per serving:** Cal 623; Net Carbs 3.2g; Fat 38g; Protein 63g

Ingredients

2 lb lamb rack, cut into quarters
2 balls fresh mozzarella cheese, sliced

4 leaves sage
4 slices thin prosciutto

2 tbsp olive oil

Directions

Preheat the Air Fryer to 350°F. Make a deep pocket in each of the lamb chops. Stuff the pockets with mozzarella cheese. Put a sage leaf on the top of every chop. Wrap each chop with a slice of prosciutto. Pour olive oil on the lamb and cook for 15 minutes. Serve and enjoy!

Sage Bresaola Wrapped Lamb

Total Time: 20 min | **Serves:** 4 | **Per serving:** Cal 623; Net Carbs 3.2g; Fat 38g; Protein 63g

Ingredients

4 slices thin bresaola
2 lb lamb rack, cut into quarters

2 balls fresh mozzarella cheese, sliced
4 leaves sage

2 tbsp olive oil

Directions

Preheat your Air Fryer to 350°F. Make a hole in the middle of each lamb chop and stuff with mozzarella cheese. Top with a sage leaf. Lay the bresaola slices on a flat surface and wrap the chops. Brush the chops with olive oil and cook in the fryer for 15 minutes.

Garlic Turnips & Lamb Chops

Total Time: 25 min | **Serves:** 2 | **Per serving:** Cal 527; Net Carbs 6.5g; Fat 41g; Protein 17g

Ingredients

2 turnips, cubed
2 lamb chops

2 tbsp olive oil
2 garlic cloves, crushed

Salt and black pepper to taste
A handful of fresh thyme, chopped

Directions

Preheat your Air Fryer to 360°F. Brush the chops with oil, garlic, salt, and pepper. Place the thyme on the bottom of the basket and top with the chops. Rub the turnips with oil and season with salt and pepper. Lay next to the chops. Cook for 14 minutes. Turn once during cooking time. Serve and enjoy!

VEGAN & VEGETARIAN RECIPES

Veggie Quesadillas

Total Time: 30 min | **Serves**: 4 | **Per serving**: Cal 796; Net Carbs 7.2g; Fat 61.4g; Protein 34.6g

Ingredients

1 ½ cups mozzarella cheese, shredded
½ cup almond flour
2 oz cream cheese
1 large egg
2 tbsp coconut oil

½ cup red onion, sliced
1 green bell pepper, seeded and chopped
½ cup white mushrooms, chopped
Salt and black pepper to taste

1 cup Pepper Jack cheese, shredded
1 avocado, mashed
½ cup sour cream
½ cup mild salsa
2 tbsp fresh cilantro, roughly chopped

Directions

Warm the coconut oil in a skillet over medium heat and sauté onion, mushrooms, and bell pepper for 5 minutes until tender. Sprinkle with salt and pepper and stir in half of the cheese; set aside.

Preheat the air fryer to 390°F. Microwave mozzarella cheese, almond flour, and cream cheese for 30-40 seconds. Remove and stir in the egg. Form the dough into a ball and cut the dough into 8 balls. Flatten each ball between two sheets of wax paper using a rolling pin to create tortillas.

Divide the veggie mixture between 4 tortillas. Scatter the remaining cheese over, and top with the remaining tortillas. Place the quesadillas in the air fryer basket and Bake for 5 minutes, turning once until the edges are golden brown. Serve garnished with avocado, sour cream salsa, and cilantro.

Artichoke, Spinach & Cauliflower Bake

Total Time: 30 min | **Serves**: 4 | **Per serving**: Cal 421; Net Carbs 4.2g; Fat 36.4g; Protein 6.8g

Ingredients

Salt and black pepper to taste
½ tsp lemon zest
⅓ cup sour cream
⅓ cup mayonnaise

1 tbsp butter, melted
1 yellow onion, diced
8 ounces cream cheese, softened
¼ cup pickled jalapeños, chopped

2 cups baby spinach, chopped
2 cups cauliflower florets, chopped
1 cup artichoke hearts, chopped
1 tbsp basil, chopped

Directions

Preheat the air fryer to 360°F. In a bowl, whisk sour cream, mayonnaise, butter, lemon zest, salt, and pepper. Stir in onion, jalapeños, cream cheese, spinach, cauliflower, and artichokes. Transfer the mixture to a baking dish. Place the dish in the fryer basket. Bake for 14-16 minutes until golden. Serve topped with basil.

Piri Piri Cauliflower Steaks

Total Time: 15 min | **Serves**: 4 | **Per serving**: Cal 121; Net Carbs 2.8g; Fat 8.7g; Protein 5.1g

Ingredients

1 head cauliflower, cut into ½-inch thick steaks
¼ cup piri piri spicy sauce
2 tbsp butter, melted

¼ cup blue cheese, crumbled
¼ cup ranch dressing

2 tbsp cilantro, chopped

Directions

Preheat the air fryer to 390°F. Brush the cauliflower steaks with butter and piri piri sauce on both sides and arrange them on the air fryer basket. Bake for 8-10 minutes, turning over halfway through cooking, until tender-crisp. Top with crumbled blue cheese and cilantro and drizzle with ranch dressing to serve.

Spiralized Zucchini & Cheese Casserole

Total Time: 20 min | **Serves**: 4 | **Per serving**: Cal 336; Net Carbs 4.2g; Fat 28.4g; Protein 9.8g

Ingredients

2 tbsp butter
¼ cup white onion, diced
2 garlic cloves, minced

Salt and black pepper to taste
½ tsp allspice
½ cup heavy cream

2 oz cream cheese
1 cup Gruyere cheese, shredded
2 zucchini, spiralized

Directions

Preheat the air fryer to 360°F. Melt the butter in a skillet over medium heat and sauté onion and garlic for 3 minutes until softened. Stir in salt, pepper, allspice, heavy cream, and cream cheese for 2 minutes.

Turn the heat off and immediately add the cheese; stir to combine well. Place the zucchini in a baking dish and pour over the cheese mixture. Fit the dish in the air fryer and cover with aluminium foil. Bake for 10 minutes, remove the foil, and bake for 6 more minutes until golden brown. Serve warm.

Cheese Stuffed Zucchini

Total Time: 35 min | **Serves**: 4 | **Per serving**: Cal 214; Net Carbs 5.2g; Fat 14.8g; Protein 10.4g

Ingredients

Salt and black pepper to taste
2 medium zucchini, sliced lengthways
1 tbsp avocado oil
¼ cup sugar-free pasta sauce

¼ cup ricotta cheese
¼ cup mozzarella cheese, shredded
¼ tsp dried oregano
¼ tsp garlic powder

½ tsp dried basil
1 tsp red chili flakes
2 tbsp Pecorino cheese, grated

Directions

Preheat the air fryer to 360°F. Scoop out the insides of the zucchini halves with a spoon. Sprinkle the zucchini halves with salt and pepper and drizzle with avocado oil. In a bowl, combine ricotta cheese, mozzarella cheese, oregano, garlic powder, basil, and pepper flakes and stir well. Spread a thin layer of pasta sauce in the bottom of the zucchini halves and distribute the cheese mixture evenly on top. Place the boats in the fryer basket and Bake for 18-20 minutes until the cheese is golden. Top with Pecorino cheese to serve.

Green Beans Frittata with Parmesan

Total Time: 15 min | **Serves**: 2 | **Per serving**: Cal 287; Net Carbs 2g; Fat 23g; Protein 15g

Ingredients

1 cup green beans, chopped
4 eggs

1 tbsp Parmesan cheese
2 tbsp warm water

Salt and black pepper to taste

Directions

Preheat your Air Fryer to 320°F. Beat the eggs, cheese, water, salt, and pepper, in a bowl. Then blend them. Grease a pan with cooking spray. Pour the egg mixture into the fryer and add in the green beans. Cook for 5 minutes.

Herby Roast Vegetables

Total Time: 25 min | **Serves**: 4 | **Per serving**: Cal 120; Net Carbs 3.9g; Fat 7g; Protein 4.6g

Ingredients

1 parsnip, sliced
5 oz broccoli florets
5 oz Brussels sprouts, halved
5 oz cauliflower florets

1 shallot, sliced
½ green bell pepper, sliced
2 tbsp coconut oil
2 tsp cayenne pepper

1 tsp garlic powder
½ tsp cumin

Directions

Preheat the air fryer to 360°F. Combine all ingredients in a baking dish and toss to coat. Place the dish in the fryer basket. Bake for 15-18 minutes, shaking the basket once until golden and crisp. Serve warm.

Curry Mixed Veggie Bites

Total Time: 40 min + marinating time | **Serves**: 16 bites | **Per serving**: Cal 160; Net Carbs 2g; Fat 8g; Protein 3g

Ingredients

1 medium cauliflower, cut into florets
6 medium carrots, diced
1 medium broccoli, cut into florets
½ cup cauli rice, not steamed
1 onion, diced
½ cup garden peas

2 leeks, sliced thinly
1 small courgette, chopped
⅓ cup almond flour
1 tbsp garlic paste
2 tbsp olive oil
1 tbsp curry paste

2 tsp mixed spice
1 tsp coriander
1 tsp cumin powder
1 ½ cups coconut milk
1 tsp ginger paste
Salt and black pepper to taste

Directions

Steam all the vegetables except the leek and courgette for 10 minutes. Set aside. Place a wok over medium heat; add the onion, ginger, garlic and olive oil. Stir-fry until onions turn transparent. Add the leek, courgette and curry paste. Stir and cook for 5 minutes. Add all the listed spices, coconut milk, and cauli rice. Stir and simmer for 10 minutes. Once the sauce has reduced, add the steamed veggies. Mix evenly. Refrigerate for 1 hour.

Remove the veggie base from the fridge and mold it into bite-sized pieces. Arrange the veggie bites in the fryer basket and close the Air Fryer. Cook at 350°F for 10 minutes. Once they are ready, it is time to serve them. Serve with yogurt dipping sauce for the best taste.

Mini Mushroom Pizzas

Total Time: 20 min | **Serves**: 4 | **Per serving**: Cal 245; Net Carbs 4.2g; Fat 18.4g; Protein 10.6g

Ingredients

4 large portobello mushroom caps
Salt and black pepper to taste
3 tbsp butter, melted
1 tsp garlic powder

¼ tsp dried oregano
2 tsp Parmesan cheese, grated
1 cup mozzarella cheese, shredded
1 cup sundried tomatoes, sliced

2 tbsp basil, chopped
1 tbsp balsamic vinegar

Directions

Preheat the air fryer to 370°F. Place the mushroom caps in the air fryer basket. Brush them with butter and sprinkle with salt, pepper, oregano, and garlic powder. Divide the mozzarella cheese between the caps and top with sundried tomatoes. Finally, scatter the top with Parmesan cheese. Bake for 10-12 minutes until the cheese is golden. Sprinkle with basil and drizzle with balsamic vinegar. Serve warm.

Pine Nuts & Roasted Brussels Sprouts

Total Time: 20 min | **Serves**: 6 | **Per serving**: Cal 112; Net Carbs 5.4g; Fat 7.4g; Protein 7g

Ingredients

15 oz Brussels sprouts, halved
1 tbsp olive oil

Salt to taste
1 ¾ oz pine nuts, toasted

Directions

Preheat your Air Fryer to 390°F. In a large bowl, pop the sprouts with oil and salt and stir to combine well. Add the sprouts to the Air Fryer cooking basket and roast for 15 minutes; check often. Remove Brussel sprouts from the air fryer and mix with toasted pine nuts.

Bell Pepper & Broccoli Salad with Pine Nuts

Total Time: 20 min | **Serves:** 3 | **Per serving:** Cal 232; Net Carbs 6.2g; Fat 16g; Protein 10g

Ingredients

1 lb broccoli, cut into florets
2 yellow bell peppers, cut and cubed
¼ cup pine nuts, toasted

½ cup Parmesan cheese, grated
2 tbsp olive oil
2 tbsp Dijon mustard

2 cloves garlic, minced
2 tbsp lime juice
1 tbsp hot sauce

Directions

Preheat your Air Fryer to 390°F. Combine the broccoli and bell peppers with 1 tbsp of olive oil. Place in the fryer and cook for 10 minutes. Remove from the heat and add in the pine nuts and parmesan cheese. In another bowl, mix 1 tbsp of olive oil, mustard, garlic, lime juice, and hot sauce. Pour the sauce over the bell peppers and serve.

Brussel Sprout Salad

Total Time: 30 min | **Serves:** 3 | **Per serving:** Cal 145; Net Carbs 5.2g; Fat 10g; Protein 3g

Ingredients

1 pound Brussels sprouts, halved
2 tbsp olive oil

A pinch of red pepper flakes
2 small halved lemons

Directions

Preheat your Air Fryer to 390°F. Spray the Brussels Sprouts with olive oil. Season with salt and a pinch of red pepper flakes. Place the sprouts in the fryer and cook for 30 minutes. Turn once during cooking time. Drizzle lemon juice. Serve and enjoy!

Creamy Egg Salad with Spinach

Total Time: 7 min | **Serves:** 3 | **Per serving:** Cal 472; Net Carbs 4.2g; Fat 41g; Protein 17g;

Ingredients

1 cup baby spinach, chopped
6 cooked eggs
2 cups tomatoes, chopped

½ cup red onion, chopped
Salt and black pepper to taste
2 tbsp mayo

2 tbsp sour cream
1 tbsp lemon juice
6 drops Tabasco sauce

Directions

Preheat your Air Fryer to 340°F. Slice the cooked egg and place them in the fryer. Add in the tomatoes. red onion, salt, and pepper, and cook for 7 minutes. Once ready, remove to a bowl. Stir in the mayo, sour cream, lemon juice, and Tabasco sauce. Garnish with baby spinach and serve.

Fluffy Coconut Bread Balls

Total Time: 30 min + resting time | **Serves:** 4 | **Per serving:** Cal 396; Net Carbs 2.8g; Fat 36g; Protein 13g

Ingredients

8 oz coconut flour
1 oz liquid stevia

3 oz water
1 egg

2 tbsp ghee

Directions

Preheat your Air Fryer to 330°F. Mix the coconut flour, stevia, and water. Add in the ghee and knead until creating a dough. Keep warm and covered for 2 hours until it grows in size. Separate dough into 16 equal portions and shape into small balls. Add them to a baking paper. Brush the balls with egg and let rest for 30-40 more minutes. Transfer to a baking tray and insert in the air fryer. Bake for 12-14 minutes until brown and crispy. Serve.

Basil Tofu

Total Time: 30 min | **Serves:** 2 | **Per serving:** Cal 187; Net Carbs 4.3g; Fat 14.4g; Protein 10g

Ingredients

6 oz extra firm tofu
Black pepper to taste
1 tbsp vegetable broth

1 tbsp soy sauce, sugar-free
⅓ tsp dried oregano
⅓ tsp garlic powder

⅓ tsp dried basil
⅓ tsp onion powder

Directions

Place the tofu on a cutting board. Cut it into 3 lengthwise slices with a knife. Line a side of the cutting board with paper towels, place the tofu on it and cover with a paper towel. Use your hands to press the tofu gently until as much liquid has been extracted from it. Remove the paper towels and use a knife to chop the tofu into 8 cubes.

In another bowl, add the soy sauce, vegetable broth, oregano, basil, garlic powder, onion powder, and pepper. Mix well. Pour the spice mixture on the tofu, stir the tofu until well coated. Marinate for 10 minutes.

Preheat the Air Fryer to 390°F. Arrange the tofu in the fryer basket in a single layer. Cook the tofu for 6 minutes. Slide out the fryer basket and turn the tofu using a spatula. Slide it back in and continue cooking for 4 minutes. Remove onto a plate and serve with a side of green salad.

Mixed Vegetables with Sesame Dipping Sauce

Total Time: 20 min | **Serves:** 6 | **Per serving:** Cal 96; Net Carbs 5.6g; Fat 5.1g; Protein 3.1g

Ingredients

2 lb chopped mixed veggies
1 ½ cups almond flour

Salt and black pepper to taste
1 ½ tbsp chia seeds

¾ cup cold water

Dipping sauce:

4 tbsp soy sauce, sugar-free
Juice of 1 lemon

½ tsp sesame oil
½ tsp xylitol

½ garlic clove, chopped
½ tsp chili sauce

Directions

Line the air fryer basket with baking paper. In a bowl, mix almond flour, salt, pepper, and chia seeds and whisk to combine. Keep whisking as you add water into the dry ingredients until a smooth batter is formed. Dip each veggie piece into the batter and place into your air fryer. Cook for 12 minutes at 360°F, turning once halfway through cooking. For the dipping sauce, mix all ingredients in a bowl.

Double Cheese Vegetable Frittata

Total Time: 35 min | **Serves:** 2 | **Per serving:** Cal 380; Net Carbs 8.4g; Fat 28.3g; Protein 24g

Ingredients

1 cup baby spinach
⅓ cup mushrooms, sliced
1 large zucchini, sliced
1 small red onion, sliced

¼ cup chives, chopped
¼ lb asparagus, trimmed and sliced
2 tsp olive oil
4 eggs, cracked into a bowl

⅓ cup almond milk
Salt and black pepper to taste
⅓ cup cheddar cheese, grated
⅓ cup feta cheese, crumbled

Directions

Preheat the Air Fryer to 320°F. Line a baking dish with parchment paper. Set aside. In the egg bowl, add the almond milk, salt, and pepper. Beat evenly. Heat olive oil in a skillet over medium heat. Add the asparagus, zucchini, onion, mushrooms, and baby spinach. Sauté for 5 minutes while stirring. Pour the sautéed veggies into the baking dish and pour the egg mixture over. Sprinkle feta and cheddar over it and place it in the fryer basket. Bake for 15 minutes. Once ready, remove the baking dish and garnish with the fresh chives. Serve and enjoy!

Mushroom Melts

Total Time: 25 min | **Serves:** 2 | **Per serving:** Cal 243; Net Carbs 2g; Fat 16g; Protein 13g

Ingredients

1 tbsp olive oil	Salt and black pepper	½ tomato
1 tsp balsamic vinegar	3 flaxseed tortillas	2 oz mozzarella cheese
1 oz mushrooms, sliced	2 oz cream cheese	
¼ large red onion, sliced	2 tbsp pesto sauce	

Directions

Preheat the Air Fryer to 390°F. Mix olive oil and balsamic vinegar. Add the mushrooms and the onion. Season with salt and black pepper. Cook for 5 minutes. Remove from the Fryer, then lower the temperature to 330°F. Brush each side of the tortillas with olive oil. Top the tortillas with cream cheese, mushrooms and onions. Spread the pesto on the tortillas and press against the mushrooms. Top with tomato, cheese and cook for 7 minutes.

Lemon-Flavored Cupcakes

Total Time: 25 min | **Serves:** 5 | **Per serving:** Cal 412; Net Carbs 2g; Fat 25g; Protein 4.6g

Ingredients

Lemon frosting:

1 cup unsweetened natural yogurt	1 lemon, juiced	7 oz cream cheese
Swerve sweetener to taste	1 tbsp lemon zest	

Cupcakes:

2 lemons, quartered	2 tbsp swerve sweetener	2 eggs
½ cup almond flour + extra for basing	1 tsp baking powder	½ cup butter, softened
¼ tsp salt	1 tsp vanilla extract	2 tbsp coconut milk

Directions

Start with the frosting: in a bowl, add the yogurt and cream cheese. Mix using a fork until smooth. Add the lemon juice and zest. Mix well. Gradually add the sweetener to your taste while stirring until smooth. Make sure the frost is not runny. Set aside. Place the lemon quarters in a food processor and process it until pureed. Add almond flour, baking powder, butter, coconut milk, eggs, vanilla, swerve sweetener, and salt. Process again until smooth.

Preheat the Air Fryer to 400°F. Flour the bottom of 10 cupcake cases and spoon the batter into the cases ¾ way up. Place in the Air Fryer and bake them for 7 minutes. Once ready, remove them and let them cool. Design the cupcakes with the frosting.

Onion Beet with Goat cheese

Total Time: 50 min | **Serves:** 4 | **Per serving:** Cal 225; Net Carbs 6.2g; Fat 16g; Protein 7g

Ingredients

¾ cup goat cheese, crumbled	3 tbsp red wine vinegar	½ tbsp liquid stevia
4 large beets, stems trimmed	¼ cup onion, minced	1 tbsp fresh parsley, minced
2 tbsp olive oil	2 cloves garlic, minced	½ tbsp fresh thyme leaves, minced
Salt and pepper to taste	1 ½ tbsp Dijon mustard	2 cups mixed baby lettuces

Directions

Preheat your Air Fryer to 390°F. Lay the beets on aluminum foil and spray with oil. Season with salt and pepper. Close the foil and transfer to the fryer. Cook for 45 minutes. Remove it and allow to cool. Whisk the onion, garlic, mustard, vinegar, and stevia in a bowl. Stir in the herbs and season with salt and pepper. Cut the beets by half. Transfer to a plate and top with goat cheese. Spray the dressing and garnish with baby lettuce.

Sunday Cooked Tomato Nest

Total Time: 20 min | **Serves:** 2 | **Per serving:** Cal 302; Net Carbs 4.2g; Fat 16g; Protein 30g

Ingredients

2 tomatoes

4 eggs

1 cup mozzarella cheese, shredded

2-3 basil leaves

1 tbsp olive oil

Salt and black pepper to taste

Directions

Preheat the Air Fryer to 360°F. Cut each tomato into two halves and place them in a bowl. Season with salt and pepper. Place cheese around the bottom of the tomatoes and add basil leaves. Break one egg in each tomato slice. Top with cheese and drizzle with olive oil. Set the temperature to 360°F and cook for 20 minutes.

Homemade Assorted Chips

Total Time: 20 min | **Serves:** 4 | **Per serving:** Cal 120; Net Carbs 6g; Fat 3.5g; Protein 3g

Ingredients

1 large eggplant

5 medium parsnips

3 medium zucchinis

½ cup arrowroot starch

½ cup water

½ cup olive oil

Salt and black pepper to taste

Directions

Preheat the Air Fryer to 390°F. Cut the eggplant and zucchinis into long 3-inch strips. Peel the parsnips and cut them into 3-inch strips. In a bowl, add the arrowroot starch, water, salt, pepper, olive oil, eggplants, zucchini, and parsnips and stir well. Place one-third of the veggie strips in the fryer basket and cook them for 12 minutes. Once ready, transfer them to a serving platter. Serve warm as a side to a meat dish or with spicy or sweet sauce.

Homemade Broccoli with Cheese

Total Time: 20 min | **Serves:** 3 | **Per serving:** Cal 432; Net Carbs 3.2g; Fat 37g; Protein 24g

Ingredients

1 head broccoli

1 egg

1 cup cream cheese

A pinch of nutmeg

1 tbsp ginger powder

1 cup cheddar cheese, shredded

Salt and black pepper to taste

Directions

Cook the broccoli on steam for around 4 minutes. Drain the broccoli and combine with one egg and the cream cheese. Add the nutmeg, ginger, salt, and pepper. Butter several small ramekins and spread the mixture. Sprinkle cheese on top. Set the timer to 20 minutes and cook at 220°F. Serve and enjoy!

Tasty Rosemary Squash

Total Time: 30 min | **Serves:** 2 | **Per serving:** Cal 68; Net Carbs 4.6g; Fat 0.2g; Protein 2.3g

Ingredients

1 butternut squash

1 tbsp dried rosemary

Salt to taste

Directions

Place the butternut squash on a cutting board and peel it. Cut it in half and remove the seeds. Cut the pulp into wedges and season with salt. Preheat the Air Fryer to 350°F. Spray the squash wedges with cooking spray and sprinkle the rosemary on it. Grease the fryer basket with cooking spray and place the wedges in it without overlapping. Slide the fryer basket back in and cook for 10 minutes. Flip the wedges and cook for 10 minutes.

Persian Garlic Mushrooms

Total Time: 20 min | **Serves:** 4 | **Per serving:** Cal 240; Net Carbs 7.2g; Fat 19g; Protein 10g

Ingredients

6 portobello mushrooms
3 oz butter, softened

2 shallots, sliced
2 cloves garlic, sliced

1 tbsp fresh parsley, chopped
1 cup Parmesan cheese, grated

Directions

Preheat the Air Fryer to 390°F. Clean the mushrooms and remove the stems. Place the mushroom stems, garlic, shallots, parsley, and softened butter in a blender. Arrange the caps of the mushrooms in the basket of the Air Fryer. Stuff the caps with the mixture and sprinkle with Parmesan cheese. Set the timer to 20 minutes.

Zucchini & Turnip Bake

Total Time: 30 min | **Serves:** 3 | **Per serving:** Cal 55; Net Carbs 2.4g; Fat 4.9g; Protein 1g

Ingredients

3 turnips, sliced
1 large red onion, cut into rings
1 large zucchini, sliced

Salt and black pepper to taste
2 cloves garlic, crushed
1 bay leaf, cut into 6 pieces

1 tbsp olive oil

Directions

Place the turnips, onion, and zucchini in a bowl. Toss with olive oil and season with salt and pepper.

Preheat the Air Fryer to 330°F. Place the veggies into a baking pan that fits in the Air Fryer. Slip the bay leaves in the different parts of the slices and tuck the garlic cloves in between the slices. Insert the pan in the Air Fryer basket and cook for 15 minutes. Once ready, remove and serve warm with as a side to a meat dish or salad.

Parsley & Cheese Stuffed Mushrooms

Total Time: 15 min | **Serves:** 4 | **Per serving:** Cal 117; Net Carbs 0.9g; Fat 11g; Protein 2.7g

Ingredients

14 small button mushrooms
1 clove garlic, minced

Salt and black pepper to taste
¼ cup cheddar cheese, grated

1 tbsp olive oil
1 tbsp parsley, chopped

Directions

Preheat the Air Fryer to 390°F. In a bowl, add the olive oil, cheddar cheese, parsley, salt, pepper, and garlic. Mix well using a spoon. Cut the stalks of the mushroom off and fill each cup with the cheese mixture. Press the cheese mixture into the caps to avoid any falling off. Place the stuffed mushrooms in the fryer basket, close the Air Fryer and cook at 390°F for 8 minutes. Once golden and crispy, remove them onto a serving platter. Serve.

Veggie Spring Rolls

Total Time: 30 min | **Serves:** 8 | **Per serving:** Cal 88; Net Carbs 7.2g; Fat 3.1g; Protein 2g

Ingredients

7 oz cooked shirataki fettuccini noodles
8 grape leaves
2 garlic cloves, chopped
1 tbsp fresh ginger, minced

2 tbsp soy sauce, sugar-free
1 tsp sesame oil
1 red bell pepper, chopped

1 cup mushrooms, chopped
1 cup carrots, chopped
½ cup scallions, chopped

Directions

In a saucepan, add garlic, ginger, soy sauce, sesame oil, pepper, mushrooms, carrots, and scallions and stir-fry over high heat for 5 minutes until soft. Add in shirataki fettuccini noodles and remove from the heat. Place the grape leaves onto a working board. Spoon dollop of veggie and noodle mixture at the center of each grape leaf.

Roll the spring rolls and tuck the corners and edges in to create neat and secure rolls. Spray with cooking spray and transfer to the air fryer. Cook for 12 minutes at 340°F, turning once halfway through cooking. Cook until golden and crispy. Serve with chili sauce.

Bell Peppers Filled with Cauli Rice and Cheese

Total Time: 40 min | **Serves**: 4 | **Per serving**: Cal 215; Net Carbs 5.4g; Fat 16g; Protein 13g

Ingredients

4 bell peppers
Salt and black pepper to taste
½ cup olive oil
1 red onion, chopped

1 large tomato, chopped
½ cup goat cheese, crumbled
3 cups cauli rice
2 tbsp Parmesan cheese, grated

2 tbsp fresh basil, chopped
1 tbsp lemon zest

Directions

Preheat the Air Fryer to 350°F. Cut the peppers a quarter way from the head down and lengthwise. Remove the membrane and seeds. Season the peppers with black pepper and salt, and drizzle olive oil over. Place the pepper bottoms in the fryer basket and cook them for 5 minutes at 350°F to soften a little. In a mixing bowl, add the tomatoes, onion, goat cheese, lemon zest, basil, and cauli rice. Season with salt and pepper. Mix well.

Remove the Pepper bottoms from the Air Fryer onto a flat surface and spoon the cheese mixture into them. Sprinkle parmesan cheese on top of each and gently place in the fryer basket. Bake for 15 minutes. Remove once ready onto a serving platter.

Roasted Pumpkin with Walnuts

Total Time: 30 min | **Serves**: 2 | **Per serving**: Cal 68; Net Carbs 4.6g; Fat 0.2g; Protein 2.3g

Ingredients

1 pumpkin, chopped
1 tbsp dried rosemary

Salt to taste
2 tbsp walnuts, chopped

Directions

Preheat your Air Fryer to 350°F. Sprinkle pumpkin with salt. Grease with cooking spray and garnish with rosemary. Spray the fryer basket with cooking spray. Place the pumpkin in the fryer and cook for 10 minutes. Do not overlap. Turn and cook for 10 more minutes. Serve warm sprinkled with walnuts.

Fall Veggie Roast

Total Time: 30 min | **Serves**: 4 | **Per serving**: Cal 77; Net Carbs 3g; Fat 3g; Protein 2g

Ingredients

1 small turnip, sliced
1 cup butternut squash, chopped
1 onion, cut into wedges

½ celeriac, sliced
1 tbsp fresh thyme, chopped
Salt and black pepper to taste

2 tsp olive oil

Directions

Preheat your Air Fryer to 200°F. Combine the turnip, butternut squash, onions, celeriac, thyme, pepper, salt, and olive oil in a bowl. Place the veggies in the fryer basket and cook for 16 minutes, shaking once.

Mediterranean Sandwiches with Pesto

Total Time: 60 min | **Serves**: 2 | **Per serving**: Cal 541; Net Carbs 8.3g; Fat 49g; Protein 16.2g

Ingredients

1 heirloom tomato, sliced
1 (4-oz) block feta cheese, sliced
1 small red onion, thinly sliced

1 clove garlic
Salt to taste
2 tsp + ¼ cup olive oil

1 ½ tbsp pine nuts, toasted
¼ cup basil, chopped

Directions

Start with the pesto: Add the basil, pine nuts, garlic, and salt to the food processor. Process it while adding the ¼ cup of olive oil slowly. Pour the basil pesto into a bowl and refrigerate it for 30 minutes.

Preheat the Air Fryer to 390°F. Remove the pesto from the fridge and use a tablespoon to spread some pesto on each slice of tomato. Top with a slice of feta cheese. Add the onion and remaining olive oil to a bowl and toss. Spoon on top of the feta cheese on the tomato. Carefully place the tomato in the fryer basket, close the air fryer, and bake it for 12 minutes. Remove the tomatoes to a plate, sprinkle with salt and top with any remaining pesto.

Nutty Broccoli

Total Time: 35 min | **Serves**: 4 | **Per serving**: Cal 140; Net Carbs 1g; Fat 7g; Protein 5g

Ingredients

1 large broccoli head, cut into florets
Salt to taste

1 ½ tbsp curry powder
½ cup olive oil

⅓ cup pine nuts, toasted

Directions

Preheat Air Fryer to 390°F. In a bowl, mix 1 tbsp of olive oil with pine nuts. Place in the fryer basket and cook for 2 minutes. Let cool. In a second bowl, put the broccoli. Stir in the curry powder, salt, and remaining olive oil. Place half of the broccoli in the fryer basket and cook for 10 minutes. Transfer to a plate. Repeat the process with the remaining florets. Add in the pine nuts and toss to combine. Serve.

Sage Parsnip & Cheese Bake

Total Time: 30 min | **Serves**: 8 | **Per serving**: Cal 131; Net Carbs 5.6g; Fat 8.3g; Protein 6.7g

Ingredients

3 tbsp pine nuts
28 oz parsnips, chopped
1 ¾ oz Parmesan cheese, shredded

6 ¾ oz crème fraiche
1 slice zero-carbs bread
2 tbsp dried sage

4 tbsp butter
4 tsp mustard
Salt and pepper to taste

Directions

Preheat your Air Fryer to 360°F. Boil parsnips in salted water in a pot over medium heat. Drain and mash them with butter using a potato masher. In a mixing bowl, mix mustard, crème fraiche, sage, salt and pepper. Add parsnip mash, zero-carb bread, cheese, and nuts and mix. Cook in your Air Fryer for 5 minutes.

Quick Fall Vegetable Delight

Total Time: 30 min | **Serves**: 3 | **Per serving**: Cal 77; Net Carbs 3g; Fat 3g; Protein 2g

Ingredients

1 small parsnip, sliced into a 2-inch thickness
1 cup butternut squash, chopped
2 small red onions, cut into wedges
1 cup celery, chopped

1 tbsp fresh thyme, chopped
Salt and black pepper to taste
2 tsp olive oil

Directions

Preheat the Air Fryer to 200 F. In a bowl, add the parsnips, butternut squash, red onions, celery, thyme, pepper, salt, and olive oil and mix well. Pour the vegetables into the fryer basket, close the Air Fryer, and cook for 16 minutes. Transfer the roasted veggies into a serving bowl.

Cauliflower Florets with Pine Nuts

Total Time: 35 min | **Serves:** 4 | **Per serving:** Cal 140; Net Carbs 1g; Fat 7g; Protein 5g

Ingredients

1 cauliflower head, cut into florets
Salt to taste

1 ½ tbsp curry powder
½ cup olive oil

⅓ cup pine nuts, toasted

Directions

Preheat the Air Fryer to 390°F. Add the pine nuts and 1 teaspoon of olive oil to a medium bowl. Mix with the tablespoon. Pour them into the fryer basket and cook them for 2 minutes. Remove them into a bowl to cool. Place the cauliflower in a large mixing bowl. Add the curry powder, salt, and the remaining olive oil and mix well.

Transfer to the fryer basket in 2 batches and cook each batch for 10 minutes. Remove the florets onto a serving platter, sprinkle with the pine nuts, and toss. Serve with tomato sauce.

Keto Sushi with Cauli Rice

Total Time: 30 min | **Serves:** 4 | **Per serving:** Cal 178; Net Carbs 5.8g; Fat 15g; Protein 2.4g

Ingredients

2 cups cauli rice
4 nori sheets
1 carrot, sliced lengthways
1 red bell pepper, seeds removed,

sliced
1 avocado, sliced
1 tbsp olive oil
1 tbsp wine vinegar

1 cup almonds, crushed
2 tbsp sesame seeds
Wasabi and pickled ginger to serve

Directions

Prepare a clean working board, a small bowl of lukewarm water and a sushi mat. Wet hands, and lay a nori sheet onto a sushi mat and spread half cup cauli rice, leaving a half-inch of nori clear so that you can seal the roll. Place the carrot, bell pepper, and avocado sideways to the cauli rice. Roll the sushi tightly and rub warm water along the clean nori strip to seal them. In a bowl, mix olive oil and vinegar.

In another bowl, mix the crushed almonds with the sesame seeds. Roll each sushi log in the vinegar mixture and then straight to the sesame bowl to coat. Arrange the coated sushi into the air fryer and cook for 14 minutes at 360°F, turning once halfway through cooking. When ready, slice and serve with pickled ginger and wasabi.

Balsamic-Glazed Beets

Total Time: 20 min | **Serves:** 2 | **Per serving:** Cal 75; Net Carbs 7.5g; Fat 4.1g; Protein 3.6g

Ingredients

4 beets, cubed
⅓ cup balsamic vinegar

1 tbsp olive oil
4 drops liquid stevia

Salt and black pepper to taste
2 sprigs rosemary, chopped

Directions

In a mixing bowl, mix rosemary, pepper, salt, vinegar and stevia. Cover beets with the prepared sauce and then coat with oil. Preheat your Air Fryer to 400°F. Place the beets in the Air Fryer cooking basket and cook for 10 minutes. Pour the balsamic vinegar into a pan over medium heat; bring it to a boil and cook until reduced by half. Drizzle the beets with balsamic glaze to serve.

Vegetables with Halloumi Cheese

Total Time: 15 min | **Serves:** 2 | **Per serving:** Cal 420; Net Carbs 8.2g; Fat 26g; Protein 22g

Ingredients

6 oz firm halloumi cheese, cubed

2 zucchinis, cut into even chunks

1 large carrot, cut into chunks

1 eggplant, peeled, cut into chunks

2 tsp olive oil

1 tsp dried mixed herbs

Directions

In a bowl, add halloumi, zucchini, carrot, eggplant, olive oil, and herbs. Arrange halloumi and veggies on the air fryer basket and cook for 14 minutes at 340°F. When ready, make sure the veggies are tender and the halloumi is golden. Sprinkle with olive oil and scatter with fresh arugula.

Thai Mixed Veggie Croquettes

Total Time: 40 min + chilling time | **Serves:** 5 | **Per serving:** Cal 160; Net Carbs 2g; Fat 8g; Protein 3g

Ingredients

½ cup okra, cut into 2-inch pieces

2 carrots, diced

1 head broccoli, cut into florets

½ cup cauli rice

2 leeks, sliced thinly

1 small courgette, chopped

1 tbsp Thai curry paste

2 tsp mixed spice

1 ½ cups coconut milk

1 tsp ginger paste

Salt and black pepper to taste

Directions

Place all the vegetables except the leek and courgette in a pot and steam for 10 minutes. Set aside. In a wok over medium heat, put in the ginger paste and stir-fry. Stir in the leek, courgette, and curry paste and cook for 5 minutes. Put in all the spices, coconut milk, and cauli rice. Cook for 10 minutes until the liquid has reduced. Place in the steamed veggies and stir. Mold the mixture into croquette shapes. Place them in the fridge for 1 hour.

Preheat your Air Fryer to 350°F. Remove the croquettes from the fridge and place them in the fryer basket. AirFry for 10-14 minutes. Turn over halfway through the cooking time. Serve with yogurt dipping sauce if desired.

Cilantro Roasted Eggplants

Total Time: 15 min | **Serves:** 6 | **Per serving:** Cal 95; Net Carbs 8.7 g; Fat 5.3g; Protein 2g

Ingredients

20 oz eggplants, sliced

1 tbsp olive oil

1 tsp cumin seeds

A handful of fresh cilantro

Directions

Preheat your Fryer to 350°F. In a bowl, mix oil, eggplants, and cumin. Stir to coat the eggplants well. Place the eggplants in your Air Fryer's cooking basket and cook for 12 minutes. Scatter cilantro over the eggplants. Serve.

Veggie Mix with Hot Sauce

Total Time: 20 min | **Serves:** 8 | **Per serving:** Cal 96; Net Carbs 5.6g; Fat 5.1g; Protein 3.1g

Ingredients

1 ½ cups almond flour

2 lb chopped mixed veggies

Salt and black pepper to taste

1 ½ tbsp flax seeds

¾ cup cold water

Sauce:

4 tbsp soy sauce, sugar-free

Juice of 1 lemon

½ tsp extra virgin olive oil

½ garlic clove, chopped

½ tsp hot sauce

Directions

Preheat your Air Fryer to 360°F. Line the fryer basket with baking paper. In a bowl, whisk the almond flour, salt, pepper, and flax seeds. Add in water and mix until smooth. Dip each veggie piece into the batter and transfer into the fryer basket. Cook for 12 minutes until crispy. Flip once during the cooking time. Whisk soy sauce, lemon juice, olive oil, garlic, and hot sauce in a bowl. Serve veggies with the sauce.

Balsamic Parsnips & Zucchini

Total Time: 30 min | **Serves:** 6 | **Per serving:** Cal 143; Net Carbs 6.5g; Fat 5g; Protein 2g

Ingredients

2 lb sliced veggies: parsnips and zucchini
3 tbsp olive oil
1 tbsp balsamic vinegar
1 tbsp stevia
2 garlic cloves, minced
Salt and black pepper to taste

Directions

In a bowl, add oil, balsamic vinegar, stevia, garlic, salt and black pepper. Mix well with a fork. Arrange the veggies into the fryer, drizzle with the dressing and massage with hands until well-coated. Cook for 25 minutes at 360°F, tossing halfway through cooking.

Tandoori Crispy Tofu

Total Time: 30 min | **Serves:** 2 | **Per serving:** Cal 187; Net Carbs 4.3g; Fat 14.4g; Protein 10g

Ingredients

⅓ tsp tandoori spice
1 tbsp vegetable broth
6 oz extra firm tofu
Black pepper to taste
1 tbsp soy sauce, sugar-free
⅓ tsp garlic powder
⅓ tsp onion powder

Directions

Line a chopping board with paper towels, align the tofu and cover with it. Pat dry to remove any liquid. Discard the paper towels and slice into 8 cubes. Transfer to a bowl. In another bowl, mix the soy sauce, vegetable broth, tandoori spice, garlic powder, onion powder, and black pepper. Pour the mixture over the tofu and stir to coat.

Marinate for 10 minutes. Preheat your Air Fryer to 390°F. Place the tofu in the fryer basket and cook for 6 minutes. Flip them and cook for another 4 minutes. Serve with a fresh salad if desired.

Cheesy Mushroom & Spinach Frittata

Total Time: 35 min | **Serves:** 2 | **Per serving:** Cal 380; Net Carbs 8.4g; Fat 28.3g; Protein 24g

Ingredients

⅓ cup ricotta cheese, crumbled
1 cup baby spinach, chopped
⅓ cup mushrooms, sliced
¼ cup chives, chopped
2 tsp olive oil
4 eggs, beaten
⅓ cup almond milk
Salt and black pepper to taste

Directions

Preheat your Air Fryer to 320°F. Line a baking dish with parchment paper. Set aside. In a bowl, beat the eggs with almond milk, salt, and pepper. Warm the olive oil in a skillet over medium heat and sauté the mushrooms and baby spinach for 5 minutes. Transfer the veggies into the baking dish and pour the egg mix over it. Top with ricotta cheese. Place the dish in the fryer basket and bake for 15 minutes. Scatter with fresh chives and serve.

Roasted Broccoli with Pine Nuts

Total Time: 20 min | **Serves:** 6 | **Per serving:** Cal 112; Net Carbs 5.4g; Fat 7.4g; Protein 7g

Ingredients

15 oz broccoli florets
1 tbsp olive oil

Salt to taste
1 ¾ oz pine nuts, toasted

Directions

Preheat your Air Fryer to 390°F. In a bowl, stir the broccoli with oil and salt. Place the broccoli in the fryer basket and roast for 15 minutes. Transfer the florets to a serving bowl and stir in the pine nuts.

Cypriot Veggie & Cheese

Total Time: 15 min | **Serves:** 2 | **Per serving:** Cal 420; Net Carbs 8.2g; Fat 26g; Protein 22g

Ingredients

1 head broccoli, cut into florets
6 oz halloumi cheese, cubed
1 large carrot, cut into chunks

1 eggplant, peeled, cut into chunks
2 tsp olive oil
1 tsp dried dill

Salt and black pepper to taste

Directions

Preheat your Air Fryer to 340°F. In a bowl, combine the halloumi, broccoli, carrot, eggplant, olive oil, dill, salt, and pepper. Place halloumi and veggies in the fryer basket and cook for 14 minutes until the veggies are tender and the halloumi is golden. Drizzle with olive oil and garnish with arugula to serve.

Cheese & Cauli Rice Stuffed Bell Peppers

Total Time: 40 min | **Serves:** 4 | **Per serving:** Cal 215; Net Carbs 5.4g; Fat 16g; Protein 13g

Ingredients

½ cup feta, crumbled
4 bell peppers
Salt and black pepper to taste

½ cup olive oil
1 onion, chopped
1 large tomato, chopped

3 cups cauli rice
2 tbsp fresh basil, chopped
1 tbsp lemon zest

Directions

Preheat your Air Fryer to 350°F. Slice the bell peppers by the half and deseeded. Sprinkle with salt, pepper, and oil. Place in the fryer basket and cook for 5 minutes until softened. In a bowl, mix the onion, tomatoes, feta cheese, lemon zest, basil, and cauli rice. Season with salt and pepper. Transfer the pepper onto a flat surface and stuff with the cheese mixture. Place again in the fryer and bake for 15 minutes.

Eggplant & Zucchini Casserole

Total Time: 30 min | **Serves:** 4 | **Per serving:** Cal 55; Net Carbs 2.4g; Fat 4.9g; Protein 1g

Ingredients

3 eggplants, sliced
1 onion, cut into rings
1 large zucchini, sliced

Salt and black pepper to taste
2 cloves garlic, crushed
1 tbsp olive oil

2 tbsp parsley, chopped

Directions

Preheat your Air Fryer to 330°F. In a bowl, add the eggplants, onion, and zucchini. Pour in the olive oil and toss. Sprinkle with salt and pepper. Transfer the mixture into a baking pan. Scatter with the parsley and garlic cloves between the slices. Place the pan in the fryer and bake for 15 minutes. When done, remove the pan and serve.

White Cabbage with Garlic Mayo

Total Time: 25 min | **Serves:** 4 | **Per serving:** Cal 52; Net Carbs 2.1g; Fat 2.6g; Protein 5.1g

Ingredients

1 small head white cabbage, shredded
Salt and black pepper to taste
1 ½ tbsp olive oil

2 tsp lemon juice
1 tsp powdered chili
3 cloves garlic

¾ cup mayonnaise

Directions

In a skillet over medium heat, place the unpeeled garlic and roast until browned. Preheat your Air Fryer to 350°F. Transfer the garlic to a plate and peel it, then crush it. Set aside. Warm the olive oil in the skillet over medium heat and sauté the cabbage. Season with salt and pepper. Turn the heat off.

Place the cabbage in the fryer basket and cook for 5 minutes. In the meantime, for the garlic aioli, combine the mayonnaise, crushed garlic, lemon juice, powdered chili, pepper, and salt in a bowl. Remove the cabbage to a serving bowl. Serve with the garlic aioli.

Homemade Root Strips

Total Time: 25 min | **Serves:** 4 | **Per serving:** Cal 120; Net Carbs 6g; Fat 3.5g; Protein 3g

Ingredients

1 rutabaga
2 parsnips
1 golden beet

½ cup arrowroot starch
½ cup water
½ cup olive oil

Salt and black pepper to taste

Directions

Preheat your Air Fryer to 390°F. Peel the parsnips and arrange on a chopping board, place the rutabaga and golden beet. Slice all the veggies into 3-inch strips. Set aside.

Combine the arrowroot starch, water, salt, pepper, olive oil, rutabaga, golden beet, and parsnips in a bowl. Place 1/3 of the veggie strips in the fryer basket and cook for 12 minutes. When done, transfer to a plate. Repeat the process with the remaining strips. Serve hot as a side dish or with spicy or sweet sauce.

Baked Parsnips with Chia Seeds

Total Time: 30 min | **Serves:** 8 | **Per serving:** Cal 131; Net Carbs 5.6g; Fat 8.3g; Protein 6.7g

Ingredients

1 ¾ oz Grana Padano cheese, shredded
6 ¾ oz heavy cream
1 tbsp chia seeds
3 tbsp pine nuts

28 oz parsnips, chopped
2 tbsp dried sage
4 tbsp butter

4 tsp mustard
Salt and black pepper to taste

Directions

Preheat your Air Fryer to 360°F. Pour water with salt in a pot over medium heat and bring to a boil. Add in the parsnips and cook for 20 minutes. Drain and mash them with butter.

In a bowl, combine the mustard, heavy cream, sage, salt, and pepper. Put in the parsnip mash, chia seeds, cheese, and pine nuts. Place the mixture in the fryer basket and cook for 5 minutes.

DESSERTS

Chocolate Topped Meringue Cookies

Total Time: 45 min | **Serves**: 4 | **Per serving**: Cal 45; Net Carbs 6.4g; Fat 0.5g; Protein 7.6g

Ingredients

8 egg whites
½ tsp almond extract
1 ⅓ cup granulated stevia

¼ tsp salt
2 tsp lemon juice
1 ½ tsp vanilla extract

Melted dark chocolate to drizzle

Directions

In a mixing bowl, add the egg whites, salt, and lemon juice. Beat using an electric mixer until foamy. Slowly add the stevia and continue beating until thoroughly combined. Add the almond and vanilla extracts. Beat until stiff peaks form and are glossy. Line a round baking sheet with parchment paper.

Fill a piping bag with the meringue mixture and pipe as many mounds on the baking sheet as you can, leaving 2-inch spaces between each mound. Place the baking sheet in the fryer basket and bake at 350°F for 5 minutes.

Reduce the temperature to 320°F and bake for 15 more minutes. Then, reduce the heat once more to 290 F and cook for 15 minutes. Remove the baking sheet and let the meringues cool for about 2 hours. Drizzle with the dark chocolate before serving.

Dark Chocolate and Peanut Butter Fondants

Total Time: 25 min | **Serves**: 4 | **Per serving**: Cal 316; Net Carbs 8.1g; Fat 22g; Protein 9.5g

Ingredients

¾ cup dark chocolate
½ cup Peanut butter, crunchy
2 tbsp butter, diced

¼ cup + ¼ cup swerve sugar
4 eggs, room temperature
1/8 cup almond flour, sieved

1 tsp salt
¼ cup water

Directions

Make a salted praline to top the chocolate fondant. Add ¼ cup of sugar, 1 tsp of salt and the water into a saucepan over low heat. Stir and bring it to a boil. Simmer until the desired color is achieved and reduced. Pour into a baking tray and leave it to cool and harden, then roughly chop.

Preheat the Air Fryer to 300°F. Place a pot of water over medium heat and place a heatproof bowl over it. Add the chocolate, butter, and peanut butter to the bowl. Stir continuously until fully melted, combined, and smooth.

Remove the bowl from the heat and allow it to cool slightly. Add the eggs to the chocolate and whisk it. Add the flour and remaining swerve and mix well. Grease 4 small loaf pans with cooking spray and divide the chocolate mixture between them. Place the pans in the fryer basket and bake for 7 minutes. Serve topped with praline.

Raspberry & Chocolate Cake

Total Time: 40 min | **Serves**: 8 | **Per serving**: Cal 317; Net Carbs 9.2g; Fat 24g; Protein 6g

Ingredients

1 cup dark chocolate chips, unsweetened
1 ½ cups almond flour
⅓ cup cocoa powder
2 tsp baking powder
¼ cup stevia

¾ cup butter
2 tsp vanilla extract
1 cup almond milk
1 tsp baking soda

2 eggs
1 cup freeze-dried raspberries

Directions

Line a cake tin with baking powder. In a bowl, mix almond flour, cocoa, and baking powder. Place the stevia, butter, vanilla, almond milk, and baking soda into a microwave-safe bowl and microwave them for 60 seconds. Let cool slightly. Whisk the eggs into the mixture. Pour the wet ingredients into the dry ones, and fold to combine. Add in the raspberries and chocolate chips. Pour the batter into the tin and cook for 30 minutes at 350°F.

Vanilla Chocolate Souffle

Total Time: 40 min | **Serves**: 2 | **Per serving**: Cal 320; Net Carbs 3.1g; Fat 25g; Protein 11g

Ingredients

¼ cup erythritol + more for garnishing

3 oz unsweetened chocolate	1 tbsp butter, melted	1 ½ tbsp almond flour
4 large egg whites	1 tbsp butter, unmelted	
2 large egg yolks	¼ tsp vanilla extract	

Directions

Coat 2 6-oz ramekins with melted butter. Add the erythritol and swirl it in the ramekins to coat the butter. Pour out the remaining sugar and keep it. Melt the unmelted butter with the chocolate in a microwave and set aside.

In another bowl, beat the egg yolks vigorously. Add the vanilla and kept erythritol. Beat to incorporate fully. Add the chocolate mixture and mix well. Add the almond flour and mix it with no lumps.

Preheat the Air Fryer to 330°F. Whisk egg whites in another bowl until it holds stiff peaks. Add ⅓ of the egg whites to the chocolate mixture and fold in gently. Share the mixture into the ramekins with ½ inch space left at the top. Place the ramekins in the fryer basket and cook for 14 minutes. Dust with the remaining erythritol.

Easy Lemon Curd

Total Time: 32 min | **Serves**: 2 | **Per serving**: Cal 260; Net Carbs 1g; Fat 16g; Protein 12g

Ingredients

3 tbsp butter	1 egg	¾ lemon, juiced
3 tbsp swerve sugar	1 egg yolk	

Directions

Add the sugar and butter in a medium ramekin and use a hand mixer to beat evenly. Add the egg and yolk slowly while still whisking. Add the lemon juice and mix it. Place the bowl in the fryer basket and start cooking at 170°F for 3 minutes. Increase the temperature to 190 F and cook for 3 minutes.

Increase the heat again to 210°F and cook for 6 minutes, then 230°F for 6 minutes, and finally to 250°F for 6 minutes. Remove the bowl onto a flat surface. Use a spoon to check for any lumps and remove them . Cover the ramekin with plastic wrap and refrigerate it overnight or serve immediately.

Pecan Baked Apples

Total Time: 35 min | **Serves**: 2 | **Per serving**: Cal 283; Net Carbs 10.2g; Fat 20.5g; Protein 4g

Ingredients

3 tbsp crushed pecans	2 tbsp butter, cold	1 tsp cinnamon
2 Granny Smith apples, cored	3 tbsp xylitol	

Directions

In a bowl, combine the butter, xylitol, pecans, and cinnamon. Mix until obtaining a crumble. Place the apples in the fryer basket and pour the pecan mixture over it. Cook for 30 minutes.

Air Fryer Crème Brulee

Total Time: 70 min | **Serves**: 3 | **Per serving**: Cal 409; Net Carbs 3.5g; Fat 32.5g; Protein 8.5g

Ingredients

4 tbsp swerve sugar + extra for topping
1 cup whipped cream
1 cup almond milk

2 vanilla pods
10 egg yolks

Directions

In a pan, add the almond milk and cream. Cut the vanilla pods open and scrape the seeds into the pan with the vanilla pods also. Place the pan over medium heat until almost boiled while stirring regularly. Turn off the heart. Add the egg yolks to a bowl and beat it. Add the sugar and mix well but not too frothy.

Remove the vanilla pods from the almond milk mixture and pour the mixture onto the egg mixture while stirring constantly. Let it sit for 25 minutes. Fill 2 to 3 ramekins with the mixture. Place the ramekins in the fryer basket and cook them at 250°F for 50 minutes. Once ready, remove the ramekins and let them sit to cool. Sprinkle the remaining swerve sugar over and use a torch to melt the swerve sugar so it browns at the top.

Mom's Lemon Cake

Total Time: 40 min | **Serves**: 16 | **Per serving**: Cal 231; Net Carbs 0.1g; Fat 27g; Protein 1.5g

Ingredients

2 cups warm butter
¼ cup liquid stevia
A pinch of salt

4 large eggs
1 grated and untreated lemon rind
2 cups almond flour

2 tbsp baking powder

Directions

Line a baking pan with parchment paper. Beat the warm butter, the stevia, and the salt. Add eggs and lemon rind; beat until the mixture becomes creamy and consistent. Sift in the flour and the baking powder. Pour the batter into the baking pan. Cook in the air fryer at 320°F for 35 minutes.

Quick Breton Butter Cake

Total Time: 20 min | **Serves**: 6 | **Per serving**: Cal 287; Net Carbs 0.8g; Fat 31g; Protein 4g

Ingredients

1 cup butter
¼ cup liquid stevia

1 tbsp pure vanilla extract
6 egg yolks

3 cups almond flour
1 large egg, lightly beaten

Directions

Preheat the Air Fryer to 350°F. In the bowl of an electric mixer, combine cream butter and stevia. Keep mixing until it becomes fluffy. Stir in the almond flour and vanilla. Add the yolks gradually, and beat well after each yolk. Now, transfer the batter into a 9-inch pan with removable bottom. Smooth the surface with a spatula. Chill the batter in the fridge before baking it for 15 minutes. Then brush it with a beaten egg. Bake for 35 minutes.

Awesome Coconut Cups

Total Time: 15 min | **Serves**: 8 | **Per serving**: Cal 75; Net Carbs 0.6g; Fat 7g; Protein 1.3g

Ingredients

1 cup coconut flour
1 tbsp baking powder
1 large egg

1 tbsp liquid stevia
¾ cup coconut milk

Directions

In a bowl, mix the flour and the baking powder. In a separate bowl, beat egg and stevia until thick. Add the coconut milk and stir until combined. Take a baking pan and line ramekins inside it.

Pour the batter evenly into the ramekins, making sure the poured mixture is thin. Cook the ramekins in the air fryer for 3 minutes at 325°F. Serve the pikelets with butter.

Minty Egg Cream

Total Time: 32 min | **Serves**: 2 | **Per serving**: Cal 260; Net Carbs 1g; Fat 16g; Protein 12g

Ingredients

1 egg white
1 egg yolk

3 tbsp butter
3 tbsp stevia

1 lemon, juiced
1 tbsp mint, chopped

Directions

With a hand mixer, mix the stevia and butter. Put in the egg white and yolk. Keep stirring. Add in the lemon juice and mint. Place the lemon mixture in the Air Fryer´s basket and start cooking at 170°F for 3 minutes.

Increase the heat to 190°F and cook for another 3 minutes. Increase the heat again to 210°F and cook 3 more minutes. Increase to 230°F and cook for 6 minutes. Increase to 250°F and cook for another 6 minutes. Transfer the bowl onto a flat surface and remove any lumps. Cover with plastic wrap and transfer to the fridge. Let chill overnight or serve right away.

Chocolate Cups with Almond Praline

Total Time: 25 min | **Serves**: 4 | **Per serving**: Cal 316; Net Carbs 8.1g; Fat 22g; Protein 9.5g

Ingredients

1 cup dark chocolate chips
2 tbsp butter

1 tbsp almonds, chopped
¼ cup + ¼ cup stevia

4 eggs, room temperature
1/8 cup almond flour, sieved

Directions

To make the almond praline, pour ¼ cup stevia in a saucepan over medium heat to melt (do not stir). Cook until lightly golden. Sprinkle with almonds, then remove to a nonstick baking sheet. Let it cool and harden, then chop.

Preheat your Air Fryer to 300°F. Place the chocolate and butter in a heatproof bowl. Microwave for 2-3 minutes, stirring in between. Let cool. Add in the eggs and whisk. Put in the flour and remaining stevia and mix. Grease 4 ramekins with cooking spray and share the mixture between them. Place the fryer and bake for 7 minutes. Sprinkle with the chopped praline and serve.

Easy Coconut Flour Bread

Total Time: 40 min | **Serves**: 6 | **Per serving**: Cal 215; Net Carbs 0.6g; Fat 22g; Protein 6.5g

Ingredients

6 medium eggs
½ tbsp erythritol

½ cup coconut oil
¾ cup coconut flour

1 tbsp baking powder

Directions

Preheat the Air Fryer to 360°F. In a deep bowl, sift coconut flour, and add baking powder. Set aside. In a separate bowl, mix the eggs, oil, and erythritol. Add the dry ingredients and mix well. Spoon the batter into a greased loaf baking pan. Cook in the Air Fryer for 35 minutes.

Blueberry Sandwiches with Chocolate

Total Time: 30 min | **Serves**: 2 | **Per serving**: Cal 256; Net Carbs 9.6g; Fat 15g; Protein 14g

Ingredients

4 slices zero-carb bread
1 tbsp butter, melted

6 oz dark chocolate, broken into chunks

1 cup blueberries

Directions

Brush the zero-carb bread slices with butter. Spread chocolate and blueberries on 2 bread slices. Top with the remaining 2 slices to create 2 sandwiches. Arrange the sandwiches into your air fryer and cook for 14 minutes at 400°F, turning once halfway through cooking. Slice in half and serve.

Air Fryer Sponge Cake

Total Time: 45 min | **Serves**: 12 | **Per serving**: Cal 183; Net Carbs 0.5g; Fat 21g; Protein 1.7g

Ingredients

1 cup butter
½ cup liquid stevia

4 large eggs
2 cups almond flour

Directions

Preheat the Air Fryer to 350°F. Grease and flour a jelly roll pan. In a deep bowl, cream butter and stevia until the mixture becomes light and soft. Beat in eggs, adding them one by one. Sift in almond flour and keep mixing until the batter becomes smooth. Spread the dough in the baking pan. Cook in the Air Fryer 350°F for 40 minutes.

Beet & Vanilla Pavlova

Total Time: 45 min | **Serves**: 4 | **Per serving**: Cal 45; Net Carbs 6.4g; Fat 0.5g; Protein 7.6g

Ingredients

½ tsp sugar-free beet juice
8 egg whites

1 ⅓ cup granulated stevia
¼ tsp salt

2 tsp lemon juice
1 ½ tsp vanilla extract

Directions

Preheat your Air Fryer to 320°F. With an electric mixer, blitz the egg whites, salt, and lemon juice until foamy. Add in the stevia and continue mixing. Pour in the vanilla extract and beat juice. Blend until stiff peaks form. Spoon in the baking sheet, previously lined with parchment paper.

Place the sheet in the fryer and bake for 5 minutes. Reduce the temperature to 320°F and cook for 15 more minutes. Reduce the heat again to 290°F and cook another 15 minutes. Let cool for 2 hours before serving.

Vanilla Rolled Cookies

Total Time: 10 min + chilling time | **Serves**: 8 | **Per serving**: Cal 341; Net Carbs 0.5g; Fat 35g; Protein 3g

Ingredients

1 ½ cups butter, softened
4 tbsp liquid stevia

4 large eggs
1 tbsp vanilla extract

4 cups almond flour
2 tbsp baking powder

Directions

In a deep bowl, cream the butter and the stevia until smooth. Beat in the eggs and the vanilla. Add in flour and baking powder. Cover the mixture and let chill for 2 hours. Preheat the Air Fryer to 390°F. Roll out the dough on a floured surface. Cut the dough into cookie shapes. Arrange them in the basket and cook for 10 minutes.

Easy Chocolate Tart

Total Time: 40 min | **Serves:** 2 | **Per serving:** Cal 320; Net Carbs 3.1g; Fat 25g; Protein 11g

Ingredients

¼ tsp almond extract

3 oz unsweetened chocolate chips

4 egg whites

2 egg yolks

¼ cup xylitol + more for garnishing

1 tbsp butter, melted

1 tbsp butter, unmelted

1 ½ tbsp almond flour

Directions

Preheat your Air Fryer to 330°F. Grease 2 medium ramekins with butter. Put in the xylitol and coat with the butter. Reserve the excess xylitol. Microwave the butter and chocolate chips until melted. Set aside. In a second bowl, whisk the egg yolks. Add in the almond extract and reserved xylitol. Keep beating.

Pour in the chocolate mixture and mix. Put in the almond flour and combine until no lumps left. In a third bowl, beat the egg whites until it holds stiff peaks. Add half of the egg whites into the chocolate mixture and fold. Divide mixture between the ramekins. Place in the fryer and bake for 14 minutes. Dust with xylitol to serve.

German Poppy Seed Cake

Total Time: 40 min | **Serves:** 6 | **Per serving:** Cal 231; Net Carbs 0.1g; Fat 27g; Protein 1.5g

Ingredients

2 cups melted butter

5 tbsp liquid stevia

A pinch of salt

A pinch of poppy seeds

4 large eggs

1 zested and juiced lemon

2 cups almond flour

2 tbsp baking powder

Directions

Preheat your Air Fryer to 320°F. Whisk butter, 2 tbsp of stevia, and salt in a bowl. Add in eggs and lemon zest. Stir until the mixture is creamy. Put in the flour and baking powder. Pour the mixture in a lined with parchment paper pan and bake in the fryer for 30 minutes.

Put a saucepan over medium heat and add in lemon juice and the remaining stevia and cook until the stevia dissolves. When the cake is ready, pour the lemon sauce all over and top with poppy seeds. Let cool before slicing and serving.

Christmas Cake

Total Time: 20 min | **Serves:** 8 | **Per serving:** Cal 215; Net Carbs 4.5g; Fat 17g; Protein 3g

Ingredients

3 tbsp heavy cream

1 ½ cups almond flour

1 tsp baking powder

A pinch of salt

1 ½ cups powdered erythritol

2 tbsp cocoa powder

3 tbsp butter, melted

2 eggs

1/2 tsp almond extract

1 oz dark chocolate, chopped

Directions

Preheat your Air Fryer to 360°F. Grease a baking pan. In a bowl, combine flour, baking powder, and salt. Add in erythritol and cocoa powder; mix to combine. Stir in the butter and stir again.

In a separate bowl, beat the eggs with the heavy cream; fold in the flour mixture. Stir in almond extract and chocolate. Pour the batter into the prepared baking pan. Place in the air fryer and cook for 10 minutes. Let cool before slicing. Serve and enjoy!

Coconut Rum Créme Brulee

Total Time: 70 min | **Serves**: 3 | **Per serving**: Cal 409; Net Carbs 3.5g; Fat 32.5g; Protein 8.5g

Ingredients

4 tbsp swerve sugar + extra for topping

1 tsp Bacardi coconut rum   ⅛ tsp salt   ½ tsp vanilla extract

1 cup half-and-half   1 cup coconut milk   10 egg yolks

Directions

In a skillet over medium heat, pour the coconut milk, vanilla extract, Bacardi coconut rum, salt, and half and half. Stir until almost boiled. Turn the heat off. In a bowl, whisk the egg yolks. Add in the sugar and stir.

Pour in the egg mixture, stirring often. Let sit for 25 minutes. Share the mixture between 3 ramekins. Place in the air fryer basket and Bake at 250°F for 50 minutes. Let the creme cool. Dust the remaining swerve sugar and serve.

Cinnamon Baked Granny Smith Apples

Total Time: 35 min | **Serves**: 2 | **Per serving**: Cal 283; Net Carbs 10.2g; Fat 20.5g; Protein 4g

Ingredients

2 Granny Smith apples, cored, bottom intact

2 tbsp butter, cold   3 tbsp crushed walnuts

3 tbsp stevia   ·   1 tsp cinnamon

Directions

In a bowl, add butter, stevia, walnuts, and cinnamon and mix with fingers until you obtain a crumble. Arrange the apples in the air fryer. Stuff them with the filling mixture. Cook for 30 minutes at 400°F.

Printed in Great Britain
by Amazon